Lauren and I first read *Age of Opportunity* almost [illegible] served as a foundation for how we have tried to parent. Through the peaks and valleys of raising our three kids, we came back to this resource several times. I couldn't be more excited about this revised and expanded version.

—**Matt Chandler**, Lead Pastor, The Village Church, Flower Mound, Texas; President, Acts 29 Network; Coauthor, *Family Discipleship: Leading Your Home through Time, Moments, and Milestones*

Paul David Tripp transforms the paradigm for parenting teenagers from one of fear and low expectations to one of hope and meaning. Parents often forget the character of God and the power of the gospel and consequently view the teenage years as a season to be survived and endured. Although raising teens has its unique challenges, Tripp reveals how remembering who Jesus is and believing in the gospel enables us to embrace this time as a hopeful, constructive opportunity with our kids. This is a game-changing book for parents of teens.

—**Cameron Cole**, Founder, Rooted; Author, *Therefore I Have Hope: 12 Truths That Comfort, Sustain, and Redeem in Tragedy*; Coeditor, *Gospel-Centered Youth Ministry: A Practical Guide*

This is a heartbreaking time for teens: suicide, depression, anxiety, FOMO, the transgender movement, isolation, and hopelessness are rife, making these difficult years even harder. This makes me that much more thankful for Paul Tripp's work in *Age of Opportunity.* In the wide world of books about parenting, there are only a few that don't push a doomed prosperity gospel ("Do it our way and your kids will be great!"); Paul's updated classic work offers the *one* hope for parents and teens: the life, death, and resurrection of Jesus. I'm eternally thankful for Paul and his heart to guide and encourage parents.

—**Elyse Fitzpatrick**, Author, *Give Them Grace: Dazzling Your Kids with the Love of Jesus*

Age of Opportunity has had a tremendous impact on my parenting, so I'm incredibly excited about this new, updated version. Paul has so helpfully applied his understanding of the gospel and the human heart to our personal walk with Jesus, our marriages, and our ministries—I am excited to see his application of the gospel to the parenting of teens made accessible to a new generation. *Age of Opportunity* avoids a formulaic how-to approach to rearing children and instead shows how to apply the gospel to the unique spiritual struggles of your child's heart. For many parents, the teen years feel like a wilderness. This book will give you a compass to guide you. Though I have read dozens of parenting books, two or three have profoundly reshaped my whole approach. *Age of Opportunity* is one of those. You'll love it and pass it to a friend.

—**J.D. Greear**, Pastor, The Summit Church, Durham, North Carolina

We need this fundamentally hopeful book about parenting teens. The hope in this book is not grounded in practical helps—although Tripp offers many. The hope in this book is not distant from the battles; it shines in the dark. The hope is grounded in the God who sent his Son to save us. Parents of teens, take up and read—and hope!

—**Kathleen Nielson**, Author, Prayers of a Parent Series; Speaker

Far too many parents enter their kids' teenage years with fear and cynicism, hoping merely to survive. But what if you viewed parenting not as a season to survive but as a golden age of opportunity? Every parent of a teen should read Paul Tripp's book. It will transform your perspective on parenting.

—**Deepak Reju**, Pastor of Biblical Counseling and Family Ministry, Capitol Hill Baptist Church, Washington, DC; Author, *Rescue Plan: Charting a Course to Restore Prisoners of Pornography* and *Preparing for Fatherhood*

Age of Opportunity

P&R Publishing Titles by Paul David Tripp

Books

Age of Opportunity: A Biblical Guide to Parenting Teens

Instruments in the Redeemer's Hands: People in Need of Change Helping People in Need of Change

War of Words: Getting to the Heart of Your Communication Struggles

Booklets

Marriage: Whose Dream?

Suffering: Eternity Makes a Difference

Teens and Sex: How Should We Teach Them?

Age of Opportunity

A Biblical Guide
to Parenting Teens

REVISED AND EXPANDED

Paul David Tripp

PUBLISHING

P.O. BOX 817 • PHILLIPSBURG • NEW JERSEY 08865-0817

Library of Congress Cataloging-in-Publication Data

Names: Tripp, Paul David, 1950- author.
Title: Age of opportunity : a biblical guide to parenting teens / Paul
    David Tripp.
Description: Revised and expanded. | Phillipsburg, New Jersey : P&R
    Publishing, [2022] | Summary: "Paul Tripp shows parents how to take
    advantage of their children's teen years, drawing on practical, hopeful
    strategies shaped by God's Word. Features a revised study guide and
    bonus chapter"-- Provided by publisher.
Identifiers: LCCN 2021056332 | ISBN 9781629958934 (paperback) | ISBN
    9781629958927 (epub)
Subjects: LCSH: Parenting--Religious aspects--Christianity. | Parent and
    teenager--Religious aspects--Christianity. | Christian
    teenagers--Religious life.
Classification: LCC BV4529 .T75 2022 | DDC 248.8/45--dc23/eng/20220112
LC record available at https://lccn.loc.gov/2021056332

To Luella

You have been
my best friend, teacher, and example.
In many ways you have taught me
what parenting is all about.
Thank you; your contribution
is greater than you will ever know.

Contents

Acknowledgments

IT WAS IN AUGUST OF 1971 that I took my first pastoral position as the youth director of Whaley Street United Methodist Church in Columbia, South Carolina. I was three months away from my twenty-first birthday. Those days at Whaley Street seem so distant, almost like part of someone else's life. Yet there is one thing that remains with me: a desire to see the gospel applied to those difficult years when a person passes from childhood into adulthood.

I couldn't have written this book in 1971. In many ways I was one of the youth that I am writing about here. But more than that, there was much work that God needed to do in me through many people whom he would raise up. It would be impossible to list all the people who have contributed to the thinking that is reflected here. This book represents the loving ministry of pastors, teachers, friends, fellow elders, and family—all who have contributed to my understanding of what it means to live biblically.

I would like to thank some people who have been significant contributors to my life, my ministry, and this book. First my children, Justin, Ethan, Nicole, and Darnay. You have given me room to learn and taught me so much about what it means to parent God's way. Thank you for the gift of forgiveness you have given me again and again. Thank you for helping me to see that the teen years are really years of huge opportunity. Thank you also for not accusing me of loving my laptop more than I loved you as I spent those many nights in the bedroom typing away. Finally, thanks for letting me tell the stories of our struggles. They help to give this book integrity.

Tedd, I am sure that you have no idea how much you have mentored me over the years. I seldom teach without your name coming up in an illustration or a quote. Thanks for encouraging me to write this book.

Ed, Dave, and John, thank you for helping me take scriptural theology and make it work where the rubber meets the road. Thanks, too, for your continuing influence as we minister together.

Sue, I cannot thank you enough for the hours of editorial work that have simply made this a much better book. Your ability to capture my thoughts with an economy and clarity of words is greatly appreciated.

Ruth, thank you for the many hours of transcription. Your willing labor gave me the jump-start I needed.

Jayne, thank you for being committed to making the things that have been planned actually happen. This book is one of the fruits of that commitment.

My prayer is that this book would give hope, courage, and insight to thousands of parents who are entering or are in the midst of the teen years with their children. May the truths of God's Word turn a time of anxious survival into a time of expectation and opportunity!

PART ONE

Clearing the Debris

1

Age of Opportunity or Season for Survival?

IT IS EVERYWHERE AROUND US—IN MOVIES and shows, in magazines on supermarket racks, on talk shows and podcasts, and yes, even in a number of Christian books on the family. Parents are afraid of their teenagers. Even as they are enjoying the early years of a child's life, they are looking over their shoulders with dread, expecting the worst, knowing that in a few short years this precious little one will turn into a monster overnight. They've heard enough stories from parents who have gone through the dark valley of the teen years to know what dangers lie ahead. They are told to expect the worst and to be thankful if they come out of the valley sane, with their teenager alive and their family intact.

I encountered this view of the teen years recently at a marriage conference. It had been a great weekend in all ways. The teaching had been engaging, convicting, and encouraging. The food and accommodations had been superb, and the conference had been held in a beautiful seaside location. Near the end of the weekend, I was looking out at the sun glistening on the waters of the bay when I noticed a couple sitting nearby. They looked very unhappy.

I was curious, so I asked them if they had enjoyed the weekend. Everything had been great, they replied. I commented that they didn't look very happy. The woman responded, "We have two teenagers, and we are dreading going home. We wish this weekend would last forever!"

"You just have to expect your teenager to be rebellious; all of us were," her husband added. "You just have to ride it out."

"Besides," she moaned, "you can't argue with hormones!"

I walked away impressed that something is fundamentally wrong with the way we think about this time in a child's life. Something is inherently wrong with the cultural epidemic of fear and cynicism about our teenagers. Something is wrong when a parent's highest goal is survival. We need to take another look: Is this a biblical view of this period in a child's life? Does this view lead to biblical strategies of parenting and biblical hope?

We need to examine what is wrong with the cynicism about teenagers that is endemic in our culture.

A Biological View of Teens

We often talk about our teenagers as if they were nothing more than collections of raging, rebel hormones encased in developing skin. We see our goal as somehow holding these hormones back so that we can survive until our teens are teens no longer. A parent recently rejoiced to me that her son had turned twenty, as if he had passed through some magic portal from danger into safety. "We made it!" she said.

This survival mentality exposes the poverty of this view of teenagers. Many parents who talk to me about their teenagers talk without hope; they see them as victims of hormones that drive them to do crazy things. Although they would never say this, the working theology that hides behind this view is that the truths of Scripture, the power of the gospel, biblical communication, and godly relationship are no match for the teen years. Yes, we believe that God's Word is powerful and effective—except if some poor soul is trying to apply it to a child between the years of thirteen and nineteen! We now even have a category of children called "preteen." These are the years when the monstrous characteristics of the teenagers begin to develop and rear their ugly heads.

Are we comfortable with a view of teenagers that says that because of the significant biological changes going on inside them, they are essentially unreachable? Are we comfortable with a hormonal view of teens that reduces them to victims of biological forces, freeing them from responsibility for their own choices and actions? Do we really want a view of teens that would have us believe that the truths that give life and hope to anyone who believes cannot reach a teenager? We cannot hold on to a robust belief in the power of the gospel if we continue to buy into our culture's cynicism about the teen years.

Particular Sacrifice and Suffering?

In 2 Timothy 2:22, Paul exhorts Timothy to "flee youthful passions." This interesting little phrase calls us to be balanced in the ways we think about teenagers and define this time of life. On the one hand, the Bible challenges us not to be naive about this period of life. There are passions, or lusts, that uniquely plague young people—temptations that are particularly powerful. These must be faced. Scripture enjoins us to be strategic, to ask the question, "What passions grip a person during this phase of life?"

On the other hand, Paul uses the qualifier "youthful" because each phase of life has its own set of temptations. The temptations of the little boy, the young man, and the old man are not identical. The temptations of the teenager are not particularly savage and severe. Each person who seeks to please the Lord at each time in his or her life must watch, pray, stand fast, and fight lest he or she fall into temptation. The teenager is called to guard against the temptations that are unique to youth, while the older person is called to guard against the temptations unique to that age. Each person, whatever his or her age, must accept each stage of warfare as a Christian living in this fallen world.

Battle of Biology or Battle of the Heart?

The 2 Timothy passage is also helpful in the way it locates and defines the battle of youth. There *is* a battle raging in the lives of young people, but it is not the battle of biology. It is an intensely spiritual battle, a battle for the heart. This is exactly what Paul wants us to be aware of as he exhorts Timothy not to let his heart be controlled by his passions. This battle is not unique to teens. It takes a certain shape during the teen years, but it is the battle of every sinner.

The tendency of every sinner, no matter what his age, is captured well by Paul in Romans 1:25: the tendency to exchange worship and service of the Creator for the worship and service of the created thing. Yes, it's there in the life of the teenager who forsakes his convictions for the approval of his peers, but it is just as powerfully present in the adult who compromises family and spiritual priorities for professional success. The battle, as Paul understands it, is a heart battle, and it is dramatically important because what controls the heart will direct the life.

There are significant temptations of the heart that greet teenagers, calling them to believe that they cannot live without some aspect of the creation. These voices call them to believe that identity, meaning, and purpose can be found in the creature rather than the Creator. These are the life-altering conflicts of the teen years. We dare not miss them because of our biologically oriented fears and our survival mentality. We must believe that Jesus came so that we would be freed from the desires of our sinful nature in order that we might serve him and him alone. This includes our teenagers.

The Struggles of Parents

The tumult of the teen years is not only about the attitudes and actions of teens but about the thoughts, desires, attitudes, and actions of parents as well. The teen years are hard for us because they tend to bring out the worst in us. It is in these years that parents hear themselves saying things that they never thought they would say. Parents find themselves reacting with accusations, guilt manipulation, and ultimatums, responding with a level of anger that they would not have thought possible. It is in these years that parents struggle with embarrassment at being related to the teen who was once, as a child, a great source of pride and joy.

It is vital for us to confess that the struggle of the teen years is not only about teen biology and teen rebellion. These years are hard for us because they expose the wrong thoughts and desires of our *own* hearts. There is a principle here that we need to recognize. As my mother said, "There is nothing that comes out of a drunk that was not there in the beginning," and the same is true for parents! These years are hard for us because they rip back the curtain and expose us. This is why trials are so difficult, yet so useful in God's hands. We don't radically change in a moment of trial. No, trials expose what we have always been. Trials reveal things to which we would have otherwise been blind. So, too, the teen years expose our self-righteousness, our impatience, our unforgiving spirit, our lack of servant love, the weakness of our faith, and our craving for comfort and ease.

Why We Miss the Opportunities

I sat recently in my office with a father who was so angry at his son that it was all he could do to be civil. He did not see the tremendous spiritual needs in his son that he had been uniquely positioned by God to meet. There was no tenderness in their relationship; there wasn't even cordiality. There was tense distance.

At one point the father rose to speak to his son about his report card. He walked to his son's chair, stuck the failing report card in his face, and said, "How dare you do this to me after all I have done for you!" To him, the bad grades were a personal affront. This was not the way he thought it was supposed to work. He had done his job; now the son was supposed to do his. He was angry at his son, but not because of his son's sin against God. He was angry because his son had taken things away from him that he valued very much: his reputation as a successful Christian father, the respect he thought he deserved, and the ease he thought he would finally achieve with older children.

This father had no attitude of ministry, no sense of opportunity, no quest to be part of what God was doing in the life of his son. Instead, he was filled with the anger described in James 4:2: "You covet and cannot obtain."

The cultural cynicism we have been discussing is based on who we think teenagers are and what we think they are going through. We tend to believe that there is little we can do to make these years more productive.

Rather, the culture says, we need to come up with positive strategies of survival that preserve our sanity as parents and the stability of our marriages and that keep our teenagers out of as much self-inflicted danger as possible.

However, it is my experience that when parents begin to recognize, own, confess, and turn from their own wrong heart attitudes and the wrong actions that flow from them, the result is a marked difference in their relationship to their teens and in the way they view the struggles of the teen years. When we look with concerned eyes toward the teen years, we need to look not only at our children but also at ourselves. Parents who are humbly willing to change position themselves to be God's instruments of change.

A Better Way

It is time for us to reject the wholesale cynicism of our culture regarding adolescence. Rather than years of undirected and unproductive struggle, these are years of unprecedented opportunity. They are the golden age of parenting, when you begin to reap all the seeds you have sown in your child's life, when you can help your teenager to internalize truth and prepare him or her for a productive, God-honoring life as an adult.

These are the years of penetrating questions, the years of wonderful discussions never before possible. These are the years of failure and struggle that put the teen's true heart on the table. These are the years of daily ministry and great opportunity.

These are not years merely to be survived! They are to be approached with a sense of hope and of mission. Almost every day brings a new opportunity to enter the life of your teen with help, hope, and truth. We should not resign ourselves to an increasingly distant relationship. This is the time to connect with our children as never before. These are years of great opportunity.

That is what this book is about. It is a book of opportunity and hope. It is time for us to come out of the bunkers of cynicism and fear and into the light, examining the plan God has for us as we parent our teenagers. This is a book about activity, goals, and practical strategies. This is a book that believes that the truths of Scripture apply as powerfully to teens as they do to anyone else.

At the same time, this book will not be naive. The teen years are often cataclysmic years of conflict, struggle, and grief. They are years of new temptations, of trial and testing. Yet these very struggles, conflicts, trials, and tests are what produce such wonderful parental opportunities.

Recognizing God's Moments of Change

It was a wintry Tuesday night. I had had counseling appointments all day and had taught for three hours in the evening. I was driving home at about ten o'clock, dreaming about an hour or so of relaxation before I hit the bed. I silently hoped that for some inexplicable reason, the whole family had gone to sleep at nine o'clock. Or, if they had not gone to bed, I hoped that they would instinctively know that I was tired and not to be disturbed. I reasoned that I had served God faithfully that day. Surely God would agree that I had the right to punch out from life! I dreamed of an empty family room, a well-iced Diet Coke, the newspaper, and the remote control. I was totally exhausted, and I had a right to relax. (You can see that I was approaching the house with a selfless attitude of ministry!)

I quietly opened the door in the vain hope that I could sneak in unnoticed. The living room lights were out, and the house was quiet. I was filled with hope. Maybe my dreams had come true and I would have an evening all to myself!

I had only put one foot in the door when I heard an angry voice. My heart sank! It was the voice of Ethan, my teenage son. I wanted to act as if I hadn't heard it. My disappointment gave way to anger. I wanted to grab Ethan and say, "Don't you know what my day has been like? Don't you know how tired I am? The last thing I need right now is to deal with your problems. You're going to have to solve this one yourself. I wish for once you'd think of somebody besides yourself. I do and do for you, and this is the thanks I get. You can't leave me alone one night?"

All these thoughts raged within me, but I didn't say a word. I listened to Ethan as he poured out his complaint. He was as angry as he had ever been at his older brother. He was cursing the fact that he had an older brother who seemed to do nothing but "trash his life." It was after ten. The issue that started this thing was petty.

I was tempted to tell him to get a grip and deal with it, but another agenda gripped me. Here was one of those unexpected moments of opportunity, one of those mundane moments ordained by a loving and sovereign God in which my teenager's heart was being exposed. It was more than an Ethan and Dad moment. This was God's moment, a dynamic moment of redemption in which God was continuing the work of rescue he had begun years ago in my son. The only question in the moment was whether I would pursue God's agenda or my own. Would I believe the gospel in that moment, trusting God to give me what I needed so that I could do what he was calling me to do in my son's life?

I asked Ethan to sit down at the dining room table and tell me what was going on. He was hurt and angry. His heart was on the table. We talked through his anger, and he became ready to listen. A petty argument with his brother had opened the door to discussing things that were far from petty. God gave me strength and patience. He filled my mouth with the right things to say. Ethan saw himself in new ways that night and confessed to things that he had never before recognized.

It was approaching midnight when I said good night to Ethan. We hugged and went to bed. What had first appeared to be an irritating moment had in fact been a wonderful opportunity of ministry, ordained by a God of love. It became very clear that God wasn't only working to change Ethan; he was working to change me as well. The selfishness of *my* heart had been revealed that evening, the same selfishness that causes parents to lash out in anger at the very teens who need them. My need of Christ, too, had been exposed. There was no way I could function as his instrument without his strength.

Little Moments, High Calling

I chose to write about this moment because it was one of those unremarkable moments that happen not only daily but many times a day. Each of these moments is loaded with opportunity. There are many, many more of these moments than the dramatic moments of adolescence—moments involving sex, drugs, and violence—that get so much press. None of us lives constantly in the grand moments of significant decision; there aren't many of them in life. No, we live in the world of the mundane. This is where we need to see our teenagers with eyes of opportunity rather than eyes of dread and fear.

The argument over the last Pop-Tart, the cry of "nothing to wear" a half hour before school, the report card crumpled in the pocket of jeans heading for the wash, the pouting expression in the face of a parent's "No," the third fender bender in a month, the constant words of discontent, the "everybody else does" and the "I'm the only one whose parents make them . . ."—all must be seen as something more than hassles that get in the way of an otherwise enjoyable life. These are the moments God made parents for. You are God's agent on the watch. You have been given an incredibly high calling. You are God's instrument of help and preparation as your child makes his or her final steps out of the home and into God's world. These moments make your life worthwhile. Here you will make a contribution that is worth infinitely more than any career or financial accomplishment.

Recognizing the Opportunities

The more I lived with my own teenage children, watched their peers, and interacted with other parents of teenagers, the more I became convinced that this is a time of unbridled opportunity. It is not a time to head for the bunkers! It is not a time to dread worst-case scenarios of total domestic chaos. This is not a time to accept a culturally dictated "generation gap." This is a time to jump into the battle and move toward your teenager. It is a time for engagement, interaction, discussion, and committed relationship. This is not a time to let a teenager hide his doubts, fears, and failures but a time to pursue, love, encourage, teach, forgive, confess, and accept. It is a wonderful time.

My wife and I have never had more of a sense of calling than during the years in which we parented our teenagers. We laughed, cried, discussed, and prayed with our teens. We struggled for them and with them.

We saw failure and trial as opportunity. We did not always respond in faith, and we needed to confess our own sin, but it was a wonderful period of family life. We were so happy to be doing what we were doing. We saw the glory of God being revealed in the midst of our own feeble efforts and weak faith.

There are three fundamental, God-given doors of opportunity that every parent of teens can walk through. Each of these problems becomes a means of helping a teenager to internalize the truths to which he or she has been exposed for years. The problems of teenage insecurity, teenage rebellion, and the teenager's widening world are actually unique points for parents to access the central issues in their teenagers' lives.

Teenage Insecurity

Teenagers are not secure people! The teenager who seems secure at breakfast can easily fall apart by supper. The teenager who goes to bed thinking she looks okay awakes, looks in the mirror before breakfast, and becomes convinced that her head is too large for her body. The teenager who is secure because he thinks he finally understands enough of the rules to be thought of as a quasi-normal humanoid is convinced he is a terminal social misfit because of an embarrassing moment at a party.

Our son Ethan was about fifteen when he came in one afternoon obviously discouraged. I asked him what was wrong. He told me that every day, people made fun of him on the way to or from school. He said, "I see them looking at me and talking and laughing." It was a tough period for him. He was rapidly growing. He was unsure of himself, his body, and his looks. He was in that limbo land between boy and man, and he projected his insecurity to everyone around him. This time of physical insecurity provided many opportunities for us to listen to him and offer him love, encouragement, and the gospel.

The teenager is flooded with questions during this period. Who am I? Do I look okay? Why is life so confusing? Will I ever remember all the rules? What is right, and what is wrong? Who is right, and who is wrong? What is happening to my body? What am I going to do with my life? Will I be a success or a failure? Do people really like me? Am I normal? Is my family normal? Is God for real?

The world of physical appearance, the world of relationships, the world of ideas, the world of responsibilities, and the world of the future all are scary and uncertain to the teenager. It is this reality that makes this time such an age of opportunity. In the midst of these questions, significant biblical themes can be discussed, such as the doctrine of creation, fear of man, God's sovereignty, the nature of truth, identity in Christ, and spiritual warfare and temptation, to mention a few. In the context of daily insecurities, we have an opportunity to help the teen make conceptual theology into functional, life-shaping theology. Each of the questions above provides an opportunity to discuss, test, experience, apply, and internalize important biblical truths.

Teenage Rebellion

The stories of gross and flagrant rebellion are one of the reasons that parents fear the teen years. The thought that the once-precious child will turn into the leader of the violent neighborhood gang is the parent's worst nightmare. We have to reevaluate our expectation of automatic teen rebellion. At the same time, we have to recognize that this is an age when children push at the boundaries, temptation abounds, and peer relationships do not always encourage right behavior.

We received one of those dreaded calls one Sunday afternoon. A mother in our church told us that our son had not stayed at her house overnight as we had thought. Our son had asked her son to cover for him, but her son was conscience-stricken and went to her for help. She called us. We were afraid and disappointed. For a moment we gave in to worst-case scenarios. How many more lies had he told? Were we living with a son we did not know? At the same time, we were deeply thankful for the Lord's rescuing mercy. We questioned our son, and he confessed. It was a watershed moment of choosing whom he would serve. We left the room so thankful that an event that we hoped would never happen had, in God's plan of mercy, taken place.

Certain desires make the teenager susceptible to the temptation to rebel: the desire to be an individual and think for oneself, the desire for freedom, the desire to try new things, the desire to test the boundaries, the desire for control, the desire to make one's own decisions, the desire to be different, the desire to fit in, and the desire to be accepted. These, with a host of other desires, all fueled by the autonomy and self-centeredness of the sin nature, can surely lead the teenager astray.

At the same time, these struggles of rebellion and submission become the context in which another set of critical biblical issues can be discussed, applied, and internalized. Biblical truths having to do with authority, sowing and reaping, truth and falsehood, wisdom and foolishness, law and grace, confession, repentance, forgiveness, and the nature and function of the heart all get put on the table. Parents with eyes of opportunity will have many, many openings to deal with central issues of biblical faith in the lives of their teenagers.

A Teenager's Widening World

One of the frightening things for parents and a source of insecurity for their teenagers is the sudden explosion of the teen's world. This world is not always exciting to the teenager. Sometimes it seems scary and overwhelming. Sometimes the teen is alive with the joy of discovery, and other times he is shy and avoidant. Sometimes he enjoys being a teenager, while at other times he seems afraid of the new expectations laid on him.

There is no stopping the widening of his world. It is a world of new friends, new locations, new opportunities and responsibilities, new thoughts, new plans, new freedoms, new temptations, new feelings, new experiences, and new discoveries. All the joys and insecurities of this widening world provide opportunities to help your teenager really understand and personally internalize fundamental truths. These include the sovereignty and providence of God, the ever-present help of the Lord, biblical relationships, spiritual warfare, discipline, self-control, contentment, faithfulness, trustworthiness, the body of Christ, the world, the flesh, and the devil, responsibility and accountability, biblical priorities, discovery and stewardship of gifts, and many other biblical truths and principles. That's quite a list! But this widening world provides wonderful opportunities for parents to prepare their teenagers for effective and productive lives in God's world.

THE PLACE TO BEGIN AS we build a biblical understanding of parenting our teenagers is to reject the dark, foreboding cynicism of our culture. Yes, the teen years are years of change, insecurity, and tumult, yet these are the very things that God uses to bring truth to light in the eyes of our children. If we are to be his instruments, we must deal with our own idolatry and bring a robust biblical faith to each rocky moment—a faith that believes that God rules over all things for our sake, that he is an ever-present help in trouble, that he is at work in every situation to accomplish his redemptive purpose, and that his Word is powerful, active, and effective.

We do not want to be driven into bunkers of survival by our teenagers' insecurity, rebellion, and widening world. Rather, we want to take Paul's call to Timothy as God's agenda for our work with our teens. "Preach the word; be ready in season and out of season; reprove, rebuke, and exhort, with complete patience and teaching" (2 Tim. 4:2). We want to approach these important years with hope—not hope in our teenagers or hope in ourselves, but hope in God who is able to do more than anything we could ever ask or imagine as we seize the opportunities he places in our paths. We want to approach these years with a sense of purpose and a sense of calling.

When people ask you what you do, say, "I am the parent of a teenager. It is the most important job I have ever had. Everything else I do for a living is secondary." Then say, "You know, I have never had a job that is so exciting! I have never had a job that is so full of opportunities. Every day I am needed. Every day I do things that are important, worthwhile, and lasting. I wouldn't give up this job for anything!"

Questions for Reflection and Discussion

1. Where have you recently seen or heard a negative stereotype about a teenager? Have you contributed to this cultural cynicism in some way, even if only privately? How can you encourage other parents of teenagers to be hopeful about this season?
2. Reflect on your adolescence and biological developments as a teenager. Were these years difficult for you physically, emotionally, or socially? How can remembering this help you to have sympathy for your child?
3. What recent challenge has your teenager experienced that created difficulty for your teenager and for you? Was your reaction to view

this as a frustrating interruption to your comfort or as a valuable opportunity?

4. In what ways is your teenager insecure? How can you comfort and encourage your teenager in his or her insecurities and remind your teenager of his or her identity as a child of God?

5. How has your teenager rebelled recently? What motivation might have been behind the rebellion? What can you do to address the deeper motivation instead of only the surface behavior?

6. In what ways do you, as an adult, still rebel against your heavenly Father? Are you more like your rebellious teenager than you wish to admit? Consider the progress that could be made if you confessed your rebellion against God to your teenager.

7. What in your life is competing with God's call to be an invested parent of a teenager? Where might you need to reevaluate your priorities, schedule, or finances to make the most of this God-given opportunity?

2

Whose Idols Are in the Way?

IF WE ARE EVER TO BE effective for Christ in the lives of our teenagers, it is important for us to be honest about our own idols and the places where we have tended to exchange worship and service of the Creator for worship and service of created things. Too often when we seek to understand the struggles of adolescence, we look only at teenagers and their problems. In reality, it is time for us to look inside and ask, "What really rules *our* hearts?"

Now, surely every Christian parent would give the correct theological answer. We are God's children. He rules our hearts. Or does he? This is not about a theological affirmation but about our day-to-day worship. At the level where the rubber meets the road—in the bedrooms, living rooms, kitchens, and hallways of life—what really controls our hearts?

Start with Your Heart

It is a waste of time for us to think about strategies for parenting our teens without first examining ourselves. If our hearts are controlled by something other than God, we will not view the golden parenting opportunities of the teen years as opportunities at all. Instead they will be a constant stream of irritating hassles brought on by an incredibly self-centered person who is neither adult nor child and who has the uncanny ability to make even the most unimportant moments of our lives chaotic.

There is an important principle here that is taught all through Scripture but enunciated most clearly in Ezekiel 14:4: "Thus says the Lord God: Any one of the house of Israel who takes his idols into his heart and sets the stumbling block of his iniquity before his face, and yet comes to the prophet, I the Lord will answer him as he comes with the multitude of his idols." The leaders of Israel have come to God to hear his words to them, but as they come, God recognizes that their hearts have been captured by idols. So God says, "Because there are idols in your hearts, the only thing that I am interested in talking about is your idolatry."

Why? There is a little phrase here that clues us in. God says that when a person sets up an idol in his heart, he also puts "the stumbling block of his iniquity before his face." The principle revealed here is the principle of inescapable influence. What controls my heart controls my life. An idol of the heart always puts a stumbling block of iniquity before my face.

Imagine that you have placed your hand, with fingers narrowly separated, in front of your face. When you attempt to look through your fingers, your vision is obstructed. As long as your hand is in front of your face, no matter where you turn to look, your vision will be altered by your fingers. So it is with an idol in my heart. It exercises inescapable influence over my life. Wherever I go, whatever I am doing, the idol influences what I do and how I do it. This is the reason God says, "It makes no sense for me to talk about anything else, because whatever I say somehow, some way, will be used to serve the idol that rules your heart. Therefore, I want to deal with your idolatry. That is my priority."

We cannot ignore this central issue. I am persuaded that our idols have caused us to see opportunity as trial and to strike back at our teenagers with bitter words of judgment, accusation, and condemnation, behaving toward them with intolerance and anger. While God calls us to love, accept, forgive, and serve, we are often barely able to be nice.

Let's consider some typical parental idols and the way they shape our responses to our teens.

The Idol of Comfort

Secretly in our hearts, many of us want life to be a resort. At a resort, you are the one who is served. Your needs come first, and you do only what you want to do when you want to do it. The only demands you deal with in a resort are the demands you put on yourself. At a resort, you live with a sense of entitlement. You've paid your money, and you have the right to expect certain things. I am afraid many of us bring this entitlement mentality to our parenting. We live for comfort. We reason that we have the right to quiet, harmony, peace, and respect, and we respond in anger when we do not get it.

Scripture warns us that life is far from being a resort. Life is war. This is clearly demonstrated in the teen years. I said to my teenagers many times as they were leaving home, "There is a war out there; it is being fought on the turf of your heart. It is being fought for the control of your soul." The tumult, chaos, and unrest of the teen years are the result not only of significant biological changes but of the dramatic spiritual war that is going on as well.

Parents who demand comfort, ease, regularity, peace, space, quiet, and harmony are ill-equipped for this war. They begin to see their teenager as the enemy. They begin to fight *with* him rather than for him, and even worse, they tend to forget the true nature of the battle and the identity of the real enemy. They act out of frustrated desire, doing and saying regrettable things, and they fail to be effective and productive in those strategic moments of ministry in which God has placed them.

The Idol of Respect

The father had stomped on every one of his daughter's CDs. He had locked her in her room every night and had publicly shared her sins with the whole church at a prayer meeting. He had slapped her in the face in front of her friends and tried to goad and belittle her into submission. He never failed to remind her that he had been a model teen. In my office, he told me with great energy and resolve, "I will get her to respect me if it is the last thing I ever do!"

Respect is what ruled his heart. He was convinced that he was entitled to it. Thus, every issue became an issue of respect. He saw disrespect where there was none. Life became a series of final exams in which he never gave his daughter better than an F. He viewed his daughter's development, insecurity, and awkwardness as a personal affront. There was no vertical, spiritual dimension to his thinking. He saw his daughter not in terms of her relationship to God but only in relation to himself. He did not see himself as an agent to lead her to a lifesaving fear of God. His heart was driven by the goal that she would fear *him* and give him the respect he thought he deserved.

Is respect a good thing? Of course! Is it something that parents should seek to instill in their children? Yes! But it must not be the thing that controls our hearts—or we will personalize what is not personal, lose sight of our role as God's representatives, and fight for and demand what only God can produce.

Sadly, the father's eyes were blind to the god that ruled him. In his quest to get respect, he encouraged the exact opposite response through his oppressive behavior.

The Idol of Appreciation

We've been there when the calls came from school. We've been there in the wee hours of the morning when the nightmares hit. We've changed the bed that was wet once again. We've gone out in pajamas and slippers to the all-night drugstore for medicine. We've made the special skateboard-shaped birthday cakes. We've cleaned up vomit from the bedroom carpet. We've sat in on meetings with the principal. We've spent hours making the papier-mâché volcano. We've provided transportation to thousands of events. We've sat through scores of painful recitals, spent thousands on memorable vacations. We've walked miles and miles in the aisles of the supermarket so mouths would be fed and stomachs filled. We've trudged through malls for hours looking for "cool" clothes. We've washed enough clothes to fill the Grand Canyon! We've given up our dreams to pay for musical instruments and braces. Isn't it about time that we get some credit?

I cannot tell you how many times I've heard parents recite this list, always with that same punch line. It seems so logical, so harmless, so right. Children *should* appreciate their parents. Yet being appreciated cannot be our goal. When appreciation becomes the thing we live for, we unwittingly look for appreciation in every situation.

Teenagers don't often burst in the door at the end of the day and say, "Do you know what I was thinking about on the bus ride home today, Mom? I was thinking about how much you and Dad have done for me over the years. You have been with me and for me from the very first moment of my life until now. On the bus I was flooded with gratitude, and I couldn't wait to get home and say thank you!" If this happens to you, erect stones as a lasting memorial or light an eternal flame!

Very few parents have headed to bed only to hear sobbing coming from their teenager's bedroom and had this conversation: "What's wrong, dear?" "Oh, I was just thinking about you and Mom and how unthankful I've been. I feel so guilty that I haven't appreciated you more, and I've committed myself to demonstrating that I appreciate you every day!" On the contrary, teenagers tend to be much more self-oriented and self-interested than aware and appreciative of others.

If parents forget their own vertical relationship with God as they minister to their teens, if they think in terms of an "I serve, you appreciate" contract between parent and child, they will struggle with discouragement and anger during the teen years. Just when parents expect their almost-grown children to give a little something back, they seem to be more selfish and lacking in gratitude than ever before. Again, every parent needs to ask, "Why am I doing what I am doing? Who am I serving? What are the things that I have come to expect and demand? Whose desires rule the moments of opportunity with my teenager—God's or mine?"

The Idol of Success

I listened as the father said to me, in the presence of his teenage son, "Do you know what it's like to go to church and know that everyone there has been talking about and praying for your rebellious son? Do you know what it's like to enter a service with all eyes on you, knowing that people are wondering how it is going and how you and your wife are coping? This is not the way it is supposed to be. We tried to faithfully do everything God called us to do as parents, and look what we ended up with! I ask myself, if I knew that this was the way it would all turn out, would we have ever chosen to have children? I cannot describe how disappointed and embarrassed I am."

That afternoon, with his son listening, that father spoke what many parents have felt but never verbalized. We tend to approach parenting as if we have hard-and-fast guarantees. We think that if we do our part, our children will be model citizens. Yet this is not the way it works in a fallen world.

When we approach parenting with a sense that our children's obedience is our right, these assumptions pave the way for our identity to get wrapped up in our children. We begin to need them to be what they should be so that we can feel a sense of achievement and success. We begin to look at our children as our trophies rather than God's creatures. We want to display them on the mantels of our lives as visible testimonies to a job well done. When they fail to live up to our expectations, we find ourselves not grieving for them and fighting for them but getting angry at them, fighting against them, and, in fact, grieving for ourselves and our loss. We are angry because they have taken something valuable away from us, something that has come to rule our hearts: a reputation for success.

It is so easy to lose sight of the fact that these are God's children. They do not belong to us. They are given not to bring *us* glory but to bring *him* glory. Our teenagers are from him, they exist through him, and the glory of their lives points to him. We are but agents to accomplish his plan. Our identity is rooted in him and his call to us, not in our children and their performance. The ultimate rejection that should make us weep is that they have rejected not us but him.

As parents, we are in trouble whenever we lose sight of these "vertical realities"—when we lose sight of God, his ownership of our children, and his call to us to be faithful parents no matter what the outcome. Whenever parenting is reduced to our hard work, our teens' performance, and the reputation of our families, it is very hard for us to respond with selfless faithfulness in the face of our children's failure. God-ordained moments of ministry become moments of angry confrontation filled with words of judgment. Instead of leading the needy teen once again to Christ, we beat her with words. Instead of loving her, we reject her. Instead of speaking words of hope, we condemn her. We are flooded much more with our own embarrassment, anger, and hurt than with grief over our wayward child's standing before God.

We need to start by examining our own hearts. Do we have attitudes of ownership and entitlement? Have we subtly become ruled by reputation? Is there within us a struggle to love our teenagers? Is there distance between us and our teenagers that is the result of that struggle? Are we oppressed by thoughts of what others think? Have we even doubted the principles of the Word and wondered why they haven't "worked" for us? These questions need to be faced if we are ever to be what God has commanded us to be in the lives of our teenagers, who are sinners living in a fallen world.

The Idol of Control

I am increasingly persuaded that there are only two ways of living: (1) trusting God and living in submission to his will and his rule, or (2) trying to be God. There is little in between. As sinners we seem to be better at the latter than we are at the former!

This spiritual dynamic hits right at the heart of parenting. Successful parenting is the rightful, God-ordained loss of control. The goal of parenting is to work ourselves out of a job. The goal of parenting is to raise children who were once totally dependent on us to be independent, mature people who, with reliance on God and proper connectedness to the Christian community, are able to stand on their own two feet.

In the early years of parenting, we were in control of everything, and although we complained about the stress of it all, we liked having the power! There was little that our infants chose to do. We chose their food, their times of rest, their manner of physical exercise, what they saw and heard, where they went, who their friends were, and the list could go on and on. However, the truth is that from day one our children are growing independent. The baby who once was unable to roll over without assistance soon can crawl into the bathroom and unravel the entire roll of toilet paper! This same child is soon driving away from the house to places well out of our parental reach.

It creeps up on us. We expect our kids to turn out just like us. I love sports, played sports in school, and like to watch them. I remember the first time my oldest son Justin said that he did not want to watch a football game with me. What? No love for football? I wanted to say, "It's not right! I raised you to be a fan of organized sports! Don't you want to be like me?"

And I remember when my daughter Nicole first announced that she did not like peanut butter. It was almost like saying that she didn't like Christmas or summer vacation. There almost seemed to be something theologically wrong with it! I determined that I would convince her that peanut butter was great. Before she left this home she would have a deep and abiding commitment to spreadable crushed peanuts!

How many parents have struggled with the friends that their children have chosen? Yes, the choice of companions is a very serious matter, but it is also a place where we surrender control to a maturing child. The goal of parenting is not to retain tight-fisted control over our children in an attempt to guarantee their safety and our sanity. Only God is able to exercise that kind of control. The goal is to be used of him to instill in our children an ever-maturing self-control through the principles of the Word and to allow them to exercise ever-widening circles of choice, control, and independence.

I regularly work with parents who want to turn back the clock. They think that the only hope is to go back to the former days of total control. They try to treat their teenagers like little children. They end up more like jailers than parents, and they forget to minister the gospel that is the only hope in those crucial moments of struggle.

It is vital that we remember the truths of the gospel: First, there is no situation that is not under control, for Christ rules over all things for the sake of the church (Eph. 1:22). Second, not only is the situation under control, but God is at work in it to do the good that he promised to do (Rom. 8:28). So I do not need to control my teenager's every desire, thought, and action. In every situation, he is under the sovereign control of Christ, who is accomplishing what I cannot. Third, I need to remember that the goal of my parenting is not to conform my children to my image but to work so that they are conformed to the image of Christ! My goal is not to clone my tastes, my opinions, and my habits in my children. I am not looking for my image in them; I long to see Christ's.

WE CANNOT CONSIDER THE TEENAGE YEARS, with their tumult and struggle, without honestly looking at what we, as parents, bring to the struggle. If our hearts are ruled by comfort, respect, appreciation, success, and control, we will unwittingly hunger for our teens to meet our expectations instead of ministering to their spiritual needs. Instead of seeing moments of struggle as God-given doors of opportunity, we will view them as frustrating, disappointing irritants, and we will experience growing anger against the very children to whom we have been called to minister.

Questions for Reflection and Discussion

1. Reflect on any idols that are currently ruling your heart—such as career, appearance, social standing, or your children's success. How have these idols informed your parenting? Can you think of a time when your own idols created trials with your teenager instead of opportunities?

2. What did you do the last time you noticed a spiritual war being waged over your teenager's heart? Did you avoid the battle? Or did you prayerfully engage in it, right alongside your child?

3. In what ways have you been tempted to see your teenager only in relation to you and your desires for him or her? How might the dynamic change if instead you viewed yourself primarily as the agent of a relationship between your child and God?

4. Can you guess or imagine what your own parents' idols may have been when you were growing up? How did these impact you as a child?

5. In what ways have you viewed your children as trophies for yourself?

6. As an agent who is leading your child toward Christ, you need to surrender your own sin and your own control to Jesus. Ask yourself the following questions: Do I have an attitude of ownership or entitlement? Have I subtly become ruled by reputation? Do I struggle at all to love my teenager? Is there distance between us that is the result of that struggle? Am I oppressed by thoughts of what others think? Have I doubted the principles of the Word?

7. In what ways have you been tempted to see your own reflection in your child instead of Christ's?

3

What Is a Family? A Definition

THE QUESTION "WHAT IS A FAMILY?" has been debated throughout human history and will be the subject of debate for generations to come. In today's world, defining the nature of the family is a particularly hot topic.

Our purpose here is not to enter into this cultural debate by trying to give a biblically comprehensive definition of the family. Our goal is to define the family in a very different way, that is, to answer the question "What is a family?" functionally. What we are really asking is "What did God intend the family to do?" This is important because our functional definition of the family shapes our goals for our children and our actions toward them. The question "What did God intend the family to do?" is the basis for asking, "What does God want us to do with our teenagers?" You will never get a proper biblical sense of your job description as the parent of a teen unless you have first understood your job description as a parent more generally.

I have listened to many of my Christian brothers and sisters tell stories of their vacations and the elaborate plans they made for many months to ensure that their families would have a good time. One day as I was listening to yet another account of a well-researched vacation package to Orlando, it hit me that many parents are more organized, more intentional, better researched, and more goal-oriented in planning their vacations than they are in raising their children.

Imagine how a vacation would go if I "sort of" understood what a vacation was supposed to be but wasn't completely sure. Imagine how it would go if I "sort of" knew where I wanted to go with my family on vacation but wasn't really committed to one destination. What if I had a bit of a sense of direction but had taken no time to study the maps? What if I knew that vacations tended to be costly but hadn't prepared financially? What possibility would there be that my family would, in fact, have any vacation, let alone a successful one?

So it is with family life. It is vital that we are biblically informed, biblically prepared, and biblically intentional.

The Family: God's Primary Learning Community

Judges 2:6–15 describes one of the saddest situations in all Scripture. It is a description that trumpets the importance of the family in what God is doing on earth. In this account we are told that the very first generation of Israelites who grew up in the promised land "did not know the LORD or the work that he had done for Israel" (v. 10). Let the words sink in. They ought to shock us! The *first* generation of children who grew up in the land God had given them did not know who God was and did not know about the amazing things he had done to deliver and sustain his people!

How could this have happened? How could Israelite children not know about God? How could they not know about the plagues, the Red Sea, Mount Sinai, water from rocks, and manna from heaven? What went wrong? How could Israelite children grow up comfortably worshiping other gods?

Did the prophets of Israel fail to do their job? Were the priests negligent? No, the failure was not there. The fundamental failure was a failure of the family to do what God intended it to do.

As Israel was preparing to enter the land of promise, God took time to talk about his purposes for the family. Deuteronomy 6 records God's plan. God essentially says this: "I have designed the family to be my primary learning community. There is no better context to teach the truths that need to be taught so that my people live the way they should live." God says, "You live with your children. You are there when they lie down; you are there when they rise up. Teach your children; the family is your classroom."

Parents have opportunities to instruct their children that no one else has, because parents live with their children. God commands us to make the most of these opportunities. Capitalize on the searching question that is asked just as you are tucking your child into bed. Make the most of the morning complaint that you feel you don't have time to deal with. Ask your school-age child what her day was like, but do it at the kitchen table over an afternoon snack rather than quickly greeting her as she comes through the door. Turn off the car radio and engage your children in conversation.

Parents have a platform for instruction that no one else has, because the family is radically different from the classroom as a setting for learning. The classroom is separate from life. In classrooms we go to elaborate lengths to recreate life so that we can study it. But family life *is* life! In the family, life is brought not only to our doorstep but into our kitchens, bedrooms, and dens. In the family, life is happening all around us, and it begs to be questioned, evaluated, interpreted, and discussed. There is no more consistent, pregnant, dynamic forum for instruction about life than the family, because that is exactly what God designed the family to be: a learning community.

The creator God who rules over all things, in whom are hidden all the treasures of wisdom and knowledge, who reveals himself in the world he made and the Word he inspired, has called parents to be his primary teachers. It is our responsibility to make sure that the family, no matter what else it does, functions as an effective learning community. This means that every moment of conflict, doubt, confusion, difficulty, unity, division, joy, sorrow, work, leisure, obedience, rebellion, hope, fear, laughter, authority, and submission that makes up family life must be seen as a teaching moment. Here it is—every moment of family life is a teaching moment! This is what makes the family a vital tool for the work the Redeemer is doing on earth.

Unlike in the classroom, teaching in the family happens spontaneously. There are no lesson plans, workbooks, or rows of desks. You have to live prepared. The moment may come on the way to the hardware store when the little boy asks if God made telephone poles. Or it may come as the teenager mutters in the bathroom that she hates her face so much she is embarrassed to leave the house. God calls us to grab the opportunities and teach, teach, teach.

Getting to Know the Students

If you are going to function as God's instrument in the life of your teen, you need to know that God intended the family to be his primary learning community, parents to be his primary teachers, and family life to be the context for life instruction to take place. Once you understand that, the next question to ask is "Who are the students?" It is not enough to say that the students are our children. We need to have a biblical description of who those children are. A good teacher not only knows his material well but knows his students well too. So it is with parenting. The more accurate our understanding of our children, the more successful we will be at doing what God has called us to do.

The Bible describes our children in a host of ways, but four descriptions are most essential. Once parents understand these, their teaching task begins to take shape.

Children Are Covenantal Beings

When the Bible declares that children are covenantal beings, it means that children were made for a relationship with God. They were made to know, love, serve, and obey him. Children were not made to live autonomous, self-oriented, self-directed, and self-sufficient lives. God purposed for everything a child thinks, does, and says to be done in loving submission to him. This is the first and greatest commandment according to Christ (Matt. 22:37–38). This is the most foundational thing that can be said about the identity of children.

The Bible says something further. It says that if children are not living in joyful submission to God, they are living in submission to someone or something else (Rom. 1:18–32). You cannot divide children into two groups: those who worship and those who do not. *Every* child is a worshiper. The question is what he worships. Everything a child does, everything he desires, every thought he thinks, every choice he makes, and every relationship he pursues is an expression of worship. When brother and sister fight over who gets the best seat, or when a teenager wants to die because of lack of peer acceptance, worship is being expressed. There is a vertical, godward dimension to every horizontal, interpersonal action.

Children are worshipers, and their lives are shaped and controlled by whatever they worship. That means that every moment is a God moment. In every moment, a child either accepts her role as a creature and lives in worshipful obedience to God or exchanges God for some aspect of the created world she is living to get. Children don't typically think of themselves this way (nor do their parents!), so they need us to faithfully point out to them the covenantal nature of their actions. There is no more important piece of the Bible's job description for parents.

Children Are Social Beings

Children were not only created for relationship with God; they were created for relationships with other people. This is the second great commandment (Matt. 22:39). Children were made for community. God always talks of people as people in relationship. The self-sufficient, self-made individualism of Western culture is foreign to Scripture. A person's goal in life is not to be a healthy individual but to be a person living in community with other people who are living in community with God!

From the very first moment of his life, a child has a moral responsibility to the people around him. He is called to love others as he does himself. Everything the child does expresses either a submission to God's call to community or a rejection of it. Sinners don't do community well. By their very nature, they are self-oriented. Sin flows out of self-worship. So sinful children living in a fallen world struggle with God's design for community.

I have never seen a child eye the last chocolate donut and say to a sibling, "I love chocolate donuts, but there is something that would give me more pleasure than eating it myself. I would enjoy it so much to know that you got the last donut and that it brought you pleasure." No, children get nervous as they watch the donut pile dwindle. They ask, "Is anybody still hungry?" "Who had the other chocolate donut?" "How many of you have had three donuts already?" Each question is born out of self-interest, out of the fear that someone else may get what they want.

When the last donut arrives on someone's plate, the tumult begins. The self-pitying child cries that nobody loves her and it's not fair. The lawyer child argues the injustice of the situation, given what has happened the last four times they had donuts. (Who remembers?!) The fatalistic child says he hates having donuts because this always happens.

Sinners struggle with God's call to love, so community must be a consistent emphasis in our homes. For a sinner, to love her neighbor as herself seems like a radical command. (And it is!) It argues against everything within her.

This hit me years ago as a kindergarten teacher. I never had to teach the children to hit one another, be jealous, speak unkindly, push to the front of the line, announce that their lunch was better than their neighbors', brag about their achievements, and turn everything into a competition. But I spent hours trying to turn that room of selfish sinners into a loving community where learning could thrive.

Such is the life of a parent. Much of your work is to help your children to live in loving community with one another, recognizing that God created them to be social beings but that sin replaces their love for others with an idolatrous love of self.

Children Are Interpreters

The Bible has so much to say about the way we think because it is such an important part of who we are as creatures made in God's image. Let me propose something that may shock you: all children think. Some of them show it more than others, but all children think, and the thoughts of their hearts shape the way they live their lives. For that reason, the Bible highlights the importance of what we are thinking. The Bible talks about truth and falsehood, wisdom and foolishness, belief and unbelief, revelation and human tradition, light and darkness, and good and evil. God says there is a right way and a wrong way to think about life, and whatever you think about life shapes the way you act.

What does it mean to say that children think? It means that children seek to make sense out of life. They try to organize, interpret, and explain the things that go on around them and inside them. Children are incessant interpreters, and they respond to life not on the basis of the facts but on the basis of the sense they have made out of those facts.

When my teenage daughter yelled from the door of her bedroom, "Someone stole my book bag!" this was not a statement of fact but an interpretation of the facts. In this case, it was a wonderfully self-serving interpretation of the facts. It was easier for her to believe that there was a book-bag snatcher in our house than for her to face the possibility that she was responsible for its disappearance. I helped her to understand that she was interpreting and explained how that interpretation served her. We found the book bag about three feet from where she was standing, under the clothes of yesteryear.

The Bible says not only that human beings are interpreters but that we need God's revelation, his truth, to interpret life correctly. That is why he gave us his Word. The very first thing God did after he created Adam and Eve was talk to them, explaining the meaning and purpose of their lives. Why did God do this? Because although they were perfect people living in a perfect world in perfect relationship with him, he knew they would not figure out life on their own. Adam and Eve needed God's words to make sense of their world. The same is true for our children.

In Genesis 3, another interpreter comes on the scene: the serpent. The serpent took the same facts that God had told Adam and Eve and gave them a very different interpretation. If Adam and Eve decided to believe the serpent's interpretation, they would be stupid to continue to obey God! They did listen, they did believe, and the result was the fall of the world into sin.

Like their first parents, children are incessantly interpreting. The sense they make out of life is based on truth or falsehood, and it will shape everything they do. Parents who understand this do everything they can to get their children to think out loud and to instill in them a distinctively biblical view of life. They realize that this is usually not done in formal times of instruction, such as family worship, but spontaneously as issues come up in the course of family life.

As important as daily family devotions are, they are not enough. It is vital that as we live in the mundane moments of life with our children, we teach them to see life from God's perspective. Parents who understand that their children are not simply reacting to facts but interpreting facts in ways that give them a particular shape and meaning ask good questions and are good listeners. For them, family conversation takes on a whole new meaning and purpose.

Children Behave Out of the Heart

Most of the parents I have worked with want their children to do what is right. Their goal is to control, direct, or guide the behavior of their children. To them, this is Christian parenting. So John, who has gotten poor grades, is forbidden to watch television until his grades are better, and Elisabeth, who didn't return her sister's blouse after she borrowed it without asking, is told that she cannot borrow anyone's clothes for six weeks. Solutions? Yes, outwardly, but there is no change of heart.

To emphasize behavior seems right and biblical, but it is not enough to place behavioral boundaries around a child. Is behavior important? Does God call us to be holy as he is holy? Are we called to obey? The answer to each of these questions is yes, but more needs to be said. Scripture not only calls us to obey but also tells us what controls our behavior: the heart. Luke 6:43–45 says,

> No good tree bears bad fruit, nor again does a bad tree bear good fruit, for each tree is known by its own fruit. For figs are not gathered from thornbushes, nor are grapes picked from a bramble bush. The good person out of the good treasure of his heart produces good, and the evil person out of his evil treasure produces evil, for out of the abundance of the heart his mouth speaks.

Like all of us, children behave out of the heart. The particular behavior discussed in Luke 6 is a person's communication, but the principle applies to all human behavior. The thoughts and motives of the heart shape the way a child acts. If the child believes things that are not true and desires what is wrong, there is no way she will do what is right.

The goal of parenting, therefore, is to focus not on getting the right behavior but on shepherding the hearts of our children. We must always seek to be used by God to expose the heart. We need to ask *why* Elisabeth thinks it is her right to take others' possessions without permission and with no sense of obligation to return them. What is it about the way she thinks about herself and others that makes this acceptable to her conscience? Or *why* is John, a bright teenager, getting such poor grades? We need to realize that his grades are a window into the thoughts and motives of his heart. What desires lead him to use the time he needs for studying on things of much less importance? We need to examine how he justifies his irresponsibility to himself. Heart response and heart change are our focus because we know that what controls the heart controls the life.

Let me use Christ's metaphor, the tree, to draw out the importance of this truth in understanding our task with our teenagers.

Pretend with me that I have a big apple tree in my backyard and that every year it buds and grows apples. But just as the apples are ready to be picked, they rot and fall to the ground. After several seasons of this, my wife says, "You know, Paul, it doesn't make much sense to have an apple tree and never be able to eat the apples. All we ever end up with is brown mush on our lawn. Can't you do something with our apple tree?" So I ponder for a while and come up with an idea. I tell my wife I am going to fix our tree and I will be gone for about an hour.

Before long I return to the yard carrying a stepladder, a pair of branch cutters, an industrial-grade stapler, and two bushels of apples. I carefully cut all the rotten apples off the tree and staple bright Red Delicious apples to it. Delighted that I have fixed the problem, I call my wife out to the yard to look at the tree.

Ridiculous? Yes! I have not solved the problem. The problem is more than a fruit problem. There is something fundamentally wrong with the tree itself, even to the level of its roots, that needs to change. I have exchanged good fruit for bad fruit, but the tree itself is still unable to produce healthy fruit. What's more, the fruit I have stapled to the tree cannot last because it is not connected to healthy roots that can give it life.

I am convinced that much of what we have called Christian parenting is nothing more or less than "fruit stapling." It is an artificial attempt to replace fruit with fruit. It focuses only on ways of changing behavior. It doesn't hunger to know and shepherd the hearts of our children. This "sin is bad, don't do it" brand of parenting forgets that sin is not only a matter of behavior but a matter of the thoughts and motives of the heart as well. It fails to recognize that if the heart does not change, any behavioral changes that take place are temporary and cosmetic, because they are not attached to roots in the heart.

Christ recognized this when he discussed the nature of adultery in the Sermon on the Mount, recorded in Matthew 5:27–28. Christ gave thoughts and desires the moral value of actions as he declared that adultery not only includes the physical act of sexual unfaithfulness but includes the lusts of the heart as well. Christ put the boundaries not at the level of behavior but at the level of the heart. As parents, we must do the same. Our ultimate goal is that God would effectively and functionally rule the hearts of our children. We work in every parental encounter as his instruments to make this happen. We cannot be satisfied with the fruit-stapling agenda of controlling behavior.

THE SUCCESSFUL PARENT UNDERSTANDS THAT the family is God's primary learning community. It is uniquely positioned by God to consistently and effectively communicate truth. Parents are God's primary teachers. If you want to do your God-given job well, then you'll want to know your students, your children. You will take the Bible's descriptions of your children seriously and seek to understand how those descriptions shape the way you approach your teaching task. This is what we will do in the next chapter.

Questions for Reflection and Discussion

1. If family is the primary learning community, what are your children primarily learning within your family? How are you taking advantage of the teaching moments afforded by your role as a parent?
2. What ordinary moments within your family routine might become teachable moments as you prayerfully watch for them?
3. If every child is worshipping something, what can you observe about your own teenager's heart? Does your child have an awareness

of what rules his or her heart? How can you gently convict your teenager about his or her skewed desires and turn him or her in the direction of Jesus—the only one who can truly satisfy?

4. In what ways has your family modeled what it looks like to live in community, Christian and otherwise? How has your sin been a barrier to community?

5. Children constantly interpret the world around them. How might you encourage yours to interpret their own worlds out loud, so that you can help to guide their thoughts from a biblical perspective?

6. When have you noticed yourself primarily concerned with your teenager's behavior instead of identifying the motivations of his or her heart? Consider your own sin as an example—what might be some of the deeper motivations behind why you do what you do?

4

What Is a Family? A Job Description

IF YOU ARE GOING TO TAKE a long trip, you need to know more than where you are going and how you're going to get there. You need to know a lot about the vehicle that will transport you. If, for some strange reason, you knew you were to travel to California, but you did not know how to start, stop, or fuel your car, there is no way you would reach your destination. The same is true for us as we parent our teenagers. If we are ever going to reach God's goals for us, we need an accurate understanding of his vehicle for doing that: the family.

In the previous chapter we defined the family as God's primary learning community. We recognized that the family provides the most consistent, comprehensive context for teaching children a distinctively biblical perspective on life. As parents, we must understand the implications of accepting our role as God's primary educators.

Perhaps you understand that the family is a learning community but are not sure how to teach God's truth in everyday life. When Joey is mocked because of his sneakers, how do you make that a teaching moment? When Sarah tells you at 9:45 p.m. that she needs poster board for a project that is due the next morning, how do you make the most of this teaching opportunity? When Josh stands in front of a well-stocked refrigerator and says there is nothing to eat, how do you capitalize on that moment? When Olivia walks in with green hair that she has just dyed with lime Jell-O at her friend's house, what truths do you teach?

I am convinced that we miss these dynamic moments because we don't know what to talk about. Our Christianity often becomes fuzzier the closer it gets to real-life, everyday experience, so we clumsily throw out-of-context Bible passages at our children in the hope that they will somehow motivate them to do what is right.

Three fundamental themes are present in some way in every human situation: (1) the existence of God and our obligations to him, (2) our responsibility to truly love our neighbors, and (3) the beauty and power of the gospel in the face of our sin. The Bible has much to say about these themes, and they should form the content of our teaching interactions with our children. With these themes in view, we will see that the family's function ought to be theological, sociological, and redemptive.

The Family as a Theological Community

It is God's plan that the family function as a theological community. Theology is the study of God, his existence, his nature, and his works. A family should be grounded in the truths that God exists and we are his creatures. Everything we do, think, and say is attached to these truths. We must never allow ourselves to view life horizontally—that is, only in terms of earthly relationships and circumstances. We must ask questions about God, his will, and his work no matter the subject or situation under discussion.

The goal of all this is to root our children's identity in the existence and glory of God. We want our children to understand that they were made by him, belong to him, and are called to live for his glory. We are called by God to *do* theology, that is, to live our lives with a moment-by-moment consciousness of God. He is the reality that gives sense and shape to every other fact we discuss and consider.

In Deuteronomy 6:20–25, the task of rooting our children's identity in the existence and work of God is placed in an everyday life context. A son comes to his father and says, "Dad, why do we have to obey all these rules?" Many parents have answered that question with "Do it because I told you to do it!" or "Do it or else!" Moses calls us to something very different. He calls us to see the opportunity within the question. He instructs us to tell the child that he is a child of a God of redemption. To tell him how God harnessed the forces of nature to fulfill his promises to his people. To tell him that God gave us his rules for our good, that his way is a pathway of blessing. To root his identity in the soil of the glory and goodness of God.

The Teacher in Ecclesiastes says it this way: "Meaningless! Meaningless! . . . Utterly meaningless! Everything is meaningless . . . under the sun" (Eccl. 1:2–3 NIV). These are powerful words that every parent needs to consider. If you cut out the heavens and act as if God doesn't exist, if you look at life only horizontally, everything loses its meaning. The Teacher in Ecclesiastes says that all labor, wisdom, achievement, pleasure, success, and toil are utterly meaningless unless they are connected to God. If there is no God who is glorious and good, who rules the earth, who has a plan, and whose will is to be done, there is no reason for anything. Why think, work, obey, love, study, discuss, serve, or give? Why? All life blows into a chaotic mass of meaningless choices unless it is rooted in the one fact that makes every other fact make sense: God. This truth must dye every encounter with our children as red dye permeates every fiber of a white cloth dipped into it.

To say that the family is a theological community means that we are always theologizing. We are always viewing everything in reference to God: who he is, what he is doing, and what he wants us to be and do. There are no unattached moments. All the stuff of our lives connects to him.

Let's talk about what to say as we theologize with our children.

Every Moment Is God's Moment

We must never allow our children to believe in a God who is distant and uninvolved, who comes to the rescue only when he hears our cries in prayer. The Bible presents God as someone who is near and active in our lives. The psalmist says that he is a "very present help in trouble" (Ps. 46:1). There is no divine emergency telephone line because God is already here and already active. There is never a moment in which God is absent or inactive. There is no situation, location, or relationship that he does not rule.

Paul told the Athenians that God rules his world in such a way that "he is actually not far from each one of us" so that we will "seek God, and perhaps feel [our] way toward him and find him" (Acts 17:27). God is near. God is involved. This moment is his moment in which he is actively accomplishing his will. What is most important in this moment is not what we desire, but what he is doing. Teenagers mistakenly believe that what they desire is most important. They see their desires as needs and express these "needs" as demands, questioning our love if we fail to meet them. We must be faithful to turn their eyes from what they desire to what God requires.

Paul says to the Romans that "for those who love God all things work together for good" (Rom. 8:28). In every situation, in every problem, in every location, in every relationship, every time, God is at work. Every moment is God's moment.

My son stood in front of the store window and said, "I just have to have those shoes! Dad, I need them!" I looked at his feet to make sure he wasn't barefoot. I knew that he had more shoes at home. What did he mean when he said that he needed those shoes?

Teenagers don't tend to live with a functional God-consciousness. They are filled with a sense of self. They know quite well what they want out of the moments of life, and they tend to wallow in self-pity, grumble and complain, or burst out in anger when their will is not done. They tend to forget God and his will. They tend to reduce life to each moment of desire. Teenagers don't tend to deal well with disappointment; they tend to live with a sense of entitlement. This means that teenagers tend to be incredibly focused on the horizontal and the present. They need us to direct them toward God, his existence, his character, and his will.

Always a Higher Agenda

In every situation of family life, there is always something more important than what we plan, desire, want, or are working for. There is always a higher purpose and a higher agenda. The higher purpose is the will of God, and the higher agenda is that we would live to please him. This means that he, rather than ourselves and our happiness, is to be the focus and reason for all we do.

If you would ask most teenagers what they want out of life, most of them would tell you that they just want to be happy. What is scary about this is not only that their definition of happiness changes almost hourly, but that there is no higher focus than their own pleasure. The "whose pleasure" question needs to be asked by parents in every situation until it is the instinctive heart response of the teenager.

My son came in one day from school with his head hanging. I asked him what was wrong, and he said, "Nothing." I told him that he was not very convincing, that obviously something was bothering him. I expressed my love for him and told him I would love to talk with him when he was ready. Later that evening, I approached him. I asked him how he was doing and told him that he had really looked discouraged earlier. He blurted out, "No one wants to be friends with a kid who has character! All the popular kids at school are jerks. They are the center of attention, they get all the girls, and here I am, a nice guy who can be trusted, and I have no friends! I'd be better off being a jerk! What sense does it make to be good if nobody notices?"

What a great moment to talk about a higher agenda! We talked about living to please God. We looked at Psalm 73, where the psalmist, too, was convinced that the wrong guys were winning. We talked about the fact that Somebody noticed. We talked of the fallenness of our world and how wrong gets applauded and right gets mocked or ignored. We made connections between the existence, glory, and plan of God and my son's high school experience. We talked about God's purpose in putting him through that trial. We had that same talk, in different situations, over and over again. We need to call our teenagers away from their own glory to a concrete understanding of what it means to live for God's glory.

Their Story in God's Story

Modern Christians have wrongly attempted to handle the Bible as if it were an encyclopedia of religious thought. We tend to have a "where can I find a verse on . . ." approach to Scripture. This approach robs the Bible of its vitality, its genius. The Bible is not put together like an encyclopedia that is organized by topic. For instance, you would not understand what the Bible has to say about marriage, government, sex, parenting, communication, work, money, the church, and so on if you looked at verses on those topics in isolation. Whatever you learned would be distorted when taken out of context because these verses cannot be understood separately from what the Bible is really all about.

The Bible is not a topical index, a dictionary, or an encyclopedia. The Bible is a *storybook*. It is God's story, the story of his character, his creation, his redemption of this fallen world, and his sovereign plan for the ages. It is the one true and unalterable story. It is *the* story. All other stories of people and nations find their life, meaning, and hope in this story. This grand, universal story is what gives all of us a reason to get up in the morning and do what we have been called to do.

To theologize with your teenagers does not mean you are to throw in an occasional Scripture verse that relates to the topic at hand. Rather, it means that every day, in every way possible, you are to embed the story of your teenager in the larger story of God. Teens live overwhelmed by their own story. They tend to live with such angst. The drama of the particular moment seems like the most significant thing in history! When we seek to help them to see that it is not as significant as they think, they fire back the quintessential "You just don't understand!"

It is the present power of their story that often gets teenagers into so much trouble. They lose focus. They live only for what they can get out of each moment. They tend to live driven by their own desires and enslaved to a quest for personal happiness. In this quest for satisfied desire and personal pleasure, they often make decisions they live to regret.

Teenagers desperately need to see the larger story. They need to see their lives as part of something that is bigger and more important than their own happiness. They need to live for a glory that is bigger than their own glory. They need to embed their story every day in the story of God. This will give them a reason to do what is right. This will give them hope. This will give them strength to endure what God calls them to endure.

The Bible has much to say about all the topics mentioned earlier, but what it has to say makes sense only when seen from the vantage point of the glorious story of God and his work. We have to be very careful that we do not "de-God" the commands and principles of Scripture. He stands in power and glory behind every one. Every command looks to him for strength to obey, every principle looks to him for wisdom, and every promise looks to him for its fulfillment. The whole system depends on the truthfulness of the story.

This is what teenagers need to understand about life. There is a God. He is alive and active! His story and his work are recorded in the Bible. The most important thing in life is to live in tune with what he is doing. As God's child, I become part of his grand, universal plan. I become part of what he is doing on earth. This is what gives meaning and purpose to whatever drama I may be living right now! As parents, we need to be faithful every day to embed the stories of our teenagers in the story of God. We must teach them always to ask questions such as

- Who is God?
- What is he doing?
- What has he promised?
- What does he command?
- How will these facts shape the way I think about and respond to the daily situations of life?

Trust and Obey

Finally, approaching the family as a theological community means getting very practical about what it means to follow God in the mundane, everyday situations of life. We don't do very many grand and significant things in our lives. Most of us will not be written up in history books. Most of us will be remembered only by family and a few friends and forgotten two or three generations after our deaths. Thus we need to teach our children to take this godward focus into the most mundane moments of life—to live for God where they live every day, in all those unspectacular moments at home, at school, or with friends.

Two questions, if regularly asked, bring God into every one of those moments. We should ask them of our teenagers until they learn to ask them of themselves. They are summarized by the words *trust* and *obey*.

Let me start with the second word. We want our teenagers to have a heart for God. We want them to have the goal of living to please him. So we must encourage them to ask in every situation, "What, in this situation, are the things that God calls me to do that I cannot pass on to anyone else?" This question requires them to be concrete and specific in the way they think about their calling from God. Once the teenager has biblically clarified those responsibilities, the only proper response is to obey.

The word *trust* points teenagers to the fact that they have limits. There are things in every situation that need to change yet are outside a teenager's control. They are not his responsibility because they are beyond his ability. These areas must be entrusted to God. So we need to get our teens to ask this question: "What, in this situation, are the things I need to entrust to God's capable and loving hands?"

Teenagers (and adults!) tend to get these areas confused. They try to do things that are God's job, and they forget to do the things that he has called them to do. A daughter said to her mom, "If it's the last thing I ever do, I am going to teach my brother that he had better stay out of my room. I'll get him to respect me and my stuff one way or the other." Although she didn't realize it, she was dead set on doing God's work and forgetting to do the simple things that God had called her to do during times of mistreatment. She would reap the disaster of attempting to do what only God can do.

The family is a theological community, so we need to teach our children that every moment is God's moment. There is always a higher agenda than their personal happiness; there is a bigger, more significant story than their story of the moment; and, in every situation, they are called to trust and obey God. The Christian family doesn't just think theologically on Sundays; it *does* theology from Sunday to Sunday.

The Family as a Sociological Community

Just as teenagers need us to root their identity in the character and existence of God, they also need us to root their identity in community. Sinners are rugged individualists. Sinners want to sing with Frank Sinatra, "I did it my way!" They are filled with a sense of self. Their thoughts are dominated by what they need and what they want. Sinners are people who are led around by the cravings of their sinful nature (Eph. 2:3). Sinners want their will to be done, and they fight whoever gets in their way. Consequently, sinners are much better at making war than they are at making peace (James 4:1–10), much better at hatred than they are at love. They are much better at causing division than they are at creating unity.

We have all experienced this in our homes. Sadly, because of sin, conflict is the norm. No, I don't mean those knock-down, drag-out fights—I mean people struggling to get along. Competition goes on where it shouldn't, unkind words are spoken, selfish acts are done, and anger is expressed. Conflict infects many of our family moments. The conflict exists because, as sinners, we tend to make our own good our highest good and the people around us seem always to be in our way.

How different life looks when we approach it biblically! You see, God's story is not just the story of his character and his work of redemption; it is also the story of his calling together a people to be the people of God. It is the story of his forming a community of love where all the old dividing lines of race, gender, nation, and economic class are broken down and God's people live as one new man in Christ (Eph. 2:11–22). A successful person in God's eyes is a person who not only loves God but also really does love his neighbor as himself.

There is no more fundamental, readily available, consistent context than the family in which to teach what it means to live in community. The family *is* a community, and it models a view of community whether it realizes it or not. The family teaches and models what it means to love your neighbor as yourself, or it violates that standard at every point and teaches a self-centered individualism. Powerful messages about the nature of relationships are taught in the way Mom and Dad talk to one another, serve one another, make decisions, and deal with their differences. It is impossible for a family to escape teaching and modeling some functional philosophy of relationship for its children.

The family is called to be the context in which what it means to love your neighbor as yourself is self-consciously taught at every turn. There are daily opportunities to do not only first-great-commandment instruction but second-great-commandment instruction as well. At the same time, amid our frenetic schedules it is very easy for us to rush by the opportunities, enforcing surface solutions rather than dealing with issues of the heart.

A mom and dad once told me that their two teenage sons constantly fought over the stereo in the family room. These fights had gotten so ugly that they had even broken a piece of furniture as they tussled over who was going play his CD. The parents' solution, which they proudly shared with me, was to devise a weekly schedule of stereo time for each son. They no longer had any conflict, and in that way the problem had been solved. But they had missed a God-given opportunity to talk about the significant issue of the heart: loving your neighbor as yourself. In arriving at a human, second-best solution, these parents had missed a God-given opportunity to shine the light of the second great commandment on the moment.

This is what Christ called "the weightier matters of the law" (Matt. 23:23). He rebuked the Pharisees for emphasizing doable behavior while neglecting fundamental issues of the heart such as justice, mercy, and faithfulness. Yet parents often respond to a situation caused by heart problems by enforcing some doable standard. This creates an instant situational fix yet leaves the more important heart issues unexposed and unchanged.

Proverbs 20:5 says, "The purpose in a man's heart is like deep water, but a man of understanding will draw it out." When selfishness, individualism, and demandingness create conflict, strife, and tension in our homes, we must thank God for the opportunity to deal with something that he has said is second in importance only to our relationship to him. If we are truly thankful, we will not opt for quick, surface solutions but will work to uncover the issues of the heart that are the real reason for the conflict.

There is no better place to do this than the family. Here children are called by God to love people with whom they did not choose to live. Here they cannot escape daily responsibilities to give, to love, and to serve. Almost everything around them must be shared. Here their desires will often conflict with another's plans. Here they will face the utter impossibility, apart from the help of Christ, of loving one's neighbor as oneself.

A teen's responses to others will be shaped by the *rule of love*: "Whatever you wish that others would do to you, do also to them" (Matt. 7:12). Or her responses will be shaped by the *rule of desire*: "What causes quarrels and what causes fights among you? Is it not this, that your passions are at war within you? You desire and do not have, so you murder. You covet and cannot obtain, so you fight and quarrel" (James 4:1–2).

In the family, the teenager's true heart toward relationships is consistently exposed. In this context, situation after situation reveals what is ruling the heart. The fight over the last drop of milk at breakfast, the shove in response to the accidental bump in the hallway, the argument over time spent in the bathroom, the discussion over borrowed clothes that weren't returned, the debate as to who gets the car, the put-down humor, the demand for assistance that is coupled with an unwillingness to help others, the lack of willing and spontaneous participation in the work of the home, the escalating duel of cruel words, and a myriad of other situations must not be viewed as the hassles of family life. These are the moments when God calls us to something greater than our own comfort and ease—to love our children with a second-great-commandment love, so that we are willing to take the time to do the second-great-commandment parenting that they so desperately need. At such moments, we need to be ruled not by the rule of personal desire but by God's rule of love, not giving in to quick, surface solutions that give us the quiet we want but rather working to form in our children the heart of Christlike love that God requires.

The Family as a Redemptive Community

Life in all its harsh realities plays out in the context of the family. Because of sin, the family is a place of unfulfilled promises, broken dreams, and disappointed expectations. The boyfriend who seemed so sensitive and attentive becomes the husband who is distant and uninvolved. The girlfriend who seemed so joyful and happy becomes the wife who is bitter and discontent. The child who seemed so sweet and responsive becomes rebellious and distant. The couple who swore that they would never repeat the failures of their parents realize they are saying and doing the very things they repudiated.

We need to face the fact that the harsh realities of the fall are depicted in everyday family life. This humble admission opens us up to one of the most wonderful functions of the Christian family, for when we humbly face the reality of our fallenness we begin to seek and treasure the riches of the grace of the Lord Jesus Christ. As we—parents and children alike—face our need as sinners, the family becomes a truly redemptive community in which grace, forgiveness, deliverance from sin, reconciliation, new life in Christ, and hope become the central themes of family life.

When God reveals sin, the Christian has only two possible responses. One is to generate some system of self-justification to make wrong desires and behavior acceptable to your own conscience. The other is to admit your sin, confess it to God and man, and place yourself once again under the justifying mercy of Christ. Parents who do the former do not have homes that function as redemptive communities. They unwittingly teach their children to hide their sin, to explain it away, to deny its existence, or to blame others for it. Parents who do the latter teach their children to rely on Christ, to confess their sin, and to believe that where sin abounds, grace abounds even more. They teach their children to grow up to be people of hope who have seen and believe that there is no pit so deep that Jesus cannot reach them!

The key to the family's functioning as a redemptive community, a family that is held together by the glue of the gospel, is parents who so trust in Christ that they are ready and willing to confess their faults to their children. Often, even the way parents talk about their childhoods is self-righteous and intimidating. "In my day," they say, "I never would have even considered . . ." It is easy for parents to relate to their children like the Pharisee praying in the temple saying, "I thank God I am not like other men" (see Luke 18:9–14). However, parents who admit their sin position themselves to model the gospel for their children daily.

If we are not compromising God's standards by accepting a human, second-best standard, God's law reveals sin. Scripture talks of the Word as a light, as a teacher to lead us to Christ, and as a mirror in which we see ourselves. As parents faithfully hold themselves and their children to God's high standard, children begin to see their utter need for Christ.

One night I walked by my daughter's room and heard the sound of crying. I went in and asked her what was wrong. In tears, she said, "Daddy, I can't do it, I can't do what you are asking me. It's just impossible!" I asked her to explain what she meant. She said, "You tell me that I should want to share with my brothers, but I don't. When you tell me to give them something of mine, I do, but I hate it and I am mad at you for asking me and mad at them for taking it! I don't want to share, I hate it! It's impossible to enjoy!" When she said these words, she burst into tears once again.

In her room that night, she began to experience something wonderful—the fact that there is no possibility of righteousness by the doing of the law. She began to realize that in her own strength, by the exercise of her own will, she could not obey God. In her room that night, she began to cry out for Christ. She began to see that he was her only hope. A struggle to share that wasn't covered over by some cosmetic human solution became the context in which Christ the Redeemer was revealed.

As the Word is held high as the standard for the family, sin is revealed for what it is. It is only then that the message of redemption in Christ Jesus makes any sense. As the Holy Spirit works through the faithful ministry of parents who forsake their own desire for comfort and ease, proud, self-defensive, self-excusing, self-righteous children become seekers after grace.

We know our children will be sinned against in our homes. They live in families populated by sinners who are not yet fully sanctified. They will hear unkind words, and they will see unloving behavior. They will experience the selfishness of others, and they will be the objects of others' irritation and anger. We need to greet these experiences with the message of redemption. We must teach our children that there is a Redeemer who forgives, delivers, reconciles, and restores. We model this when we do more than tell our fighting children to go to their rooms and leave one another alone. We model this as we require them to face one another, deal with their differences, confess sin, ask for forgiveness, and restore relationships. In so doing we teach the gospel, we testify to the presence and power of the Redeemer, and we instruct our children to be people of hope even in a fallen world.

We also know our children will experience their own sin. Cutting, hurtful words will come flying out of their mouths. Laziness and irresponsibility will be revealed. They will respond in selfishness rather than love. They will rebel rather than submit, and they will take rather than give. Each of these experiences is an opportunity to *do* redemption, that is, to bring our children to the one place of hope and help, the Lord Jesus Christ.

Often we miss these opportunities because we are too busy solving the problem at hand. We expend our energies trying to keep the siblings from fighting rather than exposing the sin behind the quarrel and leading them to Christ to experience his forgiveness and help as they seek him in confession and repentance. We also miss these opportunities because we see our children's sins as personal affronts. We get caught up in our own hurt and anger. Instead of words of hope and grace, we lash out with angry words of regret ("I wish for once you'd get your act together!") or words of condemnation ("You'll never change!").

We must not distance ourselves from the sins of our children as if they have a problem to which we can't relate. We need to identify with them. We, too, are sinners. Sin is a human condition. It is a problem that resides in our very nature. None of us is free of the disease. There is no sin that our children will ever commit that we are not capable of as well. As we admit that we are alike, we portray a personal excitement about the gospel, because it is our only hope as well. We don't respond with a "How could you?" or "Why would you?" We parent with a humble awareness of our own sin. We understand the how and why of sin, because we have been there and we *would* be there apart from the glorious grace of the Lord Jesus Christ.

We do not want to communicate to our children that they would be better off if they could somehow be like us! God forbid! Rather, we need to say that it is only through Christ that we have experienced any freedom from the things with which they now struggle. We must be willing to share our sin struggles with them so that the mercy of Christ is revealed through our story (see Paul's example in 2 Corinthians 1:8–11).

We know, too, that our children will face the fallenness and broken-ness of the world. Paul says in Romans 8 that the whole world groans as it waits for redemption (v. 22). Our children will experience a world of unfulfilled promises, shattered relationships, failed institutions, corrupted government, selfish ambition, wanton violence, and broken families. They will experience the temptations, lies, and schemes of the Enemy. They live in a world in which there really is a devil who seeks to devour them. They will be surprised and tricked. They will struggle with hurt, fear, disap-pointment, and discouragement. They will have myriad reasons for cyni-cism and hopelessness.

We will not be able to shelter them from the fallenness of their world. We cannot act as if it does not exist, because everywhere they look, they will see brokenness. Here too we must bring the gospel. This world is not a place of unmitigated chaos. Over all the brokenness rules the risen Christ, who reigns over all things for the sake of his people. He is bringing an end to all sin, sorrow, and suffering. What we face here is not comparable to the glories of eternity. There is hope! We need to find practical ways to communicate this hope to our children. There is more and better to come. There is reason to continue.

In the face of sin within and sin without, in the face of the world, the flesh, and the devil, the family needs to function as a redemptive community, humbly admitting the reality of sin. We must also consistently and expectantly point to the amazing reality of the grace of the risen Christ, who rules over all things for the salvation of his people. Each situation in which sin rears its head is an opportunity to teach grace. Each situation in which the Tempter is revealed is an opportunity to point to Christ, who is greater. Each circumstance of failure is an open door for the message of forgiveness and deliverance.

THERE IS NO MORE CONSISTENT, effective learning community than the family. The existence and glory of God, our moral responsibility to love our neighbors, and the hope of the gospel in the face of our sin must be the constant themes that interpret, define, explain, and organize family life.

As parents, we must accept our position as God's primary teachers. It is a high and lifelong calling. There is nothing more important that we will ever do. As we follow God's calling, we will pray for our children what Paul prayed for the Ephesian church:

> . . . having the eyes of your hearts enlightened, that you may know what is the hope to which he has called you, what are the riches of his glorious inheritance in the saints, and what is the immeasurable greatness of his power toward us who believe, according to the working of his great might. (Eph. 1:18–19)

Questions for Reflection and Discussion

1. If we are to point our children to God in every moment, we must practice doing the same for ourselves. Reflect on how you see God's presence and his work in even the most mundane parts of your life.
2. What is a "horizontal" problem or roadblock your teenager is

currently facing? Since every single aspect of our lives is attached to God, how can you reframe this struggle "vertically" for your child?

3. In what ways does your teenager seem overwhelmed with his or her story and place in the world? Reflect on ways you can help to thoroughly embed him or her into God's bigger redemptive story. Look to Scripture as a tool to help you to make this connection for your child.

4. How do the harsh realities of the fall manifest in your family? Pray for God's rescue and grace in those areas. Communicate your hope for redemption to your teenager.

5. Take an honest account of your own impossible sins—sins you can't escape on your own, sins only Jesus can cover. How have you dealt with these sins in the past? Do you self-justify, or do you repent? How might you model repentance for your kids when you fall short as a parent?

6. What struggles from your own life or childhood might be appropriate to share with your teenagers—struggles that show evidence of the mercy, forgiveness, and rescue you received from Jesus? Illustrate to your children the creative and loving ways God is turning all things—even hard things—in your life toward good.

7. Pray that the Lord would shape your family into a redemptive community whose central themes become grace, forgiveness, deliverance from sin, reconciliation, new life in Christ, and hope.

5

Parent, Meet Your Teenager

DO YOU REMEMBER WHAT IT was like to be a teenager? Do you remember your self-consciousness, your physical self-awareness, and your general confusion? Do you remember feeling great about yourself one day and wanting to die the next? Do you remember trying to be cool, only to make a complete fool of yourself? Do you remember doing immature and irresponsible things just at the time you were trying to win your parents' respect? Effective parents of teenagers are people who are able to remember what it was like to live in the scary world of the teen years.

I remember the time I finally got my mom and dad to trust me with the car, only to run out of gas and hitchhike home, leaving the keys in the ignition! I was crushed when my mom told me in elaborate detail how dumb that was.

I remember being in a fast-food restaurant. As I was walking to my table, I noticed three girls entering the restaurant. I had met them a few days before and was excited that they were there. Trying to get their attention as I sat down, I knocked over my soda and poured it on my lap. The girls burst into laughter. All I wanted to do was get out of that restaurant as fast as I could, but the only entrance seemed to be three hundred yards away and getting there meant walking right past the laughing trio! I will never forget that walk to the door. It must have taken three months. I was sure everyone in the place was fixated on the brown root-beer circle on my khaki pants. I had suicidal thoughts in the parking lot that night. I knew that this was it, this was the big one, it was over, I would never be a normal human being! I had failed the test, and they were still laughing!

If parents fail to remember moments like this, if we fail to recognize how huge these events are to our teenagers, we will fail to take them seriously. We will minimize things that are very important to our teenagers. We will miss opportunities to turn these moments into something more than moments of human embarrassment; we will not bring the presence, power, love, and direction of the Redeemer to a crushed and confused young person. We need to get beyond saying, "What difference does it make?" to really communicating to our teenagers that we take them and their world seriously. We want them to know that we are always there to listen to them, love them, support them, and help them. We need to communicate that we will never mock the things they take seriously.

The problem is that teenage crises sneak up on you. I was minding my business one morning when I turned around from the kitchen counter to find my son standing there. Before I had a chance to greet him, he said, "Dad, what do you think of my ears?"

"What do I think of your *ears*?" I thought. I hadn't been thinking about his ears. I hadn't thought about his ears ever. But, all of a sudden, he was very serious about his ears. He could tell I was hesitating, so I wanted to say something quasi-intelligent. "Well," I said, "what do *you* think of them?"

My son had been looking in the mirror that morning, hoping he had grown to look more like a normal human being, when he saw his ears— and they didn't seem to fit his head! I tried to talk to him about the majesty of God's creative ability and the technology of ears, but he wasn't listening. He said, "But, Dad, they're just sort of stuck on the sides of your head. They hang out so far. What do you do with them? Mine don't fit my head! They're so embarrassing, and I'm stuck with them for life!" I've never been particularly opinionated about ears, but that morning I talked longer and more seriously about ears than I had before or have since.

Maybe this is why parents approach adolescence with such apprehension. We don't like the unpredictability, the spontaneity. We get nervous about how quickly things get serious, or how rapidly things can change. So we tend to buy into the survival mentality of the culture and look for another book that will help us cope with teen chaos. I saw a T-shirt recently that said, "Of course I look tired. I have a teenager!"

We will never be able to predict what each day will bring as we raise our teenagers, but the more we understand about the age, the more we will be able to approach this time with a spirit of preparedness rather than a spirit of fear. We must reject the self-centered survivalism that sees success as making it through our children's adolescence with our sanity and our marriages intact. We must settle for nothing less than being instruments in the hands of God, who is doing important things in the lives of our children.

What the Bible Says about Teenagers

We need a biblical understanding of teenagers, but there is a problem. The Bible doesn't say anything about teens! If you looked in your Bible concordance for all the verses on teenagers, you would find none. The period of life that we call adolescence is a fairly recent invention.

Yet, at the same time, the Bible gives us wonderful descriptions of the tendencies of youth. Many of these are found in the book of Proverbs. In Proverbs 1–7, a wise father gives practical life advice to his son and describes the sorts of tendencies we find in our own teenagers. These chapters do not lead to the hopelessness so prevalent in our culture's view of teens. Rather, they simply and wisely orient you to the kinds of struggles you will encounter as you live with your teenager.

Let's look at what Proverbs has to tell us.

No Hunger for Wisdom or Correction

Proverbs emphasizes the value of wisdom and the importance of correction. The father of Proverbs essentially says to his son, "Whatever you get in life, get wisdom! It is more valuable than you will ever know." Proverbs similarly emphasizes the importance of listening and submitting to correction. It goes so far as to say, "He who hates reproof is stupid" (Prov. 12:1). These are heart-revealing emphases for teenagers (and their parents!).

Most teenagers simply don't have a hunger for wisdom. In fact, most think they are much wiser than they are, and they mistakenly believe that their parents have little practical insight to offer them. They tend to think their parents "don't really understand" or are "pretty much out of it." Yet most teenagers sorely lack wisdom and desperately need loving, biblical, faithfully dispensed correction.

Most teenagers don't walk into the family room and say, "You know, Dad, I was just thinking how wise you are and what a good thing it is that God put you in my life so that I could gain wisdom too. I thought I'd come and talk with you for a while and soak up some of the wisdom that you and I both know I desperately need." No, it doesn't happen that way. Teens don't tend to beg for our wisdom. Yet we cannot give in and let them set the agenda for our relationship with them.

Ask yourself if you respond to your teenager in ways that make wisdom appealing. Do you make the taste of correction sweet? I watch parents make correction bitter as they beat their children with demeaning words. Make wisdom attractive. Make correction something to be desired. Don't let your fear of the great what-ifs cause you to try to produce with human control what only God can produce by his grace.

Win your children for wisdom. Be a salesperson for it. You don't do this with nasty, inflammatory confrontations and ugly verbal power struggles. If you hit your kids with a barrage of verbal bullets, they will either run for the bunker or come out firing themselves. No wisdom is imparted that way.

Here is a good rule: deal with yourself before you deal with your teenager (Matt. 7:3–5). Sometimes when I would begin a conversation with one of my teenage children, I would notice my wife waving her hands back and forth at me. No, she was not flagging in ships. She was telling me that I was not ready to have the talk. I needed to prepare myself by considering the issues at hand biblically, discussing them with my wife, and praying for my child and for myself. By the time I did all that, I would be in a completely different frame of mind and more prepared to function as God's instrument of change.

After preparing yourself, talk with your teen in the right place at the right time. Get away to a quiet room in the house, preferably the teen's room where he or she is comfortable. Don't squeeze important wisdom or correction into busy moments or attempt it on the fly. Don't conduct these moments in front of other people or introduce them as you are running out to the car on the way to school or church. Take time, and in so doing say, "You are important and what God says is important, so I am willing to invest the time necessary to be his instrument of correction."

Be humble enough to admit that your teenagers do push your buttons. Get to know where your buttons are. Before you have the talk, pray that you would model the love of Christ before your teenager. If you begin to lose it, excuse yourself from the scene, pray, and get yourself together, then go back and complete the talk. Remember, giving wisdom is not hitting your teenager over the head with words. It is putting a lovely garland around his neck. It's putting gold from God's pocket into his hands. This is radically different from the way teenagers tend to think about wisdom and correction. Don't confirm their view and allow these times to be robbed of their value and beauty by your sin.

Teens tend to be defensive. They often take our loving concern and parental help as an accusation of failure. In response, they defend their thoughts and actions and engage us in debate. We need to be very careful of the words we use. We need to be sure that we come to our children with honest questions, not accusations that come out of foregone conclusions. We need to exercise God-given self-control. We need to stay out of loud arguments that have little to do with a wise perspective on the issues at hand and everything to do with who is going to win or lose the debate. Proverbs says, "A soft answer turns away wrath, but a harsh word stirs up anger" (Prov. 15:1). We must studiously avoid getting drawn into emotionally laden power struggles.

Here are three very helpful things you can do when your teenager becomes defensive.

Clarify your actions. For example, you might say, "Don't misunderstand—I'm not accusing you of anything. I love you very much, and, because I love you, I want to do everything I can to help you as you begin to move into the adult world. Don't ever think I am against you. I am for you. If you ever think that I have misjudged you, if you ever think that I don't understand, or if you ever think that I have expressed sinful anger toward you, please respectfully point it out to me. I want to be used by God to help and encourage you. I don't ever want to tear you down."

Help your teenager to examine his or her own defensiveness. Teenagers, like all sinners, suffer from spiritual blindness. They do not see themselves as they actually are, so they need our help. "You know, there is a lot of tension in this room. I haven't yelled at you, I haven't called you names, I haven't accused you of anything, but it seems like you are angry at me. Could you explain why you are so angry? I don't want this time to be uncomfortable for us. I didn't ask to talk to you because I felt like a good fight. I love you and want to help you in any way I can."

Be faithful in confessing your sins against your teenager. Expressing irritation or impatience, judging motives, name-calling, condemning, raising your voice, allowing yourself to become emotionally out of control, or hitting, grabbing, or pushing your teenager all fit under the category of "provok[ing] your children to anger" (Eph. 6:4) and must be confessed to God and to your teen. Your humility and softness of heart stand as wonderful models for your teenager. Declare, with humble assurance, your confidence in the forgiveness of Christ. By so doing, you let your children know that they are not alone in their struggle with sin, and you demonstrate that confession produces beneficial results.

Not only do teenagers tend to be defensive, but they also tend to be self-protective. Teenagers don't tend to live openly. They aren't usually walking around the house dying to talk with Mom and Dad. They are masters of non-answers. It is not unusual for them to spend an inordinate amount of time in their rooms. Sadly, I am afraid, many parents accept the moat that teenagers build around themselves. They adjust to the lack of time and relationship with a teen who, only a few short years ago, wanted to tag along with them everywhere they went. They quit talking when their teenager quits talking. Just at the point where significant things happen—things that the teenager was never meant to deal with alone—Mom and Dad are nowhere to be found.

Pursue your teenagers. Daily express your love for them. Don't ask questions that can be answered with a yes or a no—ask questions that require description, explanation, and self-disclosure. Don't relate to them only during times of correction. Don't catch them only when they are doing something wrong; catch them doing something right and encourage them. Pray daily with them, even if it makes them uncomfortable. Always find them in the house and say a warm good night to them before they go to bed. (Because this was our habit for years, our teens sought us out to say good night to us.) Enter the world of your teenagers and stay there. Don't ever let them view you as being outside their functional world. Teenagers reject grenades of wisdom and correction lobbed from afar by someone who has not been on-site for quite a while.

When you ask questions about their choices and actions, teenagers tend to respond by shifting blame. They will tell you that they didn't hear your instructions or that you did not give them enough time. They might blame a sibling. These responses can get very frustrating. Anticipate the fact that you will need the self-control that only the Holy Spirit can give.

One way that teenagers shift blame is by accusing us of being especially hard on them and unreasonably lax on their siblings. They charge us with harshness and inconsistency. In these moments, it is important for you to maintain your focus on the subject under discussion and not be diverted to elaborate justifications of your parenting. Try to respond with humility and patience. Say, "I'm sure there are times when I miss things that I should deal with. But I think you know that I love each one of you and seek to be what God wants me to be in each of your lives. I would be glad to talk about me and the pressures of parenting at another time. I'd love to let you know what it's like and hear what I look like from your end, but right now we need to talk about you."

Teenagers don't tend to be good listeners. Keep conversations interesting and to the point. Don't go into lengthy descriptions of all the ways things were different in your day. The way to deal with the short attention span of our teenagers is to make these moments of wisdom and correction *interactions* rather than lectures. Some of us carry invisible portable lecterns with us, which we are ready to set up in a moment. Leave them in the closet. Instead, ask stimulating questions that cause the teen to examine her actions, assumptions, desires, and choices. Help her to shine the light of the Word on them. Surprise her with truth. Let wisdom sparkle before her eyes. Don't give in to soliloquies or diatribes. Engage your teenager in a stimulating conversation that doesn't flash your authority or the right you have to tell her what to do. Rather, talk to her in a way that lifts up truth and points out its beauty.

Don't get sucked in. Don't get locked out. Don't engage in interpersonal war. Faithfully bring sweet words of wisdom and loving words of correction. Hold what is valuable before your teenager and trust God to produce a love for truth in his or her heart.

Legalism

Proverbs doesn't give us an encyclopedia of dos and don'ts or rights and wrongs. What Proverbs gives us is two worldviews: wisdom and foolishness. Here we find two ways of living: the way of the wise, which gets its direction from the truth of God, and the way of the fool, which gets its direction from human perspectives and desires. God is looking for more than outward behavior. He is working so that we will be nothing less than partakers of his divine nature (2 Peter 1:4)! We cannot and we must not reduce godly living to a set of rules. Godliness is humble, thankful worship that causes us to desire what God says is valuable and to do what God says will bring him glory.

Teenagers, however, tend to be dyed-in-the-wool legalists. They tend to emphasize the letter of the law rather than the spirit. Teenagers tend to push at the fences while telling you that they are still in the yard. They tend to drive you to boundary discussions. They engage you in "how far can I go" conversations and later say, "But I did exactly what you told me to do."

Teenage legalism is an opportunity to talk about what it means to have a heart for God and a heart for doing what is right. We need to be skilled at talking about the spirit of the law with our teenagers. We need to talk about the heart issues behind a command. We need to show them the difference between inner purity and pharisaic performance of duty.

My son tended to be rough in his physical play with his brother, enjoying his advantage of size and strength. On many occasions, his younger brother ended up frustrated and tearful. So I went to my son and asked him not to engage in physical play with his brother. In making this request, I summarized a lot of things that fell into the category of intimidation, using his size to take advantage of his younger brother.

A few days later, I heard his brother crying in the family room. "I thought I asked you not to do this with your brother," I said. He responded, "I didn't touch him." Do you see what happened? He kept the letter of the law, in that he did not physically touch or hurt his brother. Yet he disobeyed the spirit of the request by physically intimidating his brother without touching him.

As we point out this legalism to our teenagers and remind them of the true spirit of God's requirements, they will see their inability and begin to hunger for Christ. Otherwise, they will tend to be like the Pharisees who reduced the law of God to doable human standards. Christ told his followers that unless their righteousness exceeded that of the scribes and Pharisees they would not enter the kingdom of heaven! As we point our teenagers to the grandeur of the spirit of the law, they will say, "I can't do this. I can't love. I can't give. I am not a servant." They will begin to reach out for the help that only Christ can give.

The stakes here are high. Human legalism leads to human self-righteousness. Human self-righteousness denies the need for the saving, enabling grace of Christ. Human self-righteousness embraces the cruelest of Satan's lies: that a person can be righteous by keeping the law. If that were true, there would have been no need for the birth, life, death, and resurrection of Christ. We must help our teenagers to see their legalism, and we must not get into the endless boundary debates that legalism enjoys. We must help our children to see their rebellion of heart and take them to Christ, who *is* their righteousness.

Lack of Wisdom in Their Choice of Companions

There is a great deal of material in Proverbs about the influence that others have on you and your behavior. Teenagers often are naive and unwise in their choice of friends. Proverbs goes so far as to say that when you see certain people, you should cross the road and walk on the other side! Friendship is very important. People are known by the company they keep. It is impossible to be uninfluenced by one's friends. Yet teenagers typically assume that they won't be influenced and respond to our concern with "I can handle it."

As I was thinking about this issue, I thought of an experience from my own teenage years. As I remembered it, I was tempted to call my mother and ask for her forgiveness! Around the time I was beginning to notice the opposite sex, I had also begun to participate in a local teen ministry. In this ministry, everyone seemed to pair off into couples. I found someone I liked and brought her home after one of the weekend meetings. As I look back now, I realize that she was one of the most disreputable girls in the Christian community. I am so very glad she is not the person I married!

I remember the surreal scene as I brought her home. My mom had a pained smile on her face. She was trying to be kind and polite while at the same time wanting to rescue me from moral danger! Later that night, she asked me what attracted me to that particular girl. (It seemed obvious: she was pretty, she was fun to be around, and she liked me.) Although I wouldn't have admitted it at the time, I grew very defensive. My mother warned me of the importance of these kinds of choices, and I was offended and told her I could handle it.

We need to approach these conversations with sensitivity, patience, and love. Teenagers tend to be prickly and protective when it comes to discussions of their friends. It is as if the operational rule is "To reject my friends is to reject me." As parents, we need to be very careful about the way we have these conversations. Never resort to name-calling and character assassination. Your goal should be to get your teenager to step outside the emotion and commitment of his relationship with his friend to give it a long, honest, biblical look. He won't do this without your help. But it's also true that he won't do it if, in your own fear, you emotionally denigrate relationships that are precious to him.

This subject must be put on the table. Teenagers need to learn how to choose friends wisely. They need to understand the powerful influence that friendship has on them. It is critically important that we as parents avoid undermining our influence with our children by unwisely labeling their friends, making unwarranted accusations, judging their motives, and making assumptions about the nature and level of influence of their friendships. We need to ask good questions that help our teens to examine their thoughts, desires, motives, choices, and behaviors with respect to friendship. We want to lead our children to heart insight that will help them to make much wiser decisions about friendship. We do not accomplish anything on the heart level when we judge in fear and make decisions for them. In so doing, we miss the opportunity to see lasting heart change take place in them, yet only lasting heart change leads to basic changes in their approach to friendship.

Susceptibility to Sexual Temptation

The father in Proverbs has much to say about sexual temptation. We need to take this theme seriously, particularly in a culture that has such a distorted view of human sexuality. There is almost nowhere outside the Christian community where a teenager will get anything close to an accurate perspective of this significant area of human life. The teenage years are a time of physical awakening. For the first time, they become desirous of sexual relationships. Lust and fantasy often become the private sins of teenagers. We cannot avoid this area or respond to it with embarrassment and ambivalence. We must put this subject on the table early with our children and keep it there as a topic for open discussion.

Many parents dread having that first sex talk. They spend weeks working themselves up to it. They breathe a sigh of relief after they make it through it alive, and they never discuss the subject again. How about you? Do you know how your child is doing in this area? Do you know if he struggles with lust, fantasy, or masturbation? Do you know if she has a biblical view of relationships with the opposite sex? Do you know how many of the sexual lies of the world he has accepted? Do you understand the situations, locations, and relationships in which she is experiencing temptation? Have you brainstormed with him about ways of fleeing "youthful passions"? You cannot parent in this area if you have allowed the doors to be closed.

In order to help our teenagers with their struggle to be sexually pure, the key is to start early so that by the time a child is a teenager, parent and child alike have moved beyond any embarrassment or reticence over talking about sex. I first introduced this topic with my two oldest sons when they were eleven and nine years of age. I took them out for pizza. Little did they know what they were getting into! I asked them questions to ascertain how much they already knew. I started making explanations and drawing pictures on a napkin. My oldest son choked on his pizza and said, "Dad, are you going to draw what I think you are?" I said, "I chose a booth where no one can see," and we began to talk. They realized that I was not embarrassed by the subject, and they soon began to open up with the questions that they had wanted to ask for a while.

As the years went by, we endeavored to keep that conversation open because new questions, temptations, issues, and situations arose. A robust understanding of God's way of sexual purity is not something that can be achieved in one conversation. Learning how to recognize and flee temptation is not a skill that is mastered after one introductory talk about sexuality. Parents need to be committed to a process that begins in the preteen years and continues, with consistency, until our children are ready to leave our homes.

Do your teenagers feel comfortable raising this topic with you? Have you given them a mixed message—on the one hand saying that sex is a wonderful gift from God and on the other hand communicating fear, reticence, and avoidance? Have you agreed that this is a taboo topic? Do you know what your kids know about sex and what their source of information is? Do you know where your teenager struggles with sexual temptation and how he is doing with that struggle? Is your teenager able to embrace a distinctly biblical view of sexuality? Is she able to critique the distortions of the surrounding culture? Does your teen have a heart for sexual purity, or is he pushing the limits of biblical modesty and propriety? If you do not have ready answers for these questions, you have not kept the topic on the table as it needs to be.

There is an explosion of sexual awareness and sexual temptation in the teen years. Teenagers begin to form a sexual lifestyle that will be with them for years. At this time, many teens fall into sexual sins that alter the course of their lives, secret patterns of sexual sin that leave them in bondage for years. We must be committed to open, positive, and consistent parenting in this area. We must be committed to pursuing our children with honest questions and patient discussions. We must put the subject of sex on the table early and leave it there to be revisited until the child leaves home.

Absence of Eschatological Perspective

Eschatology—a focus on eternity—is not the strong point of most teenagers' functional theology. They don't tend to live with eternity in view. They don't think in terms of delayed gratification. Teenagers tend to live as if the present moment is the only moment of life and to put off their responsibilities until the very last minute. They don't think in terms of investment or have a harvest mentality. Galatians 6:7 says, "God is not mocked, for whatever one sows, that will he also reap." This significant spiritual principle is seldom in the typical teenager's view.

Teenagers need to be taught to think in terms of long-term investment. We need to teach them to examine the kinds of seeds they are planting and the kind of harvest those seeds will bring. We must lovingly challenge their belief that this physical moment is all that matters—that present, temporal happiness is all there is. They need to understand that God is working on something bigger than this moment. He is preparing them for something wonderful to come.

The culture around us reinforces the falsehood that life is found in present, earthly, physical treasure and that the successful person is the one with the biggest pile. Our teenagers are told, "You are the labels that you wear. You are your body size. You are your intelligence. You are your athletic ability. You are the car you drive. You are the house you live in. You are the level of popularity that you have."

Who are the heroes of Western culture? Are they people of character who invest in things of eternal significance? No, they are people with good voices, expensive clothes, hot cars, big muscles, and huge bank accounts. They live for the moment and lay up treasure on earth. They typically have no more sense of eternity than the most immature teen. In God's eyes they are, in fact, the opposite of heroes; they lead our children to believe lies and to live for what is passing away.

Our teenagers need us to be on-site, teaching them to look at life from the vantage point of eternity. Life looks radically different when viewed from that perspective! They need to see that every choice, every action, is an investment and that it is impossible to live life without planting seeds that will become the plants of life they will someday harvest.

Lack of Heart Awareness

In the book of Proverbs, this warning appears right in the middle of the father's instruction:

> My son, be attentive to my words;
> incline your ear to my sayings.
> Let them not escape from your sight;
> keep them within your heart.
> For they are life to those who find them,
> and healing to all their flesh. (Prov. 4:20–22)

He is saying, "Son, listen carefully. What I have to say is important. Don't blow off these words." Then he says, "Keep your heart with all vigilance, for from it flow the springs of life" (v. 23). In other words, "Of all that I have said, focus on your heart. Know it. Protect it. Guard it. Your heart is the control center of your life. What rules your heart will rule you."

As we saw earlier, we must not simply parent behavior. We're not just controlling decisions and ensuring our children go where we want them to go and do what we want them to do. God has called us to a higher agenda. We want to know the heart of our teenagers, to help them to see their hearts as they really are, and to be used by God to help to produce hearts ruled by nothing other than God and his truth.

Do you lead your teen to conversations that go deeper than solving problems of circumstance and relationship? Do you help her to see the heart behind those problems? Do you assist her in seeing how she has exchanged the Creator for some aspect of creation, such as peer acceptance, a certain possession, or some coveted position? Have you helped her to see the desires that rule her heart? Have you helped her to confess her true treasures? Have you taken the time to lovingly point out where her thinking is out of conformity to the truths of Scripture? Have you asked questions that expose the thoughts and motives of the heart? Have you shown her that her true worship is expressed in the way she responds to situations and relationships?

Whenever we talk about knowing the heart, we have to talk about the reality of spiritual blindness. All of us struggle with a lack of heart awareness. But teenagers seem to particularly struggle with it because they tend to think of life in such behavioral, physical, and present terms. They don't tend to spend much time searching their hearts. They don't ask themselves challenging, revealing questions. For that reason, one of our goals with our teenagers is not only to teach them about God and his will but to help them to know themselves. We want them to become aware of their particular struggles with sin, their weaknesses, and their susceptibility to temptation.

Because I wanted to help my teenagers to grow in self-awareness, I didn't burst into their rooms to announce that a rule had been broken and that a punishment would be meted out. In times of correction, we talked. I tried to ask probing questions that were designed to break through the deceitfulness of sin and expose the heart. And the more my children grew in self-awareness, the more they appreciated the things I said to them, because they realized that they needed my instruction.

Part of the defensiveness so typical of teenagers comes from their utter lack of self-awareness, their utter spiritual blindness. We must incessantly work to help our children to know themselves so that this knowledge will lead them to hunger after God. Every moment is self-revealing.

I use this illustration in counseling, but I think it is particularly true of teenagers. When a teenager plays the "video" of his story for you, he often is not in it. His version of his life focuses on the pressure of a situation or on what other people did to him. As he relates his story, he does it in a way that shifts responsibility for the things he did to someone or something else.

My daughter came home from school one day waving a report card from one of her classes. She said, "Dad, I need to talk to you about my grade in Spanish." I knew we were in trouble! She went on to say proudly, "I got the highest D in my class!"

By the time she was done talking about her grade, I thought I should post that D on the refrigerator. After all, I was the proud father of a daughter who had done well under educational duress and pedagogical incompetence. "Dad, it's the new teacher," she told me. "He's learning how to teach by practicing on us. It's like we're his guinea pigs." The more I listened, the prouder I got! What a disciplined daughter, to achieve despite the ineptitude of the rookie teacher!

In truth, as I listened to her that afternoon, I was filled with sadness because it hit me that she believed what she was saying to me. She really thought that her grade was not her fault. She truly believed that the teacher was completely to blame. Somewhere between the time she received the paper and the time she arrived home, she had generated an interpretation of events that took her responsibility out of the picture. She was spiritually blind and did not see the real issues of the heart that the report card revealed.

When I began to correct her, what would I face? She would be defensive. She would feel falsely and wrongly accused. She would probably accuse me of not understanding. She would think I was unsympathetic. She would wonder why I had taken the teacher's side rather than hers. These are the kinds of situations we regularly deal with as we seek to break through to the hearts of our teenagers.

My goal as a parent is for my children to not only come to know God but, in so doing, come to know themselves. It's only when a person knows God that he can truly know himself, and, as this happens, his hunger for God increases. We want to see this critical interplay of the spiritual life produced in our teenagers: a deep personal knowledge of God and an ever-growing knowledge of self.

This is not just a "flesh and blood" struggle in which parents try to open their teens' eyes to what they are *really* like. This is spiritual warfare. Our Enemy is a liar and a deceiver. Teenagers are particularly susceptible to his lies about the self. They believe that the problem is not with them— they have been singled out for unfair criticism and correction.

We need to stand strong and patient rather than being drawn into debilitating verbal battles that do not open a teenager's eyes but only make him more defensive and distant. With love and a humble dependency on Christ, we need to take every opportunity to expose critical issues of the heart (fear of man, materialism, selfishness, lust, covetousness, envy, unbelief, anger, self-righteousness, love of the world, greed, rebellion, and so on) and to help our teenagers look at themselves in the perfect mirror of Scripture.

ISSUES OF WISDOM AND FOOLISHNESS, legalism and true godliness, friendship, sexuality, eternity, and personal heart awareness are all on the table during the teen years, providing wide-open doors of opportunity. God uses discussions like these to help your teenagers to come to know him, to love him, and to internalize his truth in a way that gives practical direction to their lives.

These are also the things that make this a scary time of parenting. These issues can cause parental panic and dread and become the occasion of parental anger. Parents may say things about these issues that they live to regret. These issues can be used by God to form a deeper bond between parent and teen or become the thing the Enemy uses to drive a deeper wedge into the relationship.

If you respond to these issues with anxiety, irritation, and fear, you will try to control and manipulate your teen into obedience, initiating unproductive power struggles. You will take on a survival mentality in which life is a minefield and you hope for little more than getting your teenager across it with all his limbs intact. In desperation, you will give in to raging emotions and do foolish, unproductive things, all the while invoking the name of the Lord and the truth of his Word. In your self-pity over the toughness of your job as a parent, you will resort to beating your teen with words and seeking to motivate him with threats. Your relationship will disintegrate as your teenager's rebellion increases. At last, you will admit you are powerless and, in a final act of anger, you will quit parenting altogether, telling yourself you did everything you could do.

But if instead you move toward your teenager with a confident faith in the Redeemer, whose Word is true and whose sovereign presence empowers your weak and feeble parental efforts, God will use you to communicate love, understanding, grace, hope, and life. You will ask calm but probing questions that cause your teenager to examine things that she would never examine alone. You will engage your teenager in thought-provoking debate without ever becoming hurtfully personal and condemning. You will correct in a spirit of acceptance, forgiveness, and hope. You will smile when your child comes into the house, and she will not tense up when you enter her room. She will begin to pursue you to talk about things that many teens hide or ignore. And as your relationship deepens, your teen will progressively take on the character of Christ.

Questions for Reflection and Discussion

1. Take a moment to reflect on your own experience as a teenager. If you have an old journal, dig it up. Do you remember the rapid ups and downs, physical self-awareness, and general confusion? Do you remember the vulnerability, the rejection, and the never-ending stream of insecurities? Tell your children about your own experience as a teenager. Remind them that you've been in their shoes and know just how hard it is.

2. Think about the last time you offered wisdom or correction to your teenager. Did you deliver it in a way that was generous and appealing? Or were your tone and message bitter and condemning? How did your child respond?

3. Have you noticed your teenager building a moat around himself or herself? Is he or she becoming more isolated from you? Do you remember building a moat around your own teenage experience, keeping your parents at arm's length? How did it feel when an adult—a parent, a youth pastor, a teacher—tried to bridge that gap and pursue you?

4. Are you inside or outside your teenager's functional world right now? How might you lovingly and prayerfully pursue your child?

5. How might you use law-breaking events as an opportunity to point your child toward grace? Remind your teenager that his or her inability to keep the law points to a desperate need for Christ.

6. How have your teenager's friendships influenced his or her life both positively and negatively? What are some good questions you can ask your child about his or her thoughts, desires, motives, and choices that might help to illuminate the unwise relationships in your child's life?

7. Are the doors open between you and your child when it comes to discussing sexual temptation? Do you think your teenager feels comfortable coming to you with questions? Why or why not?

8. Reflect on how you might point your child beyond the present moment, with its present struggles, and give him or her a view for eternity.

9. What lies does your teenager believe about himself or herself? In what ways has he or she tended to shift responsibility and blame? As you lean on Christ for guidance, how can you gently expose your child's heart issues?

10. Take a moment to pray that God would use you to communicate love, understanding, grace, hope, and life to your teenager.

PART TWO

Setting Godly Goals

6

Goals, Glory, and Grace

I WALKED TO MY SON'S bedroom feeling overwhelmed. I was physically tired, yes, but I was also a tired parent. I was tired of my children's constant need for ministry. I didn't want to have the same conversation that I had already had ten thousand times with the same son! I wanted to tell my wife, "You do it. I'm not having this conversation again." I resented the fact that my son's immaturity and sin demanded so much of my attention and time.

I had spent some time in prayer before I went to my son's room. I thought I was prepared to have a productive conversation. Still, I was weary. He was tired too, and he immediately responded defensively. He accused me of being unloving and unkind. He said I didn't understand, and he argued with every point I tried to make. This was not how I had envisioned things going.

Somewhere in the conversation I lost it. In my anger I said words to him that were as unkind as any I had ever spoken. As I left the room, I told him I hoped to live long enough to see him really appreciate me. But, I said, I wouldn't hold my breath. He glared after me with a combination of anger and hurt.

I sat in the dark on the side of my bed, defeated and discouraged. God's call to me as a father seemed unrealistic. Impossible. I struggled with the gap between what I knew and what I had done. Would I ever get it? Torn between self-pity and conviction, I wanted my son to hurt the way he had hurt me, yet I knew that the desire was wrong. As I sat there, I realized this job was one I could not quit. There was no escape. Tomorrow I would wake up to the same demands. I cried out for God's help and forgiveness. I cried out for character and strength. I prayed for faith and perseverance. I was never more aware of my own moment-by-moment need of the Lord.

Perhaps you have been overwhelmed by what you have read in this book. Perhaps you have been filled with regret. Perhaps the sins of your heart have been exposed. Perhaps you have been tempted to say, "Paul, I will never be able to do what you have described!" Perhaps you are thinking, "Maybe this works with your kids, Paul, but it will never work with mine!"

Before we consider God's goals for us as we parent our teenagers, we need to reflect on who we are as God's children. It is important that we see that God's glory and grace are far greater than our sin and our struggle with parenting.

I want to show you three passages that have been friends to me in moments of discouragement and defeat. God has used these passages to radically alter the way I think about what he has called me to do in my teenagers' lives.

Awesome Power

Few things in life have the twenty-four-hours-a-day demand that parenting does. Few things in life have such potential for unexpected difficulty and drama. I have talked with many parents of adolescents who speak of being weary, who feel as if they do not have the strength to do what they have been called to do. It is vital in the face of this that we do not forget the strength that is ours as the children of God.

In Ephesians 3:20–21, Paul directs us to that power in a well-known doxology.

> Now to him who is able to do far more abundantly than all that we ask
> or think, according to the power at work within us, to him be glory in

the church and in Christ Jesus throughout all generations, forever and ever. Amen.

The God who is our Father is a God of awesome power. Through this power, he is able to do things that are well beyond anything we could verbalize or grasp with our imaginations. Think of the thing in your life that seems impossible to accomplish. God is able to do more! Think of the thing that the Bible says is needed in your teenager's life that seems unrealistic and out of reach. God is able to do more!

It is important for us to look at our task as parents from the vantage point of the awesome power of God—the power by which he created the world, holds the universe together, raised Christ from the dead, and defeated sin. Our God is a God of glorious power far beyond what our minds can conceive. We cannot look at our parental responsibilities only from the perspective of our own weariness and weakness. We must remember that we are the children of the Almighty. He *is* Power! He *is* Strength.

But more needs to be said here. Perhaps you're thinking, "Boy, would I like to get hold of some of that power!" but you don't know how to get it. In fact, many parents I have talked with have been *discouraged* by passages like Ephesians 3:20–21. They seem so far from their own experience.

Look carefully at the words of this doxology. It says that God is "able to do far more abundantly than all that we ask or think" (now pay attention to these words) "according to the power at work *within us.*" Where is his power? Is it off in the heavens somewhere, available only to those who have discovered the right spiritual mantra to call it into action? No, that is not what Paul says. Instead he says something that is glorious and radical, yet real. God's awesome power resides *within* his people and is actively *at work*! Parent, because you are a child of God, this glorious power lives within you, and it is not dormant. God's awesome, active power resides within you, by his Spirit, so that you can do the things God has called you to do that would be otherwise impossible.

It is in our moments of weakness, when we refuse to give up, that we experience the glorious power that resides within us as children of the Almighty. Paul tells us in 2 Corinthians 12:9 that God's strength is made perfect in our weakness. Often we miss the experience of his power because we quit when we hit the wall. It is when we are beyond the resources of our own strength and wisdom that we succumb to the emotions of the moment, saying and doing things we regret. But because of Christ's work for us, we can do something different; we can parent with courage and hope. It is important to recognize the strength we have been given as the children of God.

The Gift of Glory

In John 17, Christ is facing his crucifixion, resurrection, and ascension to heaven. In the moments before his capture, he goes to his Father in prayer for his disciples and for those who will believe through their ministry. He prays for the relationships his followers will have with one another—that his children will experience the same unity that he has with the Father and the Spirit. Imagine a family where such unity reigns! Picture that kind of relationship with your teenager!

It is tempting to look at passages such as this and say, "Come on, get real! You don't really think this is possible, do you?" But before we cast off this passage as utter idealism, too distant from our experience to be of any practical encouragement or help, we need to pay careful attention to its words:

> I do not ask for these only, but also for those who will believe in me through their word, that they may all be one, just as you, Father, are in me, and I in you, that they also may be in us, so that the world may believe that you have sent me. The glory that you have given me I have given to them, that they may be one even as we are one, I in them and you in me, that they may become perfectly one. (John 17:20–23)

In his prayer, Christ says that he has done something magnificent for his people. Knowing the brokenness of the world and our sinful hearts, he sees that, on our own, we will never experience the love and unity that he has planned for us. He sees the bitterness, anger, jealousy, greed, deceit, and vengeance that sin produces. He knows that sister would never love brother, husband would never love wife, friend would never love friend, and parent would never love child without his divine intervention. And that is exactly what he provides!

Pay careful attention to the words of verse 22: "The glory that you have given me I have given to them, *that they may be one* even as we are one." When Christ came to earth and took on flesh, the glory of almighty God was placed on him so that, through him, the glory of God would be seen by us all. Christ then says that the glory that was placed on him he has placed on his children so that *they would be one*! We need to embrace this redemptive reality. What was far beyond our grasp has been placed by Christ within our reach. He has placed the glory of almighty God on us for a specific purpose: that our relationships with one another would mirror those of the Trinity. Paul says it this way in Colossians 2:9–10: "For in [Christ] the whole fullness of deity dwells bodily, and you have been filled in him."

When you try to talk with your teenager, it is not just you and your teen in the room alone, hoping that somehow, some way you will be able to get along with each other. The glory of God has been given as a gift to you so that you will be able to be a humble, gentle, patient, forbearing instrument of the love and unity God has planned for his people. His gift of glory is your hope of unity.

Notice further that Christ doesn't pray, "May they bring themselves to complete unity." No, Christ is saying, "Father, if your children are ever going to live in unity and love, it is you who must bring them there." It is not just us who are working. God is working to produce what only he can produce. The moments you spend talking to your teen in his room are God's moments of grace, redemption, and change.

There is probably no time in our lives when we are in more need of God's gift of glory and his moment-by-moment activity than the years when we are parenting our teenagers. In these years, we are faced with our weakness, sin, and inability. In these years, the Enemy wants to turn us from the high goals to which God has called us and lead us to settle instead for human control and situational success. We need to remember that God's gift of glory was given to bridge the gap between us and our children so that his love and unity would flourish between us.

Everything We Need

There is no passage that has been more of a comfort to me as a parent than 2 Peter 1:3–9.

> His divine power has granted to us all things that pertain to life and godliness, through the knowledge of him who called us to his own glory and excellence, by which he has granted to us his precious and very great promises, so that through them you may become partakers of the divine nature, having escaped from the corruption that is in the world because of sinful desire. For this very reason, make every effort to supplement your faith with virtue, and virtue with knowledge, and knowledge with self-control, and self-control with steadfastness, and steadfastness with godliness, and godliness with brotherly affection, and brotherly affection with love. For if these qualities are yours and are increasing, they keep you from being ineffective or unfruitful in the knowledge of our Lord Jesus Christ. For whoever lacks these qualities is so nearsighted that he is blind, having forgotten that he was cleansed from his former sins.

Peter says that there are believers whose lives are ineffective and unproductive. This is because they are missing the qualities that make for a productive life: faith, virtue, knowledge, self-control, steadfastness, godliness, brotherly affection, and love. These are the essential qualities of a Christian's effectiveness. They are also the essential qualities of productive parenting. We need these qualities in those tough moments with our teenagers.

Peter tells us why some people lack these essential qualities: they are nearsighted and blind, forgetting that they have been cleansed from their past sins. In short, they have forgotten their *identity*. They have forgotten who they are as the children of God. Peter argues that if you forget who you are as a child of God, you will quit pursuing the qualities that make your life effective and productive.

The first few verses of the passage lay out the glories of our identity as God's children. Peter says we must not forget these. He says that God "has granted to us *all things* that pertain to life and godliness." God has given us *everything we need*—not only for eternal life but also for the

God-honoring life to which we have been called until he returns. Notice the tense of the verb. Peter says God *has granted* us everything we need. It has already happened! This is a fundamental gospel truth. God will not call us to do anything without providing a way for it to be done. If he calls us to cross the Red Sea, he will send a boat, build a bridge, part the waters, or enable us to swim!

Peter says, "Don't forget who you are. You are a child of God who has inherited riches beyond your ability to conceive. You have been given everything you need to do what God has called you to do. Don't give in to discouragement. Don't quit. Don't run away from your calling. Don't settle for a little bit of faith, virtue, knowledge, self-control, steadfastness, godliness, brotherly affection, and love. Get everything that is your inheritance as God's child."

As we walk into the rooms of our teenagers, we need to say to ourselves, "I have everything I need to do what God has called me to do." In these moments we can experience a little more of the inheritance of character that Christ has provided to us through his death.

WE HAVE AWESOME POWER DWELLING within us. God has given us glory so that we can be agents of love and unity. We have everything we need to do what God has called us to do. This is the gospel. This is our identity as the children of God. These are the truths that can lift us out of our weariness and discouragement so that we can parent our teenagers with faith, courage, and hope. They call us to hold on to God's high goals and to fight the hopelessness that the Enemy wants to rule our hearts.

We have not been left alone. God has given us rich resources of grace. He is active in us and through us to produce what we could never produce on our own. The gospel says that we can parent with hope. It tells us that we can grow, we can change, we can do more and better. When we are at the end of our strength, we can experience his power to love, to be self-controlled, to be steadfast, to do what is good, and to be kind, even in the face of our teenagers' resistance.

God knows our weakness. He is aware of our sin. And he has given us glorious gifts of grace so that we can be his tools of change in our children's lives. We cannot give in to discouragement and hopelessness. Christ gives us reason for hope—hope that we can be effective and productive as we parent our teenagers. The gifts of grace that he gives turn weak and failing sinners into effective and productive children of the almighty God. We can hold to his high goals with hope as we look at parenting through the lens of his grace and glory.

After I left my son's room that dark night, my mind went to these passages. I recited them once again to myself. I confessed my disobedience and unbelief and prayed for a heart of faith. The truths of these passages renewed my hope and my courage. They helped me to reach once more toward God's goals. As I went to sleep, I was anxious for the morning to come. I couldn't wait to talk with my son, to express my love for him, and to ask for his forgiveness. I knew I would face many more moments of challenge and struggle, but I had hope. I was able to look at those moments from the vantage point of God's grace and glory.

Questions for Reflection and Discussion

1. When was the last time you felt defeated as a parent? What drove you to this point of mental and emotional exhaustion?
2. When you feel overwhelmed, where do you turn for life and energy and hope? Do you try to escape your responsibilities or numb yourself to the challenges with food, entertainment, or other forms of pleasure?
3. How has the Lord done far more abundantly than you have thought or asked in the past (Eph. 3:20)? Does his work produce an optimism in you that you are able to carry into parenting your teens? If not, why the particular cynicism?
4. Do you parent with the confidence that "his divine power has granted to us all things" (2 Peter 1:3)? What are some of the parenting "things" that you predict you will need his power for this week? What can you do to prepare for these?
5. How has parenting your teenager revealed weaknesses in your spiritual life? Have you tried to hide these weaknesses from your teen, family, or peers? Are you creating a social media parenting facade that contradicts 2 Corinthians 12:9?

6. What other Scripture passages can comfort you in challenging times as a parent of a teen? Where can you store these so they are readily available in moments of discouragement?

7

There's a War Out There

IT HAPPENED UNEXPECTEDLY, AS IT almost always does. She said very hesitantly that she needed to talk with me about something. She said that it was about school, that she was in trouble. Even while she was making her introduction, my heart began to race. What had she done? How serious was it? How long had it been going on? What was I about to hear? I invited her to sit down with me and talk.

With her head bowed in an attempt to avoid eye contact, she handed me a crumpled piece of paper. "I got caught in English class giving this note to Samantha," she said. "The teacher was very upset when he read it and made us go to the principal's office right away. The principal said I had to show you the note tonight, then she wants to see you tomorrow. Then she will decide what she is going to do with us."

I unwrinkled the paper and read its contents. The note was brazenly offensive. It was disrespectful of authority. It used language that I could not believe would ever be in the mind of my sweet little girl, let alone written down to be passed to a classmate in a Christian school! I flushed with a volatile combination of emotions.

I was angry. How dared my daughter be so boldly rebellious and insensitive? We had faithfully schooled her in the truth. Was this the way she was going to thank us? At the same time, I was grieved. A simple, sweet, uncomplicated world had suddenly died. My daughter was no longer the innocent little girl who climbed up on Daddy's lap, begging to be told a story. I wanted the power to turn back the clock. I didn't want to have to parent the person who wrote that note. I wanted my little girl back.

There was, however, a third thing I felt. I was embarrassed. I was well known in the Christian community. I was a pastor, seminary teacher, and counselor. I spoke at conferences about the Christian family and parenting. What would people think of me now? Some expert! Some example! I was filled with self-pity. I wondered what the administration at the school had thought when they saw that note. I wondered what they thought about me.

I kept reading and rereading the note as she sat there. I could not bring myself to believe that she had written it. I asked her again if she had. I guess I was hoping she would say that she hadn't, that she was covering for somebody else. But she *had* written it. The words had come from *her* mind and been written with *her* pen. She had written exactly what she wanted to say to her friend. There was no mistake here.

Was this the tip of the iceberg? What other things was she into that I and my wife didn't know about? What language did she use with friends that she wouldn't think of using at home? Who was she hanging out with in school? How bad was her crowd? Where had she gone? What else had she done that we would soon hear about, that would further shatter the image of our girl we carried in our hearts? I felt conflicted. I wanted to know it all, yet I was afraid to ask for fear of what I might hear.

I don't know how many minutes went by before she asked, "Dad, are you just going to sit there and stare at the note? Aren't you going to say something?"

I said with emotion, "Right now I don't know what to say." I asked her if there was anything else she needed to tell me.

It is because of these kinds of situations—the unpredictability of the teen years and our own heart struggles in the face of them—that parents need a clear set of biblical goals that function as God-given guardrails to keep us on the road he wants us to travel. We can't wait to decide what to do when these moments suddenly come on us. We cannot expect that when tensions and emotions are high, we will be able to think clearly, biblically, and concretely. We can't expect to set long-term goals when we're dealing with the powerful feelings of sadness and disappointment. We have to enter these times with our children with a precommitment to a concrete set of goals. Failure to do so will keep us from accomplishing the good things that are possible when God enables us to turn a sinful situation into a redemptive opportunity.

I want to use this situation with my daughter as a real-life context for discussing five foundational goals for parenting teenagers. But let me first point out what our goal should *not* be.

Regulating Behavior

I am afraid that most parents of teenagers have the regulation of their teenagers' behavior as their most basic goal. They fear the big three vices of the teen years: drugs and alcohol, sex, and dropping out of school. They want to do anything they can to keep these from happening. So they do whatever is necessary to maintain control of their teenagers' choices and activities.

These people spend much of their time doing detective work. They are more like police than parents. They seek to motivate by *guilt* ("After all we have done for you, this is how you are going to thank us?" or "What do you think the Lord feels as he looks down at what you are doing?"), *fear* ("Do you know the diseases that you can get out there?" or "You do that, and there is no telling how I will respond!"), or *manipulation* ("If you _____, we would be much more willing to get you the car" or "We'll make a deal: if you _____, we will _____ for you").

It is a short-term victory at best to control the behavior of a teen whose heart is not submissive to God. The moment he is out from under your system of control, he will act in ways that are more consistent with his heart's true thoughts and motives. He will no longer do what is right, because the right that he did was forced on him by external parental control. His heart never changed. We see this again and again as teenagers go to college and seem to throw off everything they "learned" in their Christian homes.

Colossians 2:20–23 warns us against this behavior-control strategy:

> If with Christ you died to the elemental spirits of the world, why, as if you were still alive in the world, do you submit to regulations—"Do not handle, Do not taste, Do not touch" (referring to things that all perish as they are used)—according to human precepts and teachings? These have indeed an appearance of wisdom in promoting self-made religion and asceticism and severity to the body, but they are of no value in stopping the indulgence of the flesh.

The rules-and-regulations approach that focuses on keeping the teenager out of trouble will ultimately fail because it does not deal with the heart. As Paul so powerfully states, it is of "no value in stopping the indulgence of the flesh." What he means is that it does not deal with the source of a person's wrong behavior: the sinful desires of the heart. Peter says that the corruption in the world is caused by evil desires (2 Peter 1:4). We have to work at the level of the heart desires of our teenagers, or we will win lots of battles and ultimately lose the war. It is not enough to be detectives, jailers, and judges. We must pastor the hearts of our children with the kind of faithful, watchful care for their souls that we receive from our heavenly Father.

The parent who has a pastoral model of parenting will do more than hand down regulations and enforce punishments when they are broken. Pastoring parents will befriend their teens. They will probe and examine. They will engage their children in provocative discussions. They will be unwilling to live with distance, avoidance, and non-answers. They will not let their teenagers set the agenda for their relationship. In times of trouble, they will have discussions rather than cross-examinations. They will not be there simply to prove their children wrong and to announce punishment. They will seek to expose the true thoughts and motives of their teenagers' hearts by asking heart-disclosing questions, such as

- What were you thinking and feeling at the time?
- Why *was* that so important to you?
- What were you seeking to accomplish when you did that?
- What was the most important thing to you at that moment?

- What was it that you were afraid of in that situation?
- What was it that you were trying to get?
- Why did you become so angry?
- If you could go back and do something differently, what would you change?

They will help their teenagers to look at themselves in the accurate mirror of the Word, which is able to expose and judge the heart. And they will do all of this in a spirit of humble, gentle, kind, forgiving, forbearing, and patient love. In so doing they will incarnate the love of Christ, who is the Great Shepherd (Pastor) of their teenagers' souls.

Colossians 3:12–14 gives us a wonderful description of the attitudes that need to shape the ministry encounters we have with our teenagers.

> Put on then, as God's chosen ones, holy and beloved, compassionate hearts, kindness, humility, meekness, and patience, bearing with one another and, if one has a complaint against another, forgiving each other; as the Lord has forgiven you, so you also must forgive. And above all these put on love, which binds everything together in perfect harmony.

Parents who approach their teenagers with these attitudes of heart will demonstrate the presence of the One who is truly ever-present and whose redemptive love is boundless. He, the great Changer of Hearts, is then able to use them as instruments in his restorative hands. How different this is from the anxious anger, fearful control, and desperate manipulation that many parents exercise in an attempt to get their teenagers to do what is right! James says that this anger "does not produce the righteousness of God" (James 1:20).

Attempts to control your teen get in the way of what the Lord is seeking to do in her life. Ezekiel states very clearly that God's agenda is to "lay hold of the hearts of the house of Israel, who are all estranged from me through their idols" (Ezek. 14:5). God says, "I am working to recapture the hearts of my people so that they serve me and me alone." Can we have a lesser goal as we parent our teenagers? We must work to see the underlying idols of the heart that have shaped their behavior. They will be exposed as the Spirit works through us to shine the light of Scripture on our teens' lives.

All that we do with our teenagers, from the casual encounters to the crisis moments, must be shaped by a basic commitment to heart change. This parental pastoring of the heart can be summarized with five fundamental goals that offer practical guidance in all that we do with our teenagers. These goals will form the discussion of this and the next four chapters.

GOAL 1:
Focus on the Spiritual Struggle

Teenagers' lives tend to be dominated by concerns about the world that can be seen, touched, and tasted. They fret tearfully about how they look. They long to be accepted by peers. They hold their "stuff" possessively. They talk in dramatic terms about what looks beautiful or tastes appealing to them. They are crushed when someone mocks an outfit they are wearing. They anguish over perceived rejection. Teenagers tend to be intensely materialistic—that is, focused on the physical world. Often the more significant unseen world of the spiritual seems unreal to them.

Teens tend to believe two deadly lies. First, they tend to believe the physical is more real than the spiritual. Present, physical, personal happiness seems more important to them than eternal blessing. Second, they tend to believe in the permanence of the physical world. It doesn't seem to be passing away. It seems always to be there, and it seems to be "where it's at."

How different this is from the biblical perspective! Asaph, in Psalm 73, says the prosperity of the wicked is like a dream. What a powerful analysis! A dream seems real yet is not. It passes away the moment the body wakes. The earthly goods that a person acquires are passing away even as they are collected. The physical world is destined to perish.

In 2 Corinthians 4:16–18, Paul says it this way:

> So we do not lose heart. Though our outer self is wasting away, our inner self is being renewed day by day. For this light momentary affliction is preparing for us an eternal weight of glory beyond all comparison, as we look not to the things that are seen but to the things that are unseen.

> For the things that are seen are transient, but the things that are unseen are eternal.

Paul is preoccupied with the unseen. He is focused on the spiritual. He is not invested in the physical and material world. Why? Because it is passing away. Christ said, "What will it profit a man if he gains the whole world and forfeits his soul? Or what shall a man give in return for his soul?" (Matt. 16:26). John warns us in his first letter not to "love the world or the things in the world" (1 John 2:15). The theme is everywhere in Scripture. The wise person lives for what cannot be seen; the fool lives to build another barn to store away what is perishing and useless in the world to come. The wise person longs for spiritual blessing; the fool craves physical reward. The wise person looks to eternity; the fool lives for the moment.

Not only do teenagers tend to live with a physical focus—missing or minimizing the significance of the spiritual world—but they also tend to live with a peacetime mentality. In times of peace, people give themselves to luxury, leisure, and pleasure. They focus on wants and desires. However, in times of war, people live with another focus. The factory that produced high-end tech is converted to produce electronic equipment for battle. The assembly line that produced luxury cars begins to produce tanks. Young men go to military training instead of college. War commands the focus not only of the professional soldiers but of the whole society.

Here's the point. Scripture says that *life is war*! As I have said many times to my children, "A war is being fought on the turf of your heart. It is being fought for the control of your soul. Each situation you face today is a skirmish. Be aware of the battle. Don't forget you have a scheming enemy who is out to deceive, divide, and destroy you. To win, you must fight. You must not relax." We cannot say this enough to our teenagers (or ourselves).

Wise, mature, godly people live with awareness of the spiritual; they see it in every situation of life. They never view life "*under* the sun," as Ecclesiastes repeatedly says. They see the spiritual implications in everything they do and in every situation they are in. This is the mindset we must aim to produce in our teenagers. To do this, we must be spiritually minded ourselves. We must live in awareness of the war.

Two things keep us from teaching our children to face and fight in the spiritual struggle.

Misplaced Worries

As parents, we tend to be more worried about the world of the seen than the world of the unseen, especially when it comes to our teenagers. We are more upset about how their lost jobs will affect their collegiate futures than we are about the inner spiritual issues that God is revealing. We are more concerned about their poor grades than about what those grades reveal about the spiritual condition of our children. We get angry when a room is a chaotic litter of dirty clothes, and we do not see the heart behind the mess. We are more upset over the physical damage of our possessions than the spiritual damage that may be taking place at the same time in a teen's life. We tell her that her outfit looks ridiculous or complain that he drank the last of the milk, and we miss what is of eternal importance.

Because of this, we do not take advantage of daily opportunities to remind our teenagers of the spiritual struggle present in every situation in this fallen world. If we are going to produce teenagers who engage in the spiritual struggle, we need to start by asking ourselves what is really important to us. Are we, by the things that concern us and the way we solve problems, demonstrating the opposite of what we say we believe? Are our own lives consistent with what we say that we would like to produce in our teenagers?

Cultural Misunderstanding

The second thing that gets in our way is a cultural misunderstanding. Our Christian culture has tended to misunderstand spiritual warfare. By most Christian thinking, if spiritual warfare were a movie, the movie would be produced by Steven Spielberg and written by Stephen King! Spiritual warfare makes us think of demon possession, horrific demonstrations of satanic control, and dramatic exorcisms. But Scripture presents spiritual warfare not as the violent, bizarre end of the Christian life but as what the Christian life *is*!

When Paul introduces the subject of spiritual warfare at the end of his letter to the Ephesians, he is not changing the subject to talk about the dark side of spirituality. No, he is summarizing everything he has said up to that point. Where does spiritual warfare take place? In the body of Christ, in the marriage relationship, in the parent-child relationship, in the relationship between slave and master, and in every location in the culture around us. Our teenagers need to learn how to fight the war and use the battle equipment the Lord has provided. Paul's description needs to shape the way we think about this every-day, every-situation war.

> Finally, be strong in the Lord and in the strength of his might. Put on the whole armor of God, that you may be able to stand against the schemes of the devil. For we do not wrestle against flesh and blood, but against the rulers, against the authorities, against the cosmic powers over this present darkness, against the spiritual forces of evil in the heavenly places. Therefore take up the whole armor of God, that you may be able to withstand in the evil day, and having done all, to stand firm. Stand therefore, having fastened on the belt of truth, and having put on the breastplate of righteousness, and, as shoes for your feet, having put on the readiness given by the gospel of peace. In all circumstances take up the shield of faith, with which you can extinguish all the flaming darts of the evil one; and take the helmet of salvation, and the sword of the Spirit, which is the word of God, praying at all times in the Spirit, with all prayer and supplication. To that end, keep alert with all perseverance, making supplication for all the saints. (Eph. 6:10–18)

If our teenagers are going to stand strong in the spiritual war, they need to know that there *is* a spiritual world where war is taking place. They need to know who the enemy is (and who the enemy is not). They need to know the weapons of this war and how to use them, and they need to know what victory looks like in everyday life. This is vital because not only does spiritual warfare take place *where* we live, *it is what we are living.*

That is why Paul summarizes his letter to the Ephesians this way. He does not want us to think about our situations and relationships horizontally. He wants us to realize that dramatic vertical struggles are taking place in them all. So he tells us to be aware of the devil's schemes, to stand fast in the Lord's power, to put on the whole armor of God, and to pray.

There is a war going on out there. It is not an *aspect* of the Christian life; it *is* the Christian life.

Sadly, because they have bought into the cultural misunderstanding, most Christian parents have not constantly reminded their teenagers of the battle or prepared them for the daily victories that can be experienced by the children of God.

Qualities of a Spiritual Warrior

Our goal is to raise children who are very aware of the spiritual world and understand the spiritual implications of everything they do. What will these teenagers look like? Let me list several qualities that will be evident in their lives.

Heartfelt Fear of the Lord

Teenagers who live as spiritual warriors have a heartfelt, internalized fear of God. This is the foundation of a spiritual life. The fear of God is the beginning of a truly wise life (Prov. 1:7). The fool has no fear of God in his heart, so he lives for what the moment can deliver and what his eyes can see.

What is this fear of God? It is the nonnegotiable motivator of the spiritual person. God, his presence, his will, and his glory are the reason the spiritual person does what he does. He has a single motivation in his life—to live so as to please his Lord. He does not live for his own pleasure or the pleasure of others. He does not live for what he can possess. He does what he does not because someone is watching or out of fear of the consequences but ultimately because of a deep, worshipful love and reverence for God. To knowingly and purposefully disobey God is unthinkable.

A heartfelt fear of the Lord is the only thing that will keep our teenagers pure in times of temptation when we are far away and the pressure is on them to step outside God's boundaries.

Submission to Authority

Second to the fear of God, but directly related to it, is submission to authority. One of the sad things that I hear parents say is "Come on, Paul, you have to expect teenagers to rebel. It's just part of growing up." I don't think that we should ever come to casually expect or accept rebellion from anyone.

If a person fears God, she will be submissive to the authorities that God has placed in her life. A person who disregards, argues against, or seeks to skirt the authorities in her life is not taking advantage of God's help in fighting the spiritual battle. God places authority in our lives to restrain sin. A person who is aware of her sinfulness and who wants to live a godly life will not chafe against authority. She will appreciate it and submit to it. This is the spirit we want to see in our teenagers.

Something is wrong when a teenager views authority as negative and punitive. Our goal is to teach our teenagers to admit their need of God-ordained authority and the importance of willing submission to it. We want them to grow to see the authority figures in their lives as instruments of help, guidance, protection, and restraint who are lovingly given by a God who knows their hearts and the nature of their struggle in this fallen world. Ultimately, we want them to say, "Authority—I need it, I want it, and I am thankful God has put it in my life."

This goal may seem unrealistic for two reasons.

We have become so used to accepting negative responses from our teenagers that we are surprised when they respond with acceptance, respect, and willing obedience. Rather than expecting respect and being grieved in the face of rebellion, we have succumbed to the cultural belief that rebellion is an acceptable norm for the teen years.

We did not fight and win essential authority struggles while our children were young. We spent too much time indulging their demands and giving in to their misbehavior. We explained away their rebellion, saying that they were teething, overtired, or just trying to get attention. Now that our children are teenagers, they don't appreciate our authority. They see no need to submit to it. They don't understand why we are not excusing their rebellion as we once did and why we are now standing in their way. As teenagers, they are now all too willing to take us on when we try to exercise parental authority.

Rebellion against parental authority is never okay, at any age. Rejection of parental authority is a rejection of God's authority. And the rejection of God's authority is, in fact, claiming his authority as one's own. It is an attempt to *be* God. Whether your teenager realizes it or not, the stakes could not be higher!

Separation from the Wicked

Let me start by stating the next quality in positive terms. The teenager who fears God wants to be with other teenagers who fear God. It is true that a person is known by the company he keeps! If a teenager is serious in his desire to participate in the spiritual struggle, if he is seriously seeking to live a life pleasing to the Lord, and if he is living in a willing submission to the authorities in his life, then he will want to spend his time with people who share his values. Rebellious teenagers will not be attractive to him. Teens who have no desire for spiritual things will not draw him. Rather, wherever he is, he will instinctively seek out those who have a heart for God. He will feel strangely out of place with kids who have no interest in the things that God says are most important. This is separation from the wicked, and it is a quality of the spiritual warrior that the book of Proverbs discusses liberally.

Thorough Knowledge of Scripture

It is impossible to participate in the spiritual struggle if you do not have the ability to think through your faith and apply it to the situations of life. What a teenager needs, if she is going to live a God-honoring life, is a thorough knowledge of Scripture that allows her to apply its commands, principles, and perspectives to the many different situations that arise in everyday life. She needs to be more than a person who has acquired biblical knowledge; she needs to be a person who is able to approach life with biblical wisdom.

Many teenagers are unprepared for the spiritual struggle because they have never been taught to think biblically. They have been in Sunday school, so they know all the familiar Bible stories and have memorized all the favorite Bible passages, but these are not much more than isolated, unconnected biblical factoids to them. They haven't been woven into a consistent, distinctively biblical view of life. To these teenagers, the Bible is a book of moralistic stories, a book of dos and don'ts, rather than a way of thinking. As a result, although they have lots of biblical knowledge, they have little biblical wisdom. They do not have a functional, useful, biblical view of life that keeps them from living foolishly.

We must disciple our children to think biblically, to interpret all the facts of life from a biblical perspective. We must teach them to always ask how the Bible can help them to understand whatever they are considering. They must learn to look at themselves and everything else in their lives from the vantage point of Scripture. This consistently biblical view of life will enable them to recognize what is wise to think and do in every situation.

We will not accomplish this by barking orders at our children. This takes time, patience, and love. It also assumes that we have taken time to think through the issues ourselves. We cannot mentor our children into something we ourselves do not have.

Biblical Self-Awareness

The final quality of a teen who recognizes the spiritual struggle around him is biblical self-awareness. Maybe it is obvious, but teenagers don't tend to be very self-aware. They are very aware of how *others* respond to them. They focus on how they look and how they feel, but they tend to lack the essence of biblical self-awareness: an awareness of the heart. This is powerfully demonstrated when parents point out a wrong attitude in their teenagers. Most often, teenagers respond with hurt, feeling that they have been falsely accused or wrongly singled out.

We want to be used by God to produce teens who can regularly examine themselves in the perfect mirror of the Word of God and humbly accept what is revealed there. A teenager who has an accurate view of himself will not only respond well to the help of his parents but also seek it out. He will be aware of his spiritual weaknesses and will welcome the resources that God has placed in his life. He will not excuse his sin, defend it, argue about it, or shift blame when it is pointed out. He will "not . . . think of himself more highly than he ought to think" (Rom. 12:3). It may sound unbelievable, but it is true.

Many teenagers do not take protective measures against sin ("flee youthful passions") because they believe that they are much stronger and more mature than they are. They really do believe they can play with fire without getting burned. When they get burned by their choices and behavior, their inaccurate view of self leads them to conclude that what happened was the fault of others or of the circumstances.

How important it is for us to take every opportunity God gives us to hold the mirror of the Word in front of our teenagers so that they can begin to see themselves as they actually are! So often in the moments when their hearts are being revealed, our own anger and frustration cause us to beat them with words and mete out harsh punishments. We forget to function as God's instruments, and our anger leaves our children only more defensive, closed, and self-deceived.

Each of us sins, yet we do not all sin in the same way. A teenager who is biblically self-aware will live with an accurate, practical knowledge of personal themes of weakness, temptation, and sin. The spiritually aware teenager knows the ways he is susceptible to temptation, and that knowledge helps him to take protective measures against it.

One Sunday as we were traveling to church, I inadvertently drove into a rather large pothole. After the car quit bouncing, my wife said that she was confused. I asked her why. She said she didn't understand why I drove into the same pothole Sunday after Sunday! It was in the same place each week. The road had another lane. Why didn't I anticipate and avoid the pothole?

Teenagers often drive into the same spiritual pothole again and again because of their blindness to the themes of their hearts. One of the most helpful things we can do for them spiritually is help them to look down the road of life, anticipating where temptation will hit them and teaching them how to avoid it. As we do this, they will grow in self-awareness and in appreciation for the mercy and grace of the Lord, who helps them in their time of need. They will also begin to see their parents not as judges and jailers but as God-given resources to assist them in fighting life's most significant battles.

In times of struggle and failure, we need to do more than pronounce judgment and enforce punishment. We need to talk, discuss, engage, and interact with our teenagers, hoping that God will use these moments of opportunity to open their eyes a little more to who they really are and to their constant need for Christ.

THAT NIGHT WHEN I HELD that awful note written by my daughter, I needed to keep this first goal in mind. Here was a wonderful, God-ordained opportunity to talk with her about the nature of the spiritual struggle. My daughter's note was about more than bad language and disrespect. It pictured the spiritual war that was raging in her life. By God's grace, the war had broken out into the open, yet she didn't see it. She was much more focused on the fact that she was in trouble at school and at home, and she wondered what consequences she would receive for her behavior.

My daughter didn't need me to tell her that I was crushed, that I was ashamed of her, that I would never have thought of doing such a thing when I was young! She didn't need me to announce a punishment and leave the room, missing a golden opportunity to do the work of the Lord. No, she needed her mom and me to take her to a deeper level of concern and understanding. What had motivated her to write such a note? What desires had led her to do so? What did the whole situation reveal was important to her? What did the note reveal about her relationships with peers and her response to authority? What could she learn from this situation about her own personal susceptibility to temptation?

In thinking through these questions with her, my wife and I were helping her to understand and participate in the spiritual struggle. The discussion gave us an opportunity to talk to her about the fear of God, submission to authority, separation from the wicked, the ability to think through and apply her faith, and biblical self-awareness. It provided an opportunity for us to help our daughter to know herself more accurately, to know God more personally, and to be much wiser in understanding the schemes of the Enemy. In the midst of real failure, she took one more step toward becoming an active participant in the spiritual struggle. She would have never taken these steps without our help.

Questions for Reflection and Discussion

1. Have your own unplanned and emotional responses to your teen's sinful behavior driven a wedge into your relationship? Sit down and prayerfully build a concrete set of goals—deeper than behaviorial change induced by guilt, fear, and manipulation—that will better prepare you to handle your child's sin with biblical wisdom and grace.

2. What are your worst fears as a parent? Can you name them? As you look back over your past, can you see how those fears have led you to grasp for control, to do God's job for him? How would your life and your parenting look different if you put your trust in him and *his* work in your teenager's heart?

3. What parenting model do you primarily follow—pastor, detective, jailer, or judge? Is your primary goal as a parent to see behavioral change in your teenager or a heart for God? Reflect on the heart-disclosing questions on page 111 and consider implementing these into daily conversations with your child.

4. As we aim for our children to live for "what is unseen," are you modeling this as a parent for your family? Are your eyes fixed on the eternal?

5. What do you think of when you hear the term *spiritual warfare*? How do you think spiritual warfare plays out in your life and in the life of your teenager? Notice the ways the Enemy may be out to deceive, divide, and destroy both you and your child.

6. Reflect on the five qualities of the teenager who understands and participates in the spiritual struggle: fear of the Lord, submission to authority, separation from the wicked, knowledge of Scripture, and biblical self-awareness. Pray these qualities over your teenager, and consider how you might be a redemptive instrument in his or her life.

8

Convictions and Wisdom

MY WIFE AND I WERE going away to a weekend conference. Our son, a young teenager at the time, asked if he could stay with a family from our church who had children his age. We agreed, dropped him off, and went on our way. It seemed as though it would be a nondescript, uneventful weekend. Little did we know that God had something else planned. For our son, this would be a weekend of temptation, decision, and difficult exercise of faith.

Before our son arrived at our friends' house, the kids in the family went to the video store to rent a couple of movies. After our son arrived and the parents left the house for the evening, the videos came out. It wasn't long before our son realized that the videos contained content he should not be watching.

What would he do? He could watch the videos—probably neither we nor his friends' parents would know. But instead he decided to try to convince the others *not* to watch them. They said he was "being stupid" and put the first video in. Not knowing what else to do, and having nowhere else to go, he spent the evening in the kitchen, eating more chips and drinking more soda than he ever had in his life. He had made a choice. He had exercised conviction. He had taken the heat for his faith.

113

When the parents of the house came home and found him in the kitchen, they asked him why he wasn't with the others. When he explained, they had two reactions. First, they were upset at their children for the video choices they had made and for their insensitivity to their guest. Second, they were amazed at our son for the choice he had made to live out what he thought was right.

I am afraid that many of us are so busy making decisions for our children in order to keep them safe that we do not teach them to develop their own set of internalized biblical convictions. It is one thing for a teenager to do what is right under a watchful eye or under threat of punishment. It is quite another thing for a teenager to exercise independent, unpressured, heartfelt personal conviction. As we prepare our teenage children to go out into this darkened, fallen world and live godly lives, it is mandatory that we make the development of their internalized convictions one of our primary goals.

GOAL 2:
Develop a Heart of Conviction and Wisdom

Along with developing convictions, developing wisdom—the second half of this goal—is necessary if our teenagers are to live God-pleasing lives. Let me illustrate with another story.

The call came to me at work in the middle of the day. It was my son calling from his part-time job. He had been asked to do something that was dangerous and not part of his job description. It was not a moral issue—there was no clear right or wrong—but a decision needed to be made. He called me and asked if he could fax me his job description so that we could discuss what he should do.

We talked about the people who were in authority over him and why they were making the request. How should he deal with those over him? In a way, he wanted me to make the decision for him, but I would not, because I thought this situation was sent by God to develop him. There were many wisdom issues involved here. My son was open, seeking, and thinking well. After discussing the situation, I told him I would pray for him. I was confident that he had what he needed to make a wise decision.

What happened? He got fired! I couldn't believe it. He had done all the right things, yet he lost his job. I was tempted to question God. Couldn't he encourage him just this once? But in the firing there was an opportunity to talk about life in a broken world, the blessing of doing things God's way, and what it means to entrust yourself to God's sovereign care. A couple of months later, he was hired back. The regional manager was very angry over the way the situation had been handled and instructed those under him to offer our son the job again.

Notice that this situation was very different from the Friday night video incident—but no less important. The first situation had to do with what I will call *clear-boundary issues*. These are issues to which God has plainly spoken, in which there is an obvious right and wrong. They require us to exercise personal, biblical, internalized conviction. The second situation had to do with what I will call *wisdom issues*. These are issues with no direct "thus says the Lord" but to which Scripture speaks with a myriad of balancing principles so that we may live wisely in a fallen world. What is needed in such situations is readily applicable biblical wisdom.

When your teenager encounters clear-boundary issues, she does not need to pray for wisdom. For example, in a department store she does not need to pray that God would give her the wisdom to know whether she should steal or not! What your teenager needs is a heart that submits to God's will as revealed in his Word. She needs a heart more controlled by love for the Creator than for the created thing.

But when a teen encounters wisdom issues, he will never solve them by treating them as though they are simple boundary issues. If he tries to do this, he will begin to lose confidence in Scripture, thinking that it does not speak clearly to his life. Then, in his lack of confidence in Scripture, he will move toward one of two extremes: (1) legalism, in which he makes everything a rigid boundary issue, or (2) foolishness, in which he concludes that anything that is not an obvious boundary issue is unimportant and not addressed in Scripture.

I fear that many of us do an inadequate job of preparing our children to deal with wisdom issues. For some of us, this is because we live with a secular-spiritual dichotomy in our own lives. Many of us think of our lives in a two-worlds way. There is the world of the spiritual that includes our devotional, church, and formal worship lives and those issues on which God has given us clear commands. Attention to these things makes up our definition of what is spiritual.

The other world in this two-worlds way of thinking is the secular world. It is the world outside God's clear commands in Scripture and our devotional-worship-church lives. In a two-worlds way of thinking, Scripture has little if anything to say about life in this second world. Unfortunately, this world tends to be vastly larger than the spiritual world. It tends to be the world where we live every day and expend most of our productive effort. How can we teach our teenagers to exercise biblical wisdom there if we are not accustomed to doing it ourselves? How can we teach wisdom when we have failed to realize that *all* of life is spiritual and that Scripture speaks in some way to *every* situation of the human experience?

There is another reason why parents fail to prepare their children well for the wisdom decisions they will face as they leave home. It is, sadly, that many parents simply do not have a fluid, functional, situationally applicable knowledge of Scripture themselves. Many of us have little more than a Sunday-school knowledge of the Bible. We know the popular stories, we have some grasp of the major doctrines, and we know phrases from the most-quoted passages, but we have not meditated on or mastered the Word. We don't know how to use its wisdom to guide us in matters of everyday living, and our own lack of knowledge keeps us from discipling our children to live in a biblically wise way.

As parents, we cannot give what we don't have ourselves. We can teach our children to be practically obedient to the Word, exercising decisive biblical conviction, only if we are doing the same. We can teach our children to wisely apply the principles of the Word to the issues of life only if that is what we ourselves are seeking to do. Obedient students of the Word tend to produce the same kind of children.

Understanding Clear-Boundary Issues

Let me define further what I mean when I talk about clear-boundary issues versus wisdom issues. Clear-boundary issues are situations that involve the plain commands of Scripture. The call to speak the truth, to

honor father and mother, to not steal, and to not commit adultery or for-
nication are all examples. To live God's way in these situations, a teenager
needs two primary things. First, she needs to know the commands of Scrip
ture. She cannot stay inside God's boundaries if she doesn't know what they
are. Second, she needs personal conviction—that is, a heart committed to
doing God's will regardless of the consequences.

I am persuaded that it is very important to define the concept of convictions for our teenagers. Too often, what we call convictions are actually
preferences. Real convictions are based on the revealed truth of Scripture.
Preferences are based on personal desire. Convictions are constant; preferences change with desire. Convictions demand faith; preferences rely
on the emotions of the moment. Our teenagers need to understand the
difference between a conviction and a preference.

Here are six characteristics of biblical conviction:

- *A biblical conviction is always based on the study of, submission
  to, and application of Scripture.* Our knowledge of the will of God
  combines with a heart to obey that we carry into the situations of
  everyday life.
- *A biblical conviction is always predetermined.* You do not arrive at
  biblical convictions on the spur of the moment or in the heat of
  the circumstances. Biblical convictions are predetermined first by
  God. He has made the decision for us; our job is simple—to obey.
  Second, they are predetermined by us. Long before we enter the
  situation, we have decided that we will live according to the clear
  commands of the Word. We bring this heart commitment, made
  long beforehand, to each new situation.
- *A biblical conviction will not change with the circumstances.* It does
  not respond to outside pressure. We see this powerfully demonstrated by Christ, the apostles, and the martyrs of old. Conviction
  is based on an inner commitment, not on external pressures such
  as peer opinion or potential consequences.
- *Biblical convictions are inflexible.* True convictions are nonnegotiable. They will not be offered up, dealt away, or compromised in
  order to get or achieve something else.

- *True biblical conviction is bold.* There is a foundational confidence to it because it is based on the clear word of the Lord as revealed in Scripture. When we have conviction, we realize that the God who made the world and who controls each moment has spoken; therefore, there is no safer choice than to actively do his will! True conviction is not timid and doubting. It results in courageous acts of faith.
- *True biblical conviction is always lived out.* Conviction that is not lived is not really conviction. If our hearts know, understand, acknowledge, and submit to what is right, our convictions will show in the decisions we make every day.

A person who does not have biblical convictions does not have an internal restraint system. This person will do right when under a watchful eye or external pressure. However, when external motivators are removed, that person will behave very differently. Think, once again, about the note my daughter wrote in chapter 7. She lacked personal, internalized, biblical convictions. Her problem was not lack of knowledge. It wasn't even that she failed to acknowledge that God's standard is right. What she lacked was a personal *commitment* to obey God no matter the cost. Lovingly, God revealed this gap dramatically so that she would have a turning of heart.

Understanding Wisdom Issues

As important as biblical conviction is, and as important as it is to pay attention to the boundary issues, a believer spends most of his time grappling with wisdom issues. Because a true believer has decided to live in submission to the lordship of Christ, he lives a basically obedient life in which he does not test God's boundaries. Yet there are myriad situations in which he needs wisdom—that is, he needs to apply the principles, perspectives, and themes of Scripture so that his practical everyday decisions express God's will for his life.

Let's look back at the decision my son had to make in his part-time job. We'll consider a few of the many scriptural principles that apply to the situation and define what living wisely looks like in such a circumstance.

Authority

Scripture clearly presents the authorities in my son's life (parents, bosses, government officials) as ordained and appointed by God—as God's servants for my son's good. Whenever he appeals to or disagrees with these authorities, he must do so in a spirit of honor, thankfulness, and submission.

Grace

Proverbs says that "a soft answer turns away wrath, but a harsh word stirs up anger"(15:1). In a time of disagreement and controversy, the way my son speaks is very important.

Truth

It is important that my son avoid the temptation to trim or embellish the truth. At the same time, it is vital that he not use the truth vengefully as a weapon. He must speak the truth as he would want it spoken to him: with love.

The Higher Agenda

As a believer, my son is called to work in such a way as to make the gospel attractive. Even at work he is to function as an ambassador of the Lord and living spokesperson for his truth.

Wise Counsel

The Scripture warns my son against impulsive, independent decision-making. God will give wisdom to those who ask, without showing favoritism (James 1:5). Scripture also tells him that in the multitude of counsel there is wisdom (Prov. 15:22). It is important for my son not to respond hastily but to take the time to receive the wisdom God has promised.

Faithfulness and Integrity

It is important for my son to examine his job description because he has to accept the obligation to do the work he has promised to do in exchange for his wages. Scripture calls us to be careful of the promises we make and to be faithful to what we have promised.

God's Sovereignty

It could be tempting for my son to look at his situation as "rotten bad luck" that somehow has befallen him. He needs to see that this event is under the careful control of God, who rules over everything for his sake. He does not need to panic or gain control of the situation somehow. He is free to act wisely and entrust the outcome to his heavenly Father, who judges all things justly.

Values

In situations like this, we express what is really important to us. It would be tempting for my son to live for things that can be seen. A job is important, but Scripture enjoins him not to live for earthly treasure or for what can be seen, touched, tasted, and quantified. Rather, it calls him to live for things that have eternal value. Even in this job situation, my son is being called to live for God's glory, to keep his own heart pure, and to seek God's kingdom and his righteousness. Where the rubber meets the road, this means doing what is right and trusting God to provide.

The Heart

Scripture teaches us that what we do expresses the thoughts and desires of our hearts. It is important for my son to be aware of his heart in this situation. To what temptations is he particularly susceptible? Is he tempted to give in to the fear of man? Is he tempted to anger? Is he doubting God? Is he giving in to discouragement? Is he succumbing to time pressure or the pressure of his peers? It is very important in this kind of situation for a teenager to operate with heart awareness so that he can protect himself from the temptations to which he knows he is particularly weak.

God's Glory

My son is called to live for something grander than his own good, comfort, success, affluence, and ease. The most important thing he must do is respond to the situation in a way that pleases God. This is more important than solving the situation, pleasing the boss, pleasing himself, or retaining his job. He will never do what is right at the practical, every-day level unless he has the glory of God as his ultimate goal. Whenever we disobey God, it is because our own glory and good are more important to us than the glory of God.

These ten principles bring focus to the job situation our son encountered. Each principle helped him to know more clearly what he should do and how, when, and why he should do it. There are many, many more principles that apply to this situation, each giving light to the heart and a lamp for the feet.

The truths of Scripture are like the music of a great symphony orchestra. In an orchestra, each instrument is made more beautiful by the other. You do not understand or experience a symphony by hearing the separate notes of one violin, oboe, or drum. It is only as you hear all the instruments play together that you understand the beauty and majesty of the symphony. Each complements and balances the other. Similarly, Scripture gives us a symphony of truth. Not just one note but many contribute to the rich, harmonious tones of truth.

As parents, we need to have a symphonic mentality as we train our children for godly living. We cannot hammer away at one note. We must introduce them to the whole symphony of biblical wisdom so that they can make biblically sound decisions. To do that, we must know the symphony ourselves, and we must be committed to take the time to talk to our children daily about the principles that apply to their life situations. We need to get away from the quick and easy "do this, don't do that" that we dispense with little or no discussion or explanation. We need to invite our children to examine and discuss these principles, seeing difficulty and trouble as an opportunity to help them to hear more of God's symphony of truth and to understand how its notes make sense of life. It is of paramount importance that *we* do not think for our children but teach *them* how to think about life and employ the symphony of perspectives God has given us in his Word.

Strategies for Developing a Wise Heart

To raise children of conviction and wisdom, we need a strategy. Let me list some things that you can do to help to develop a sensitive conscience and a wise heart.

See Problem Situations as Opportunities

This is the theme of this book: God, who loves us and who is in control, is accomplishing his wonderful purposes in our problems.

Several years ago, a brokenhearted parent told me that she had found pornography in her son's bedroom. She was crushed, and her husband was angry. They had been getting ready to go after their son when they decided to call me first. I was thankful they did. They needed perspective. Yes, I shared their sadness, but I saw something else very wonderful: I saw the rescuing hand of God. Their son could have gotten away with it and moved a little deeper into that world of enslaving secret sexual sin, but God, in his glory and goodness, had another plan.

I said to this mother, "Don't you see that God's work of rescuing your son from this temptation has already begun? Thank him for his awesome love, and be a part of what he is doing. Don't go in with guns blazing. Tell your son that he is loved by God and that today that love is being demonstrated in the way God ordained that the pornography be found. Then help him to understand the thoughts and motives of his heart that led him into this sin."

If you look at these situations as irritants that ruin your plans for your morning, afternoon, or evening; if you respond to them impulsively with impatience, irritation, and verbal put-downs; if you fail to reflect a biblical mind ("I couldn't care less what you do when you're out of here, but you do this again, and you're on the street!"), your teenager will grow up to do the same. Instead, stop, thank God for your high calling as a parent, and have a patient and heart-engaging conversation with your son or daughter.

Resist Making the Decision for Your Teenager

Remember, we need to have a goal more fundamental than keeping our teenagers safe by regulating their behavior. Take the time to teach your teenager how to make a wise decision. Teach her the biblical content that applies to each situation and teach her the biblical process of decision-making. Our goal should be to put more and more decisions into our children's hands as they mature. To do this, you have to deal with your own fear, desire to control, and reluctance to place your life and the life of your teenager in the capable hands of God.

You will also need to be patient and to persevere in the face of resistance. Ephesians 4:2 provides the model for us. It says, "Be completely humble and gentle; be patient, bearing with one another in love" (NIV). "Bearing with in love" means being patient in the face of provocation. Teenagers say wild things. They give weak excuses and offer illogical arguments. They make extreme statements ("No one has ever . . ." "You always . . ." "This happens to me every time"). They compare you to the parents of their friends. They do all this because teenagers don't tend to think that they need help. They tend to see your loving intervention and instruction as unwelcome interference. It is your job to win them for the way of the Lord. You are called to be an instrument of wisdom in your teenager's life. To do so, you must be gentle, humble, patient, and persevering.

Draw Out the Heart of Your Teenager

Ask open-ended questions that help him to communicate what he really thinks and what he really wants. As you do this, don't scold the teenager for his honesty. You don't need to lecture someone who is open, communicative, and teachable. Ask your teenager what he wants to do and why he wants to do it. Ask him what is important in his situation and why. Ask him what he fears most when he thinks about what could happen. Ask him to describe what would make him happy in a situation. Ask him what he thinks God thinks about the circumstances he is in.

The goal is to get your teenager to look at himself. You need to ask good questions that he cannot answer without examining his own heart. In problem situations, resist making pronouncements about what your teen did, why he did it, and what he is going to get as a result. Resist doing all the thinking and talking as you examine the situation. Resist turning a discussion of choices and decisions into a lecture in which you preach at him with pointed fingers, red face, and loud voice while he sits silently, waiting for you to leave. If we consistently handle things this way, it is not long before our teenagers determine to avoid these "talks" at any cost and feel a sense of dread when we approach their rooms. Sometimes we have unwittingly driven our teenagers into the very silence that we say we hate.

Be Persistent

Don't settle for grunts, groans, lack of eye contact, silences, and yeses or nos that are given without explanation. Be positive, friendly, and encouraging—but be persistent. Few teenagers will draw you out. Often teenagers have many questions and much to say, but they say nothing unless given the opportunity to talk with someone who really does appear to care. Seek out your teenager and patiently engage her in conversation. Don't take personal offense at her resistance but remind her of your love and commitment. Make sure that she understands that the conversation you are having is not about catching her in the wrong and dispensing punishment but about helping her to identify and do what is right.

Help to Distinguish between a Clear-Boundary Issue and a Wisdom Issue

Your teenager needs to determine what kind of issue he is dealing with. Discuss the difference between the two. If he is dealing with a clear-boundary issue, discuss the nature of true, personal, biblical conviction with him. Make sure that this conversation is held not in the abstract but in the context of the particular circumstances in which he finds himself. If together you determine that he is dealing with a wisdom issue, then brainstorm with your teenager about the passages, principles, and perspectives that may apply to him. Share examples from your own life of how you seek to exercise biblical wisdom as you make decisions.

Don't Try to Fit Everything You Have Learned into One Conversation

As you talk, be sensitive to how you are being received. Is your teenager a willing and active participant? Or is she trying her best to end the conversation and get out of the room? Have you talked so long that her attention has waned? Remember, you will have another opportunity to get at the issue again. Be wise, and use a few well-thought-out and strategically positioned words. Your goal is not to demonstrate the breadth of your own wisdom but to teach your child to think and live wisely. Take advantage of the moment, but realize that you will have many more opportunities.

Questions for Reflection and Discussion

1. Do you exercise biblical wisdom over the secular parts of your life? In what specific ways can you engage the Word more deeply, use its wisdom to guide you in matters of everyday living, and model this behavior for your children?

2. Does your teenager understand the difference between his or her convictions and preferences? Does he or she understand the commands of Scripture and long to stay inside God's boundaries? Pray for your teenager's growth in this area.

3. Look back at the list of biblical wisdom principles on pages 119–21. What principles do you see positively reflected in the life of your teenager? Consider in what ways he or she is lacking in the "symphony of godly living" and how you might invite him or her to examine and discuss how God's truth helps to make sense of life.

4. Are you often tempted to think and make decisions for your teenager, instead of gently leading him or her toward God's truth and a better understanding of his or her own heart motivations? Pray for the courage to place your fears and your desire for control into the capable hands of Jesus.

9

Life in the Real World

YOU SEE IT IN THE SNEAKERS. You hear it in the music. You encounter it when your teenager speaks to you in English that you barely understand. You observe it in the way teenagers relate to one another and to you. It beams into your home through the internet, television, and radio. It tells you what to think, desire, and do. It is inescapable and very powerful, often unnoticed but everywhere visible, always new yet ancient in its influence, often recognized by its power to shape our actions but more significant in its ability to shape our thoughts. It is something we create, yet daily it shapes us.

What is it? Human culture.

Where there are people, there is culture. Where there are fallen people, there is fallen culture. This is life in the real world.

One of the most important skills for teenagers to develop is *cultural awareness*. By this I don't mean an appreciation of classical music or expertise in cross-cultural relations but an understanding of the way the spiritual struggle is played out in the culture in which we live. To do this, we need a practical understanding of the nature of the believer's struggle with culture.

Two Typical Responses to Culture

It's a Saturday evening church supper, and the Smith and Jones families find themselves together in the food line. Both families are hoping that they do not have to sit together for supper, but, alas, they end up sharing the last available table. There aren't any real problems between these families—they just don't understand each other at all!

Let's look around the table. The Smith children are dressed very conservatively, and their conversation is about a book they are reading together as a family. Their children have little interaction with non-Christians because of the negative influence. No modern music is played in their home, and the Smiths do not go to the movies. They do own a television, but the children watch only educational programming.

Mr. and Mrs. Smith operate within a very small sphere. Mr. Smith works with two other Christian men, and Mrs. Smith's contacts with other women occur mostly within a tiny support group of Christian friends. On the surface, the Smith children look unlike their peers and act very differently from them. The Smiths' model for relating to the outside world is "Go out from their midst, and be separate from them" (2 Cor. 6:17).

It doesn't take long to see that the Joneses have taken a very different approach. Their children are dressed much differently from the Smith kids. For one thing, there are a lot more jewelry and earrings on the Jones children—and that includes the boys! The Jones daughter has her phone on the table beside her, although she doesn't check it during the meal. The Jones children participate in many public-school activities. They stream a lot of shows online. The oldest son plays in an alternative rock band. On the surface, the Jones children look and act like their non-Christian peers. The Joneses' model for relating to the world outside is "Be in the world but not of the world" (see John 17:11–16).

Rejection

The Smiths illustrate a rejection-isolation response to culture. This strategy's basic philosophy is *Evil is in the thing, so avoid the thing*. It usually includes a list of cultural activities to be avoided, such as movies, music, and dancing. The Smiths interpret being separate to mean that the

Christian family must avoid participation in the secular world wherever possible. On the surface, this response may not seem so bad, yet it carries inherent dangers and deficiencies.

Rejection may subtly deny the goodness of creation. The doctrine of creation declares that all that God made was good (Gen. 1:31; Ps. 139:14). Evil is not an organic presence within certain things but the result of the way things are used to express the thoughts and gratify the desires of sinful man. We need to be biblically precise in the way we think about cultural issues.

For example, modern music is not in itself evil, as if evil were a substance present within in it. After all, God created the melodic and rhythmic structures that it employs. No, modern music becomes problematic because it is a powerful medium for the worldview of individuals who are living in rebellion against God. Because of this, it is important for us to teach our children to resist the way it panders to their sinful hearts without letting them think they win the battle with sin simply by avoiding it.

Rejection may miss the core issue of the struggle with evil. The core of our struggle is not with evil outside us but with evil within. There *is* a war being fought: the war in our hearts. The rejection-isolation response may miss this.

Peter says that God has given his children everything they need to escape "the corruption in the world caused by evil desires" (2 Peter 1:4 NIV). As parents, we need to teach our children that we do not solve the struggle with evil by avoiding certain things, although there are times when fleeing certain situations, locations, and relationships is a principal means of avoiding sin. Nevertheless, Paul says that such restrictions "are of no value in stopping the indulgence of the flesh" (Col. 2:23). Avoiding external temptations alone does not restrain sin because it does not deal with the sin already in the heart. We want to teach our children that avoidance is not a cure, though it can be used by God to limit the damage of sin in our lives.

Rejection may promote self-righteousness. In the isolation response, righteousness may become equated with keeping "the list." People who keep it are considered righteous and mature, and people who don't are considered carnal and immature. Christ pounded away at this view of righteousness when he attacked the spiritual pride of the Pharisees (Matt. 5:20; 23:1–36; Luke 18:9–14; see also Isa. 29:13). It is possible to keep this list rigidly while still having a heart that is far from God and totally reliant on self.

Assimilation

It is clear that there must be a better way to teach our teenagers to respond to culture than modern, conservative-evangelical isolationism—and the Joneses would say that they have found it: assimilation. The philosophy of assimilation is *Things are neutral, so there is no harm in participating in the thing.* This approach, too, has defects.

Scripture teaches us that nothing is ever neutral. In this world, things always carry moral freight. Christ said it very plainly: "Whoever is not with me is against me" (Matt. 12:30). For example, you could argue that language is in itself neutral. Individual letters, individual words, and the sounds that they make are neutral, but we never, ever encounter them that way. Language is always used to convey some kind of meaning. When employed, language is no longer neutral.

So there are certain things we must acknowledge as we think about the institutions, relationships, media, and products of the culture around us:

- All things that God created are good.
- All things that we encounter have been put together, or are used, in a way that carries meaning.
- Everything can be used for good or evil.
- Everything in culture expresses the perspectives of its creator and the user.
- Nothing appears in culture in a neutral context or setting.

Just as the rejection-isolation response to culture has its weaknesses, so does the assimilation response common in the evangelical church. Our children need a third way to respond to the culture around them, one that is the result of good biblical thinking. They need to understand what culture is and the nature of its power and influence and need to form a biblical plan for living within it.

What Is Culture?

God never intended for people to have a passive relationship with his creation. In the beginning, he created us with the capacity to interact with the world, and he gave us the responsibility to do so in a way that images him. He made us in his image with creative abilities that he gave to no other creatures, and he commanded us to use them (Gen. 1:26–31; 2:15–20). Thus people are always instinctively interacting with the world. We are always organizing and reorganizing, interpreting and reinterpreting, creating and recreating, building and rebuilding. We never encounter the world in its original state. People have always had their hands on it.

When people made in the image of God interact with the world God made, culture is what results. Where there are people, there is culture. If a family isolates itself from the surrounding culture, it does not escape the cultural struggle, because it forms a family culture. If an individual isolates himself from both the surrounding culture and the family, he still does not escape the cultural struggle, because he creates an individual culture. There is no way for us to escape dealing with the relationships, customs, institutions, structures, media, products, and beliefs that make up culture. We all live our lives in the environment of human culture.

Something more needs to be said here: the fall is the reason for the cultural struggle. Before the fall, Adam and Eve interacted with the world God had made. They expressed their godlike creativity without any problems because all they did and said, all they created, and all their customs and ways of relating were based on the words of God. Tragically, another voice, the serpent's, came on the scene to give another interpretation to what God had made and said. By following this voice, Adam and Eve created the cultural struggle.

Since the fall, people build culture on the basis of many varied and competing authorities. Gone are the simple days of Genesis 1 and 2. Now the cultural canvas is stained with sin, and until eternity human culture will not perfectly reflect the will of God. This is why our response to culture is so important. It is one of our primary moral struggles. Teenagers need to grow up understanding this and being prepared for it.

The struggle with culture is inescapable, and it is always moral. People always interact with the world in a spirit of submission to God and his Word or in rebellion against him and dependence on their own minds. The cultural struggle is always about right and wrong, true and false, good and bad, belief and unbelief, human desire and God's will. Isolation is impossible. Assimilation is capitulation. We need a better way.

The Need for Protection

You can see the influence of culture in the way we dress. Few of us wear the same style of clothing we wore ten years ago or maybe even five. Skirt lengths go up and down, and tie widths go from narrow to wide and back again. Have you ever looked at a family photo album and said, "I can't believe I wore that!"? Fashion is a pointed example of the influence of culture. It shapes not only what we do but also the way we think and the way we see.

The example I used with my teenagers to capture the insidious influence of the surrounding culture on them (and us) is air. Like the air we constantly breathe, culture is the spiritual air that our hearts constantly absorb. Many of the pollutants in the physical air are unseen. The same is true with culture.

We as parents have made a great error in our tendency to emphasize obvious issues (sex, drugs, violence, abortion, and so on) while neglecting the more deceptive, unseen pollutants in the cultural air around us. The result is that although our children may not participate in the "biggies," they end up serving the idols of the surrounding culture. (See the figure on pages 134–35 for examples of these idols, their impact on our teenagers, and their biblical alternatives.) Surely, these idols are more to be feared because they creep up on us unseen, appearing harmless and attractive (see Col. 2:8). They also powerfully play to the desires of the sinful nature—that is, they feed the very thing that God, by his Spirit, seeks to destroy.

Another error we have tended to make as parents is to blame the vehicle rather than focus on the idol themes these vehicles promote. A variety of vehicles—internet, social media, government, music, movies, education, television—all transmit and promote the philosophy of the culture. None of these vehicles are in themselves bad or dangerous. The danger is in the way they are used to promote the things they promote.

The point is not to slay the messenger—these vehicles are used for both good and evil. We must be aware of the power of the media to transmit a culture's ideas, but it is the ideas that are dangerous, so it is the ideas that must be the focus of our attention. For example, many Christian parents will not let their teenage children go to R-rated movies but will permit them to scroll for hours through social media, which is also a vehicle that transmits the perspectives, relationships, and values of the surrounding culture.

This is where the pollution metaphor helps us. When there are poisons in the physical air, people wear protective equipment that filters them out. In the same way our teenagers need spiritual filters against the unseen poisons in the cultural air. They need the protection of a biblical world- and life-view, and, as parents, we want to begin giving them one from the very earliest moments of their lives. We also want to have eyes of faith to see that every situation, relationship, and problem in their lives is an opportunity for us to encourage them to rethink and carefully apply a biblical view of life to concrete situations.

Talking to Your Teenager about Culture

In light of this, don't be hesitant to talk, talk, talk to your teenager. This cannot be a time when your relationship grows distant. Your child needs your parenting as much as ever, so seek him or her out.

Let me suggest some strategies for these conversations.

- *Don't wait for your teenager to talk to you.* Seek your child out in a way that is warm, friendly, and affirming. Teenagers who are on the defensive won't talk freely and won't listen well.
- *Don't settle for non-answers.* Follow up the yeses and nos. Ask questions that your teenager cannot answer with a yes or no and that require him to disclose what he is thinking, feeling, and doing.

Theme	Definition
RELATIVISM	• No absolute standard for life. • Each person determines what is right for himself or herself. • What is right changes with the situation.
INDIVIDUALISM	• No higher goal than happiness and pleasure. • No higher purpose than meeting one's own needs, wants, rights, and desires.
EMOTIONALISM	• Feelings are the most influential, most important indicator of what is right and best. • Feelings treated as personal guidance.
PRESENTISM	• Focus on the present—living for the moment. • Focus on present personal happiness. • No sense of delayed gratification or investment.
MATERIALISM	• No recognition of the spiritual world. • Goal of life is experiencing physical pleasure and possessing material goods. • Focus on what is seen.
AUTONOMY	• No sense of innate, natural responsibility to a higher authority than self. • No functional recognition of the existence of God and his call to live to his glory.
VICTIMISM	• No sense of personal responsibility for one's actions. • Belief that people are what their experiences have made them. • Belief that people's defects are the result of others' actions and situations outside their own control.

FIGURE 1. Themes (Idols) of Modern Culture

Fruit in Teen	Biblical Alternative
• No consistency of lifestyle or conviction. • No internal restraint. • Susceptibility to influence of others. • Dislike of rules.	*Truth.* Willing submission and obedience to the commands and principles of Scripture.
• Selfishness, self-centeredness, focus on rights. • Lack of commitment to others. • Laziness, irresponsibility. • Grumbling, complaining.	*Two great commands.* A life that is shaped by practical commitment to love God and to love one's neighbor.
• Focus on feeling good. • Disinclination to act against feelings. • Sensitivity to approval or disapproval.	*Biblical faith.* A commitment to test everything by the truths of Scripture.
• "Got to have it now" mentality. • No focus on long-term investment. • No sense of consequences. • Impulsive decisions.	*Eternity.* A personal commitment to do everything with an eye toward the reality of eternity.
• No independent pursuit of the things of God. • No focus on character and attitude. • Focus on clothing, beauty, friends, things.	*Spirituality.* A life that is shaped by seriousness about issues of one's heart and relationship with God.
• Tendency to rebel against authority. • No real godward focus in life. • Negative view of authority and correction.	*Creaturehood.* A way of life that is guided by recognizing the Creator and pursuing his glory.
• Regular patterns of blame shifting. • Excusing and rationalizing bad behavior; defensiveness. • Lack of confession. • No sense of need for personal change.	*Sin.* Humble recognition of the struggle with sin within and temptation without. Thankfulness for Christ's forgiving grace.

- *Be positive.* Don't be like a detective hunting for what is wrong. The purpose of these talks is not to "catch" the teenager but to help her to understand, desire, and do what is right. So much of the talking that goes on between teenagers and their parents is negative and discouraging to the teenager.
- *Lovingly seek to expose the faults in your teenager's thinking without making him feel ignorant or stupid.* Teach him, in an affirming way, to see where he has breathed in the pollutants of his culture.
- *Become a partner in your teenager's struggle by sharing your own struggle to live a godly life in an ungodly culture.* Admit to the places where you have been influenced. Ask your teenager to pray for you as you promise to pray for her in her struggle.
- *Always point your teenager to Christ.* Remind your child that Christ daily gives us mercy and grace in our moments of need and patiently continues to work in us until his work is complete.
- *Always keep in mind that you cannot protect your children from culture.* The only effective strategy is to prepare them to deal with culture in a biblical fashion. This will take years of loving commitment on your part.
- *Model the character of Christ.* Don't be drawn into negative verbal power struggles. Greet anger, negativity, and accusation with soft-spoken strength. Don't beat your teenager with words but win him with Christlike love.

What Is the Influence of Culture?

Have you ever cringed at the outfit your teenager was wearing? Is sixteen a magic year in your home because that is the year your teenager can get a license to drive? Have you ever contemplated retirement at sixty-five? Have you ever succumbed to buying the latest piece of exercise equipment, only to have it gather dust in your home? These things depict the distinctive influence of modern culture on the way each family thinks about life.

If we understand the ways that we are influenced by our culture, we can teach our teenagers to live wisely, alertly, and redemptively. To be *wise* is to be able to apply the principles of Scripture to practical decision-making in the context of one's culture. To be *alert* is to live with an awareness of the "hollow and deceptive philosophy" (Col. 2:8 NIV) of the surrounding culture and not give in to the temptation to serve its idols. To be *redemptive* is not to be satisfied with isolation or live protectively but rather to follow the command of Christ to be salt and light in a corrupt and darkened world.

Don't look at your teenager and settle for survival. Thank God if your teen is sexually inactive and drug-free, but set your aim higher. God's will is that your child would "[partake] of the divine nature" and "[escape] from the corruption that is in the world because of evil desire" (2 Peter 1:4) and "in the midst of a crooked and twisted generation . . . shine as lights in the world" (Phil. 2:15).

The influence of the surrounding culture is much more pervasive than the obviously offensive content found online, on television, in movies, and in music. Yet we all are tempted to make these the focal points of our debates and skirmishes with our teenagers. Sometimes we even respond negatively to cultural things our teenagers bring home not because they are morally corrupt but because they are different from the culture of our own youth. We say, "You're not gonna play that racket around here!" (which expresses the exact sentiment our parents had toward *our* music). But is it morally wrong for our teenagers to enjoy music that we find unlistenable? At other times we say, "There's no way that you're gonna wear that!" (which expresses the bewilderment our parents felt at the clothing *we* thought looked good). But is it *morally* wrong for my son to wear pants that are so big that he can take three steps before his pant legs move?

When we respond to issues of taste in the same way we respond to moral issues, we cheapen the whole cultural discussion and weaken the positive influence that we can have with our teenagers. We need to accept that in many ways they will be different from us. The issue is not whether they are participating in things that are enjoyable to us but whether they are participating in things that are pleasing to God! That requires an awareness of the subtle and pervasive influences of the culture in which they live.

The powerful influence of culture can be summarized in four areas. These areas, when taken together, describe all of life. The surrounding culture will influence every area of your life in some way. This is why we must live vigilantly and teach our teenagers to do the same.

Culture Will Set the Pace of Life

Have you ever complained about how busy you are or how fast-paced your life is? How much time for quiet meditation or personal reflection do you have? How many moments of family activity do you have when all the members of the family are present? Is there at least one meal a day—a week? a month?—when you all eat together? Do you wonder how you and your children can participate in all the expected activities of church, school, Little League, and music lessons? Have you ever wondered who told you to live this way? Have you ever wanted to stop the world and get off? The pace of life in our culture is directly related to what the culture thinks is important. It is the direct result of a culture that has acquiring and achieving as two of its highest values.

The culture influences not only the daily schedule of our lives but the order of events in our lives as well. There is an unspoken but mandatory order to life in Western culture. The order moves toward the big dream, retirement, and the ultimate in personal success—early retirement. The order is high school, college, house, career, promotion, bigger house, and retirement, with marriage somewhere in there. Certainly, there are variations, but there is a remarkable similarity to the order of events in the lives of most people.

Who gave us this order? What are its strengths and weaknesses? How does it get in the way of God's revealed plan for us? In what ways does it enslave us rather than serve us? In what ways do we see ourselves and our teenagers following it blindly?

One of the things I enjoy doing is eavesdropping on the conversations around me in the supermarket checkout line. I find these conversations informative and enlightening even if I do get a sore neck from trying to listen without being conspicuous!

I overheard two older men a few months ago. One said, "Hey, Joe, I haven't seen you for a while."

"I retired last year."

"Must be nice," the friend replied.

"I don't know why I did it," Joe said. "It seemed like the thing to do, but I hate it—it's driving me crazy! I've already begun looking for a job."

"Man, Joe, you're raining on my parade," the friend said as he walked away.

Such is the influence of culture. It dictates the conventional passages of life, and we often follow them without even knowing why we have made the decisions we have.

Culture Will Set the Agenda for Life

An agenda is a plan. It is what we are doing and why. An agenda always expresses priorities and values. We form a life plan by determining what we value and making a strategy to acquire it. The agenda for a person's life in any culture expresses what is important to that culture. If you had to list the priorities of our culture, what would they be? How different are they from your own priorities? How different are they from biblical priorities?

Our culture always expresses its perspective on what is important, valuable, and "true." For example, when your teenager can follow television shows, social media, podcasts, and online video content for a week and never hear God mentioned or the Bible included in the discussion, the culture is powerfully telling him what is important and what is not.

Imagine the influence of television or the internet on a teenager who spends just three hours with it each day, every day. That equals nearly 7,700 hours over her teen years. During these hours of cultural bombardment, she is usually relaxed and not thinking critically. She is breathing in the cultural air with little thought of protection. It would be the height of naivete to think she will remain uninfluenced by it. Her life view and her life plan will be shaped by the culture if she uncritically breathes it in and accepts its priorities.

How many Christian families are so committed to the teaching, relationships, fellowship, and ministry of their local church that they would refuse a promotion or a job offer because it would take them away from the body of Christ to which they are committed? Most Christian families would jump at the job and hope they would be able to find a good church wherever they went next. The Western church has become so transient that it is hard for relationships to develop and gifts to be recognized within it so that God's people can do what he has called them to do. Is it wrong to move? No, but we must make this decision from the vantage point of biblical values and not blindly follow the surrounding culture. We won't teach our teenagers to live with their eyes open if we are not doing the same.

Culture Will Define and Shape Our Relationships

Such things as our views of authority and government, of men and women and their roles, of children and their place in society, of the relationship between men and women, of sexuality, of the family and its role in and importance to the culture, and of the elderly are examples of the ways in which culture shapes our relationships.

An example of the powerful influence of culture on our relationships is the radical redefinition of the family that has occurred. *Family* was once a term that was used to describe a husband (male) and wife (female), who were married (to each other), and their children. It now has an endless and often disturbing variety of meanings. It is tempting to think that this radical redefinition of the family will never influence us, but we need not look much farther than the vast number of divorces and single-parent families in the church to humbly remind ourselves that we *are* being influenced.

For teenagers, the influence of culture is no less powerful. There is a pressure in our culture for boys and girls to pair off ("I'm going out with . . ."). There is a strongly physical emphasis to these relationships—evident in the reasons a person is considered attractive—that encourages sexual expression. "Sexy" tends to get a higher billing than "mature." And in a physically focused culture, to say someone has a nice personality is the kiss of death.

Our task is to make sure that the styles and rules of relationships that we promote to our children, by word or by example, meet biblical standards (Matt. 5–7; Rom. 12; Eph. 4; Col. 3:12–14).

Culture Will Powerfully Influence Our Spiritual Lives

Culture will always exert its influence on a person's religious or spiritual life. Either a person's spiritual life shapes the way he thinks about and responds to his culture, or a person's religious or spiritual life becomes enculturated—there is no middle ground.

Again, begin by becoming aware of where your culture stands on key issues. First, religion has virtually been barred from the cultural debate. Those representing religious institutions are rarely welcomed into the discussion of significant cultural issues. Second, religion is often presented in a negative light by the popular media. Third, psychology has taken its place as the dominant "religion" of our culture. It defines who people are. It defines the meaning and purpose of our existence. It defines what is normal and what is not. It defines why people do the things they do and how they can change. It is an understatement to say that these things have influenced the church and our personal spiritual lives.

Our teenagers need to understand that they do not live in a vacuum. They live in a culture that exercises its influence on every area of their lives. It is important that they learn not only to protect themselves from their culture's pollutants but also to influence the culture with the truth of Jesus Christ.

As we seek to prepare our teenagers, we need to be humbly honest about the ways in which our own lifestyles have been shaped more by cultural norms than by biblical principles. We cannot disciple our teenagers into a consistently biblical lifestyle without being willing to evaluate inconsistencies in our own lives.

Responding to Culture: A Plan for Our Teenagers

Do you remember the Smiths and the Joneses? Each family had chosen a radically different strategy for dealing with culture.

The Smiths were convinced that *isolation* was the right strategy. They failed to realize that it is impossible to escape the struggle with culture, because where there are people, there is culture. They failed to realize that culture starts with the heart. The institutions, media, relationships, and products of a culture are the fruit of what that society craves and serves. The cultural struggle is really a struggle with the evil desires of the heart, and although separation is at times the right choice, a child will not be safe just because a family avoids the physical locations, situations, relationships, and institutions of the surrounding culture. Further, the Smiths did not prepare their children to obey Christ's call to be salt and light in a corrupt and darkened world.

The Jones family was convinced that it had found a better, more sensible way to respond to culture: *assimilation*. They regarded most things in their culture as neutral and saw no harm in allowing their children to actively participate in it. The mistaken view of neutrality led them into an involvement with their culture that lacked analysis or evaluation. Like the Smiths, the Joneses failed to teach their children to function as salt and light.

Parents need a third way to guide their children that does not give in to the weaknesses of isolation or assimilation. I call this third way *redemptive interaction*.

GOAL 3:
Teach Thoughtful, Redemptive Interaction with Culture

The purpose of this goal is to raise teenagers who are fully able to interact with their culture without becoming enslaved to its idols. And the aim of the interaction is not to achieve personal pleasure and satisfaction but to redeem their culture for Christ. Matthew 5:13–16 gives us the biblical basis for this strategy.

> You are the salt of the earth, but if salt has lost its taste, how shall its saltiness be restored? It is no longer good for anything except to be thrown out and trampled under people's feet.
>
> You are the light of the world. A city set on a hill cannot be hidden. Nor do people light a lamp and put it under a basket, but on a stand, and it gives light to all in the house. In the same way, let your light shine before others, so that they may see your good works and give glory to your Father who is in heaven.

In their assimilation, the Jones family lost their saltiness, and in their isolation, the Smith family hid their light. We want to teach our children to do neither but rather to move out and be involved, protected by truth and ready to redeem.

The redemptive interaction strategy has two fundamental objectives. First, we want our teenagers to thoroughly know and understand God's truth as a protection against becoming enculturated. Second, we want to teach them what it means to live truth in their everyday lives in a way that points to their heavenly Father.

These two objectives give us the inward, outward, and upward face of Christian living in a fallen world. The *inward face* is a personal commitment to truth that protects our teenagers from the surrounding culture's subtle falsehoods and deceptive idols. The *outward face* is their commitment to witness to the reality of Jesus Christ by the way they live, even when they are not verbally interacting with the culture. And the *upward face* is their commitment to do all this so that people would give God the Father the glory that is his due. We do not want to be afraid to set high goals, and we don't want to let the agenda be set by the reticence of our teenagers. These objectives will not be accomplished in one sitting but are achievable as the Holy Spirit empowers your faithful, day-by-day commitment to use the opportunities God gives you to prepare your teenagers to be people of God.

Let me suggest five strategies for preparing teenagers for redemptive interaction with their culture.

Prepare

The first step is to instill in your teenager a biblical view of life. Many Christian families have years of unfocused family devotions. What their children receive during these times is not totally without merit, but it would be so much better if parents had a goal of instilling a biblical world-view. Without that goal, children end up familiar with popular Christian stories and random doctrinal facts without ever assembling them into a usable system of truth that reflects God's way of thinking about life.

The aim of all family Bible instruction must be to equip our children "for every good work" (2 Tim. 3:17) by attaching what we learn from Scripture to a biblical system of thinking. We can help our teenagers to do this by asking the following questions of each passage we study together.

- What does this passage teach about God, his character, and his plan?

- What does this passage teach us about ourselves, our nature, our struggle, and the purpose of our lives?
- What does this passage teach us about right and wrong, good and bad, true and false?
- What instruction does this passage give us about relationships, love, authority, and so on?
- What does this passage teach us about life—its meaning and purpose?
- What does this passage teach us about the heart and how it functions?
- What have we learned from this passage that should guide the way we live and make decisions?
- How does this passage help us to understand and critique our culture?

As we teach our children to ask and answer these questions, we show them how to use the things they read in the Bible to think in practical terms about their own life situations. Knowing the truth will help our teenagers learn to be "in the world but not of the world" (see Christ's prayer in John 17:15–18).

Test

In this step, we teach our teenagers to critique, evaluate, interpret, and analyze the surrounding culture from a biblical perspective. This is why they must first be well grounded in their knowledge of biblical truth.

Here is where many Christian parents make a decision that seems right on the surface but that I believe is all wrong if they hope to prepare their teenagers to be a redemptive influence in the cultural struggle. Like the Smiths, many Christian parents try their best to keep the surrounding culture out of their homes. In so doing, they lose a wonderful, focused opportunity to teach their children how to use a biblical view of life to understand and critique their culture.

It is important not always to say no to your child's requests but to sit with her as you listen to the music and watch the content that interests her, to engage her in a discussion about it, and to share your evaluation with her. Help your teenager to understand what attracts her to the media (the artist, the message, the music, the visuals, the action, the pressure of peers, and so on). The easiest way to critique the content is to apply to it the same set of questions that you have been using to study the Bible in your family devotional times.

Parents are tempted to overreact to issues of taste that really shouldn't be the focus of a critique. For example, resist getting into an argument about how something is "not really music." Don't initiate debates over clothing, hair, and jewelry. You want to get to the heart of the matter, that is, the view of life promoted by the piece of media. All the externals are expressions of the *heart* of the artist, director, or producer. Spend your time looking at that.

Whenever we go to movies and concerts with our teenagers, listen to music with them, or watch videos or shows together, we are making the most of a huge opportunity to raise teenagers who can think with biblical and cultural clarity. Our goal is to sensitize them to be alert and watchful. We want them to be insightful and wise, so we look for opportunities to help to produce these results. We are interested in doing more than protecting them; we want them to influence the culture in a redemptive way and, in so doing, bring glory to God.

Identify

Next we teach our children to recognize common ground they have with the culture around them. The struggles of life in this fallen world are a universal experience. In modern music, we discover anger, fear, disappointment, and loneliness. We hear disillusionment and distrust. We hear of the quest for real love, the breaking of trust, the failure of friends, family, and government. We hear of lust and greed, selfishness and hypocrisy. The cries of the rap artist and the rock star are our cries as well. The difference comes in the way we interpret and respond to our struggles.

We share common ground even with the performer who offends us the most, who represents the very things from which we want to protect our children. Our families have fallen apart, our promises have been broken, we have acted out of greed, we have seen government and church fail. Our beliefs have been challenged and our hopes dashed. We and the world have been broken by sin, and all of us have felt the pain. In fact, this is one of the reasons this material is attractive to our children. Whether we are comfortable with admitting it or not, performers, writers, directors, and media influencers give voice to the cries of our own children, who have also experienced the harsh realities of life in the fallen world.

This is important. Many Christians buy into the lie that they have nothing in common with their culture. Yet if we look at our own sin and our own experience of being sinned against, we humbly recognize common experience and common grief. This recognition of common ground moves us toward ministry to the culture. In the context of this common ground we are called to bring the message of the gospel.

So we want to raise teenagers who have learned to identify with their culture—not agreeing with its interpretations and responses but identifying with its struggle and humbly acknowledging why these responses seem logical to someone who does not know Christ and his Word. ("The world is broken, so get angry!" "The world is broken, so party, party, party!" "Take care of yourself and get all you can get.") Identifying means recognizing common ground. As we teach our teenagers to acknowledge their own struggle to live in this fallen world, they will build platforms of ministry to their culture.

Decide

We want to teach our teenagers how to know when they can be redemptive participants in their culture and when they must separate from it. Scripture teaches us to do both, yet it also pictures how God's people have struggled with this participation-separation issue (Rom. 14; 1 Cor. 8; 10; 2 Cor. 6:14–18).

As a Christian parent, you have many ways to help your child to work through these issues. Don't settle for a bald no to their requests to participate. Don't resort to saying, "Because I told you so!" Don't get into loud arguments over Friday night's proposed activities. Calmly help your teenagers to learn how to think through these decisions. Require them to be part of the discussion and thinking process. Many parents not only protect their teenagers from the world but block them out of the decision-making process as well. In so doing, they leave them unprepared for the myriad of decisions they will have to make as adults. These moments are opportunities to prepare your teenagers to respond with biblical wisdom to the many choices they will face.

Redeem

Finally, we teach our teenagers to take back turf that has been lost to the world by witnessing to the good news of Jesus Christ. God has not ordained that we use our voices in the culture to always speak *against* something. Our goal is to declare positively what God had in mind when he designed things in the beginning, to be part of rebuilding the culture his way, and to proclaim that this rebuilding can be done only by people who are living in proper relationship with God through Christ Jesus.

The church of Jesus Christ, the Christian family, was never meant to exist as an isolated ghetto in the middle of a darkened and broken culture. We are called by Christ to participate in the world as his agents of redemption.

SO WE NEED TO PREPARE our teenagers. We need to train them in truth and to teach them evaluative and analytical skills. We need to model how to think and interpret life biblically. We need to engage them in the decision-making process. We need to teach them to recognize common ground and to speak to the cries of the culture in language it understands. We need to teach them how to recognize the idols that underlie what the culture produces. We need to teach them to participate in the cultural debate, to be people of influence, and to be rebuilders. And we need to teach them to do all this without giving way to self-righteous isolationism or the personal compromise of assimilation.

It is exciting that we can do this without fear. God has given us his Word, he has filled us with his Spirit, and he has surrounded us with the resources of the body of Christ. He will give us daily opportunities to engage our children in fruitful, wisdom-building conversations about the nature and struggles of the world and the nature of their own struggles of heart. We are not alone. He is with us, giving us everything we need to produce teenagers who approach the world with more than a list of dos and don'ts.

With hope we can hold on to our goal of raising teenagers who can think biblically, understand their culture, and deal with anything it produces from a biblical perspective. These teenagers will become adults who know when to separate and when to participate. They will know when to tear down and how to rebuild. They will be people of influence. They will be salt and light.

Questions for Reflection and Discussion

1. Reflect on the ways you, your children, and your family as a whole engage in the culture around you. Are you entirely separate from the world, or are you blindly a part of the world without considering the cost of doing so? Have you landed on one extreme of this spectrum? What would it look like for your family to live "in the world but not of the world"?

2. Think of both positive and negative influences that your culture has had in your own life. What about in the life of your teenager? Do you see the presence of sin and evil both outside culture and inside culture? Do you view evil as outside yourself, or can you also see it within?

3. How has your culture set the pace of your family life? How has it set your agenda? How has your culture defined and shaped your teenager's relationships? How has it influenced your spiritual life? What about your child's?

4. Do you tend to focus on the more damaging aspects of your culture that influence your teenager? Reflect on specific ways you can enjoy and engage in culture *with* your child. Whether it's positive or negative—a song, a movie, a celebrity he or she admires—how can you help your child to gain a biblical perspective? How can you lead him or her to influence the culture redemptively and bring glory to God?

5. What are some principles of biblical wisdom that might equip your family to live wisely, alertly, and redemptively within the culture, to "in the midst of a crooked and twisted generation . . . shine as lights in the world" (Phil. 2:15)?

6. Does your child understand his or her own struggle to live within a fallen world? Does he or she identify with the surrounding culture and its struggles and acknowledge that other people's wrong interpretations and responses seem logical to someone who does not know Christ and his Word?

10

A Heart for God

We had dreams for them before they even came into the world. Before we were married, we talked about how many children we wanted, how we would raise them, and what we wanted for them. I felt such excitement when I knew there was a child growing within my wife. I remember resting my hand on her stomach because the only connection I could make with our first son was when I felt his movement. I would wonder about him as I drove to work. Who would he be? What would he look like? Would he be healthy? Would he be a scholar, a preacher, an athlete, a mechanic? Would he have a good career, go to the mission field, find a decent wife—what would his journey be?

The moment our son was born, I held him in my hand with a thunderous collision of absolute joy and powerful fear. We had a son! He was healthy, alive, and warm! Yet I was confronted with the length, the importance, the awesomeness of the task ahead of me. I was his father! No one else would be in the position of his mother and me. God had chosen us to be his primary agents of love, care, instruction, and training.

Over the years, we dreamed dreams and bought books. We loved him, fed him, instructed him, played with him, and disciplined him. There were myriad firsts and lasts. We had thousands of after-school what-happened-today conversations. We spent thousands of moments in instruction. We said yes and no innumerable times. We bought clothes, skateboards, books, and furniture. We enrolled him in schools and took him out of schools. We met his friends and welcomed them into our home. We greeted girlfriends and heard the stories of tough bosses. We went through science projects and SATs. We sat again and again with him in his room and had discussions about things that really matter—and my wife and I had many, many late-night conversations after he went to bed. We prayed for him and with him. We instructed him daily in the Word and took him to places where others would do the same.

We worked and worked and worked. We prayed and prayed, many nights going into his room as he was sleeping, putting a hand on him, and once again committing him to the Lord. We did all these things with each of our children.

Yet we fell short of the kind of parents we hoped we would be. We gave him irritated looks, said unkind words, and fell into weary silences. We did many things—none of them perfectly. In all this we were confronted with our weaknesses and the ever-present resources of God's strength.

What were we doing? Were we simply walking through the passages of family life? What was our goal? What was our focus? What did we want to produce?

Our Highest Goal

All of us want things for our children. We want them to have a good education, a suitable and satisfying job, a loving marriage, healthy children, a good home, and a life that isn't torn by tragedy. But if we could wish one thing for our children, what would it be? What central wish should give focus to all our labors and dreams?

David captures what should be the paramount focus of all our parenting efforts as he describes his own desires.

> One thing have I asked of the LORD,
>   that will I seek after:
> that I may dwell in the house of the LORD

all the days of my life,
to gaze upon the beauty of the LORD
   and to inquire in his temple. (Ps. 27:4)

How lovely is your dwelling place,
   O LORD of hosts!
My soul longs, yes, faints
   for the courts of the LORD;
my heart and flesh sing for joy
   to the living God. (Ps. 84:1–2)

Even the sparrow finds a home,
   and the swallow a nest for herself,
   where she may lay her young,
at your altars, O LORD of hosts,
   my King and my God.
Blessed are those who dwell in your house;
   ever singing your praise! (Ps. 84:3–4)

For a day in your courts is better
   than a thousand elsewhere.
I would rather be a doorkeeper in the house of my God
   than dwell in the tents of wickedness. (Ps. 84:10)

What David expresses so beautifully is a *heart for God*. Above all else, this is the goal of our parenting efforts. This is *the* quality we want to see in our teenagers as they prepare to leave home. This quality will give a godward focus to all their other character qualities and to their lives as well. We cannot let ourselves elevate any other quality over this one. We cannot be too busy to invest in seeing this developed. We cannot follow cultural norms that elevate education and career far above everything else; the Bible says that someone who lives only to be successful in these things is a fool. This goal of having a heart for God reflects the purpose for our creation as human beings. As the first answer in the Westminster Shorter Catechism says so well, the chief end of man is to "glorify God and to enjoy him forever."

Perhaps for many of us, this goal seems unrealistically high. We have become used to feeling good because our teenagers are willing to go to church without putting up a fight or are fairly respectful around the house. Yet this is God's goal for each one of us—can we settle for anything less for our children? Maybe this goal seems unrealistic for our teenagers because we haven't had it for ourselves. We lack the faith to seek it for them because we haven't seen it as a possibility for ourselves.

GOAL 4:
Develop a Heart for God in Your Teenager

It is a sad reality that many children leaving Christian homes do not have a heart for God. Whether or not they profess to be Christians, they are worldly in the way they approach life. There is little evidence in their day-by-day living of a hunger for God. They may not consciously deny God, but their love of God has been replaced by love of other things. His rule no longer plays a functional role in their lives. Although they may not be overtly rebellious, at the heart level they have a greater love for the world than for the Father (1 John 2:15). They worship and serve created things rather than the Creator (Rom. 1:25).

What Has Gone Wrong?

Why is this situation so common? If the Lord is the central focus of our lives, why is this value not passed on to our children? This question haunts many heartbroken Christian parents, but I believe it is a question all of us should ask. We should search our hearts and examine our family lives as we do so.

Let me suggest some possible answers to the question.

Familiarity
As the old saying goes, familiarity breeds contempt. As fallen human beings, we tend to take for granted the things that have been regular parts of our lives. We don't live with a sense of appreciation for the lavish food, clothing, housing, and health we enjoy in the Western world. We are

incredibly rich by the standards of many, yet we do not live with a sense of privilege. In fact, we often grumble and complain because we think we don't have enough! Our teenagers will open the door of a fully stocked refrigerator and moan that there is nothing to eat!

This dynamic is surely present in the spiritual realm as well. Somehow we need to break through the ordinariness that characterizes Christianity for our teenagers. We need to help them to appreciate what a gracious privilege it is for them to be born into a family of faith. We need to help them to see that the "normality" of their Christian home is anything but normal in this world. Rather, it is the act of a sovereign and loving God, who has harnessed the forces of nature and the course of human history so that we would come to know him and his truth.

Further, our teenagers need to see that God continues to be present, daily working in us so that we do not wander away and so that we live with his glory as our highest goal. We need to faithfully point to his existence and power and evidences of his hand at work. We cannot let ourselves or our teenagers forget the most glorious facts of our existence: that God really does exist, that he is glorious in power and goodness, and that he has made us to be his children! There will never be anything more important or wonderful than these truths.

We have failed our children if we don't do everything we can to equip them to leave our homes with a sense of awe over God and the glories of his grace. We cannot relax if our teenagers do not appreciate knowing God, being loved by him, and being chosen to live for his glory. We need to recognize humbly that one reason we have not passed this on to them is because we may have lost it ourselves. Many of us have become "nearsighted" and "blind" because we have "forgotten that [we have been] cleansed from [our] former sins" (2 Peter 1:9). Our teenagers will not understand that redemption is a gift and a privilege if we do not appreciate it ourselves.

Many of us need to hear these words not only with humble, convicted hearts but with hearts that find comfort in the forgiveness Christ has purchased for us. Our Redeemer not only convicts but forgives. He not only forgives but delivers. He not only delivers but restores. Forgiveness, deliverance, and restoration are all offered to us as Christian parents. Christ's work for us means that we do not have to be paralyzed by regret. We confess our sins; he forgives and delivers. As we step forward in faith, he does more than we could ask or imagine by the power of his Spirit that is within us. The gospel allows us to look back in peace and look forward in hope.

Lifestyle

Deuteronomy 6 envisions a lifestyle in which parents are *with* their children: "You shall teach [God's commands] diligently to your children, and shall talk of them when you sit in your house, and when you walk by the way, and when you lie down, and when you rise" (v. 7). In an agrarian culture such as the Israelites', the family was together all the time. Parents mentored their children in practical skills, life, and faith. A family's lives and activities focused on the family home and property. In cottage industry or family farming, a need or crisis in the family caused their work to give way to this personal pressing need. Members of the family were physically present with one another much of the time. Parents could talk with their children literally from the time they awoke to the time they fell into bed.

It is important to recognize how radically different today's typical family lifestyle is from that of the time when Deuteronomy was written. With the industrial revolution and the rise of modern education, the family home and property are no longer the focal point for the lives of family members. In fact, family members rarely spend time together. Our homes tend to be like motels where we all arrive at night to sleep, only to go our separate ways the next morning. Go out in public and notice how few families you see together. Look around at the worship service at your church and notice how few families even sit together. The point is not that we should demand that our teenagers be with us every waking hour or wish that we were parenting hundreds of years ago. Rather, we must recognize that the word that captures modern family lifestyle is not *togetherness* but *separation*.

The degree to which most modern families live separate lives surely does affect our ability to communicate redemptive awe to our children. From the age of five or six, most of our children spend most of their waking hours outside the home. As they mature and begin developing friendships, participating in outside activities, and seeking employment, their time spent outside the home and apart from the mentoring influence of their parents only increases. In our culture, it is almost considered weird for a teenager to spend time with her parents. When you see families together, the parents usually have younger children. At eighteen (hardly the age when most children reach full maturity!), most teens leave home for some distant college, never to live with Mom and Dad again.

I am not suggesting that we should all homeschool our children or forbid them to get jobs, participate in outside activities, or go away to college. We simply need to recognize how the lifestyle of separation affects our ability to nurture our teenagers. If we are to prepare our children for adulthood, we need to be focused and disciplined. We need to manufacture opportunities to talk in relaxed ways about significant things with our teenagers. We need to evaluate the choices we make for our families and the degree of busyness we permit to be our norm. You cannot mentor, pastor, disciple, or develop children whom you are seldom around.

This means turning away from the screens that distract us. It means sharing our personal lives and hearts with our children. It means simplifying our lifestyles, and it means making an effort to talk daily with each of our children—going to our teenagers' rooms, showing interest in their lives, and sharing ours with them. It means traveling less and being less focused on career development. It means confessing our own selfishness when we have lived closed and isolated lives while falling back on the ever-available excuse of a busy schedule. It means asking whether we have passed down to our teenagers a love for God and a commitment to live to his glory—and if this has not happened, it means asking if busyness and separation are part of the reason why.

Hypocrisy

The final reason we may not have passed an appreciation for God down to our children is hard to face, but it must be considered. It is hypocrisy. Children whose parents have vocalized a strong commitment to their faith but have not lived consistently with it tend to despise that faith. Living consistently with the faith does not mean living perfectly but rather living in a way that makes it clear that God and his Word are the most important things to you. You can honor God even in your failure by humbly confessing it and showing a determination to change.

Parents who talk about sin but live self-righteously ("I get up and go to work every day, and you don't see me complaining!") are functionally denying the gospel. Parents who talk about the sacrificial love of Christ but live selfishly ("Turn off that infernal racket—it's driving me crazy!") are functionally denying the gospel. Parents who talk about the grace of Christ but are verbally condemning as they discipline their children ("What are you trying to do? See how many stupid things you can do in one day?") functionally deny the gospel. Parents who talk of the forgiveness of Christ but live with an angry, unforgiving spirit toward their children ("The next time you want something from me, remember how you treated me today!") functionally deny the gospel. Parents who talk of seeking God's kingdom but get swept up into their culture's materialism (living for what money can buy) functionally deny the gospel.

God's call is for us to live lives that are worthy of the gospel that we have received (Eph. 4:1). If we don't do this as parents, our teenagers will dismiss or even despise the very gospel we say is of paramount importance. They may reject the God we have so poorly represented, and they, too, will end up serving the idols of the surrounding culture (Judges 2:6–15).

Search Your Heart

How do you react to what I am saying? Are you defensive? Ashamed? Discouraged? Don't be! To be these things is to functionally deny the gospel too. If you see your sins and failures, you don't have to justify yourself to me, your child, or God. You don't have to live with the heavy burden of regret or be tempted to give up. The gospel gives you hope not only for your children but for yourself. Christ lovingly invites you to repent and let him do a new work in your life.

As parents, we need to be willing to search our hearts and examine our lives. We need to be willing to confess and repent of ways that our lives have contradicted our words about the most important thing in our lives. And we need to confess our sins—not with bitter feelings of defeat and failure but with the joyful recognition that there is forgiveness and deliverance in Christ! He who forgives will also empower us to live in a new way!

If you look at yourself and say, "Yes, the life that I have lived before my teenager is in many ways a contradiction of the gospel," don't despair. Go to your teenager and confess. Say, "You know, the way I have lived and responded to you has often contradicted how I have taught you to live and how God has responded to me. I know this has often discouraged you and made you angry. I know I have been self-righteous, unloving, condemning, and unforgiving, and I am here to ask for your forgiveness. I have come to realize that I have not represented God very well to you as a parent. I ask that you pray for me, and I would welcome you to come to me whenever you think I have treated you in a hypocritical or unloving manner. I have committed myself before God to live in a way that makes him and his Word attractive to you and your siblings. Please pray for me."

I am convinced that these are healing words that God can use to fundamentally alter your teenager's appreciation for him. It is never too late to confess and repent! Don't give in to defeatism. Recognize that God is able to restore what the locusts have eaten (Joel 2:25). He is the God of restoration, the Creator who is able to tear down and recreate! Humbly take part in his work of rescue and restoration.

Signs of a Heart for God

What does a heart for God look like in a teenager? The central characteristic of a heart for God is its deep, sincere hunger to know and honor God. This needs to be contrasted with a pharisaical performance of Christianity's external duties or a life lived for Christianity's temporal benefits. God communicated his rejection of the heartless "obedience" of the Israelites using the strongest of terms:

> What to me is the multitude of your sacrifices?
>   says the LORD;
> I have had enough of burnt offerings of rams
>   and the fat of well-fed beasts;
> I do not delight in the blood of bulls,
>   or of lambs, or of goats.

When you come to appear before me,
    who has required of you
    this trampling of my courts?
Bring no more vain offerings;
    incense is an abomination to me.
New moon and Sabbath and the calling of convocations—
    I cannot endure iniquity and solemn assembly.
Your new moons and your appointed feasts
    my soul hates;
they have become a burden to me;
    I am weary of bearing them.
When you spread out your hands,
    I will hide my eyes from you;
even though you make many prayers,
    I will not listen;
    your hands are full of blood.
Wash yourselves; make yourselves clean;
    remove the evil of your deeds from before my eyes;
cease to do evil,
    learn to do good;
seek justice,
    correct oppression;
bring justice to the fatherless,
    plead the widow's cause. (Isa. 1:11–17)

And the Lord said:
". . . This people draw near with their mouth
    and honor me with their lips,
    while their hearts are far from me,
and their fear of me is a commandment taught by men." (Isa. 29:13)

Christ had the same kind of response to the heartless, self-righteous duty performance of the Pharisees.

Woe to you, scribes and Pharisees, hypocrites! For you clean the outside of the cup and the plate, but inside they are full of greed and self-indulgence. You blind Pharisee! First clean the inside of the cup and the plate, that the outside also may be clean.

Woe to you, scribes and Pharisees, hypocrites! For you are like white-washed tombs, which outwardly appear beautiful, but within are full of dead people's bones and all uncleanness. So you also outwardly appear righteous to others, but within you are full of hypocrisy and lawlessness. (Matt. 23:25–28)

For I tell you, unless your righteousness exceeds that of the scribes and Pharisees, you will never enter the kingdom of heaven. (Matt. 5:20)

The warnings of these passages can help us to look honestly at ourselves and at our teenagers. Every Christian community has a received list of dos and don'ts that typically combines biblical injunctions and prohibitions with many man-made standards of conduct. Godliness is more than keeping that kind of list of behaviors. True godliness flows out of the heart and produces a harvest of good fruit in a person's life. This is what we seek for our teenagers.

What you *will* see in a teenager who has a heart for God is a catalog of behaviors, attitudes, relationships, and activities that reflect a *personal pursuit of God*. This is not the begrudging performance of duty. It is not motivated by threats, guilt, ultimatums, and parental manipulation. All such parental interventions are attempts to produce what only God can produce. They will not produce a lasting harvest of godliness, only fruit that decays as soon as the pressure is removed.

Notice the terms I have used. We want God to use us to develop in our teenagers a *personal* pursuit of God, a seriousness about relationship with him that is internally motivated. Such a teenager is a spiritual self-starter. He does not need to be coerced or manipulated. He involves himself in spiritual things because he genuinely wants to, because they are important to him.

Notice further that what we are describing is a personal *pursuit* of God. A teenager with a heart for God is a seeker. She is hungry. She looks for situations, locations, and relationships that help her to do what is most important to her: to know God. She finds time. She goes out of her way.

She is decisive and intentional in her faith. She is open and teachable. She is not looking for excuses to miss a worship service or Bible study. She reads, studies, and memorizes Scripture and meditates on it. She independently, of her own volition, runs after God.

Lastly, we seek to foster a personal pursuit of *God*. A teenager with a heart for God is not hanging around the body of Christ because the "cool" relationships are there. He is not placating his parents by participating in the stuff going on at church. Rather, he has come to know and love God and wants to know and love him better. He has a real desire for fellowship with God, a real desire for his life to be pleasing to him. He really does love God, and his lifestyle reveals that love.

Signs of a Pursuit of God

A teenager's personal pursuit of God reveals itself in the behaviors, activities, and relationships in her life. If your teenager does have a heart for God, these are the things you will see.

A Life of Independent Personal Worship and Devotion

A teenager with a heart for the Lord spends personal time with him. He wants to read the Bible and pray. No, he probably won't be getting up at five in the morning to read and pray for two hours, but he will be developing a life of personal devotion.

I remember going into my teenage son's room to look for something and noticing a well-used New Testament next to his bed. He had been daily reading his way through it. He had not been dramatic or vocal about his devotional life, but his hunger for God had driven him to find time in his often chaotic schedule to study Scripture.

A Desire for Corporate Worship and Instruction

A teenager who is glad to go to church services will be there for two primary reasons. First, she enjoys worship—it expresses her heartfelt love and thanksgiving for God and the basis of her hope. Second, she enjoys being with people who share her desire to praise God. She finds that corporate worship helps her to focus on the most important thing in her life:

God and his glory. She may not be able to verbalize these things, but she will be there because she wants to be there.

One Sunday I had recently returned from a lengthy overseas trip. Our family was heading into what looked like a very busy time, so I decided that we would hibernate for the weekend. We would have a quiet time of family worship and then have lunch together. My oldest son told me that he wanted to go to our church's morning worship service. He asked if I would be offended if he took the train to the service and joined us for lunch afterward. Would I be offended? I was delighted! I wanted to do nothing that would dampen his desire to participate in the corporate gatherings of the church. In fact, his desire for worship caused me to reexamine the choice I had made.

A Hungry and Teachable Spirit

A teen's desire to participate in the gatherings of the body of Christ points to another positive sign of a heart for God: a hungry and teachable spirit. As we saw in chapter 5, teens often don't recognize their need for instruction. They can get defensive when you seek to advise them. They think they know much more than they actually know and assume they are much more prepared for life than they actually are.

It is a sign of God's grace at work when a teenager seeks out instruction. It is a sign of spiritual hunger when a teenager has a teachable spirit. Teenagers who have a heart for God will not avoid teaching or preaching; they will look for it. And they will not be in the back row of the church, slouched in their seats, looking as if they are barely able to endure the boredom. No, they will demonstrate a hunger to learn more about God, his will, and his way. They will appreciate the teachers whom God has raised up in the body of Christ, and they will want to be in a place where biblical instruction is offered.

Fellowship with the Body of Christ

A teenager who has a heart for God wants to spend time with others of like mind. He looks for peers who share his faith and his desire to be involved in the Christian community. When he goes to college, he immediately begins checking out the Christian student fellowships that are available on campus. He finds the fellow Christians in his high school. When he is out and about, he is excited to meet fellow Christians. He also values the help, prayers, encouragement, experience, insight, and wisdom of the older members of the body of Christ.

I remember one teenager who obviously didn't want to be sitting in my office. He was slumped in the chair in that "okay, do something that will impress me" posture, and I was doing my best to get inside his defenses. In the middle of my efforts, he said, "I gotta get out of here. This is driving me crazy! It's not enough that Mom has brought God into every discussion we have ever had! Now she forces me to come here so you can do more of the same. Just tell me what you want me to do and I will do it, so I can get out of here!" These were sad words spoken by an angry young man who had no time for the things of the Lord. Sadly, too, his reaction revealed the wrong way the Word had been used in his home.

Openness to Discussions about Spiritual Things

We should not expect our teenagers to be closed and defensive, unwilling to listen to the Word of God, nor should we accept such behavior. We are seeking to produce young adults who love the Lord and his Word, who understand that it speaks in some way to every situation of life, and who hunger to be guided and corrected by it. We do not want to produce teenagers who are spiritually defensive; rather, we want to produce teens who are humble and open, who know that they need God's help and who seek it.

Evaluate your teenager. How does she respond when the Bible or the Lord's will is mentioned in a conversation? Does she talk about the truths of the Word in any way? Does she ever talk about praying or seeking biblical direction for a decision? Does she seek out your help with a morning conversation, with a text in the middle of the day to see what you think about an issue, with a late-night discussion in which she bares her heart, or with a request for you to pray for her about something coming up? Is she an increasingly devoted consumer of the things of the Lord, one who is hungry, needy, seeking? Is she relaxed and at home with God's truth and with people who hold it dear?

My daughter was in a tough situation with a very competitive and often catty group of friends. She faced a real temptation to give in to anger, bitterness, and gossip and to return evil for evil. One night she shared some of the things that were going on with the group. Then she said, "I've thought about this a lot, and I know what is right to do."

Maybe this doesn't seem like a remarkable statement to you, but it was very encouraging to me. My daughter was saying that she hadn't gone with the flow of the group. She had stepped back to take a look, and she had sought to determine what was right to think, say, and do.

A Biblical Approach to Decision-Making

Teenagers who have hearts for God have hearts for what is right. In the example above, our daughter wanted to do what was right and took time to consider God's will. We cannot be content to raise teens whose decisions are impulsive, emotion-driven, and self-centered. We must hold a higher standard before them. We want to be used by God to develop in them a constant godward reference for everything they do—to raise young people who really do live for God's glory. We want them to believe that the most important question in any situation is "What does God want me to think, desire, say, and do?" And we want them to see the Bible as their most important tool for making the critical and practical decisions of life.

Our highest goal as parents must be for our teenagers to have hearts for God. This is the root that produces all other fruits of godliness in their lives. We do not want to give in to thinking that this is impossible for our teenagers. The gospel is for teenagers! The Holy Spirit can work godliness in the heart of a teenager as well as anyone else! If we believe these things, we will try to function as God's instruments of godliness in their lives.

Strategies for Encouraging a Heart for God

What practical things can we do to encourage a heart for God in our teenagers? As in anything else, if we are going to be successful, we need to know where we are going and how to get there. Let me suggest several things you can do to encourage a hunger for God in your teenagers. Keep in mind that all these things apply to younger children as well but are particularly important during the teen years.

Make Engaging Family Worship a Priority

To engage your teenager first of all means to hold her attention. It means to draw her in and get her involved. It also means to attract her and win her over to God's will and way. In order to do this, our times of family worship need to be enjoyable, relevant, challenging, and interactive. Family worship needn't be a boring drudgery for our children; it can be an enjoyable family time that is Scripture-centered. Let me mention some things my wife and I did to engage our teenagers.

First, we tried to keep our children interested and challenged by using good Christian books as the basis of our instruction and discussion. Much of the Christian devotional literature aimed at teens is fluffy and over-psychologized. For example, much of it deals with self-esteem, a category you do not see heavily developed in Scripture. So we looked for good, practical, fun-to-read books that were aimed at adults—books by excellent storytellers who would build bridges from the truths of God to everyday life. I would bring the vocabulary down to the level of the youngest child who was participating in the devotions. Thus each book was understandable to the youngest, yet conceptually challenging to the oldest.

Second, we found that spending time in Proverbs and the Gospels was very helpful for keeping our teens engaged. You could not find a more readily practical portion of Scripture than Proverbs! It is impossible to read a chapter of that book that does not speak directly to things that each of us encounters. Proverbs often sparked good discussions. Likewise, the Gospels bristle with real life. God comes in the flesh and engages the people around him to consider the truths of the kingdom of God. Christ, the master questioner, the master storyteller, the master illustrator, can hold the attention of your teenagers as you help them to understand the important issues he discussed.

Third, we found it important not to enter the family worship time with rigid expectations and a rigid plan. We wanted an atmosphere of freedom in which our teenagers would feel free to ask questions, verbalize doubts, express confusion, debate applications, and try to draw inferences and applications—all without the fear of being silenced, rebuked, or ridiculed. We wanted the truth to connect, to convict, and to capture our teenagers, so we were in no hurry. We wanted to give them time to understand and the Spirit time to work. Our family devotional time was for them. We had no expectations about the amount of material we covered, and our goal was not to get our teenagers to agree with us. Our goal was to stimulate in them a hunger for God, so we wanted to be relaxed, patient, and creative. Make these times conversational. Draw your teens out to see if they understand, if they have doubts or confusion, and if they can connect the things being discussed to what is happening in their own lives.

Look for Opportunities to Point Your Teenager to God

Don't let your teenager live in *functional atheism*, a view of life in which God is functionally absent. Look for natural ways to identify the presence, power, and provision of the Lord. We know he is there, we know he is active, and we know that whatever he does is good, so there should be many opportunities for us to point him out to our teenagers. Protect your teen from a view that God is distant and passive. Many teenagers believe in a God who simply doesn't make any difference, so their faith and their lives exist on two completely different levels.

Point out direct answers to prayer. Talk about situations in which the Lord has given you or others strength and wisdom. Help your teenager to recognize instances of his protection and provision. Note the places where Scripture can prepare your teenager for something that he is facing. Discuss the guidance and direction Scripture offers in times of decision. Point out the good gifts that God lovingly supplies. Don't let your teenager live in a world where God functionally does not exist.

Be Positive and Christ-Centered in Your Use of Scripture

Many teens develop a negative attitude toward Scripture because of the way it has been used by their parents. Don't use Scripture as a club to inflict guilt, to put your teenager down, or to condemn him. Don't embarrass your teenager with Scripture. Don't beat him with the Bible. Remember that the truth must always be spoken in love. The purpose of the Word in your teenager's life is not to beat him down and discourage him but to prepare him to be "complete, equipped for every good work" (2 Tim. 3:17).

Your use of Scripture with your teenager should be drenched with hope because Scripture always moves from human failure and sin toward forgiveness and deliverance in Christ. Don't use the Bible in a way that causes your teenager to run and hide from God. Use it in a way that encourages him to run to Jesus for the help that only he can give.

Be Willing to Use Yourself as an Example of Christ's Grace

Our story as parents is the story of God's work; it is very important that we do not take the credit for what he has done. Refrain from those all-too-typical "In my day . . ." or "When I was your age . . ." conversations. We should not see ourselves as pictures on which our children are to gaze but rather as windows through which our children can see the glory of Christ. We powerfully point to Christ when we humbly admit to our teenagers that we were and are people in need of the Lord's help.

Be Willing to Ask for Forgiveness, Accountability, and Prayer

Even your parental failure can be used by God to soften the heart of your teenager! What hope there is in the gospel! Don't let selfishness, irritation, harsh words, impatience, and anger just fade away. Go to your teenager and confess your faults. Ask her to pray for you, and invite her to come to you any time she has been hurt by the things you have said and done. Be a picture of humility, dependence on Christ, and hope.

I saw my son's progress report from school at the end of the day and was immediately angry. Although the grades were not terrible, I knew he could do better. Lashing out at him, I told him how hard we worked to get him through school (guilt). I told him I sometimes wondered if he would ever get his act together (condemnation). And I told him that when I was his age, I was very serious about school (self-righteousness). He sat across from me with his head down. He said nothing. When I was done, he went to his room.

At once I was convicted by how I had behaved. I prayed and asked the Lord to forgive me. Later that night, I asked my son to sit down with me. I told him I had come to realize he was not the only sinner in the house! He smiled. I asked for his forgiveness. I confessed my need for God's help and for his prayer. I told him that I was his father, but I also wanted to be a faithful friend. I told him that I wanted to leave him with hope even in moments of correction. He thanked me for talking with him, and he went to bed.

When my son came home from school the next afternoon, he grabbed my arm and said, "I want to be your friend too." Precious words. They represented a softening of his heart, and they represented God's redemptive work through my failure. Remember, it is not your weakness that gets in the way of God's working through you but your delusions of strength. His strength is made perfect in our weakness! Point to his strength by being willing to admit your weakness.

Model Prayer without Ceasing

Make prayer a regular and important part of your family's life. Pray with your teenager constantly. If he tells you he is facing a tough test, don't promise to pray for him; pray for him right then and there. If she shares with you that she is struggling with a relationship, don't simply tell her how to handle it; pray with her. When you are starting out on a family trip or vacation, gather as a family and pray. When your teenager is struggling to get along with his siblings, don't give in to constant yelling; sit down and pray with him. Ask your teenager in which areas she struggles with doubts, fears, anger, discouragement, and other temptations, and pray with her. Go back later and tell her you have continued to pray, and ask her how things are going. Pray, pray, pray, pray. In family life, there are a thousand natural opportunities to pray with and for your teenager.

Be an Example of Hunger for God

Let your teenager see your commitment to personal and family Bible study, to being under the regular teaching of God's Word, and to being in robust fellowship and ministry with the body of Christ. Ask yourself, "Do I hunger after God, and does my teenager see it?" Are you a model of the thing you are seeking to instill in your teenager?

My father was very faithful in gathering us for daily family devotions. He was not a teacher, but he would read a passage to us and we would all pray. During one period of time, my older brother Tedd was working first shift at a factory. He had to be there between 6:00 and 6:30 a.m. Dad got us up at 5:00 a.m. so that we could read and pray together. Then the rest of the family would go back to bed as Tedd went off to work. I don't remember much of what we read, but I remember how the unaltering commitment to family worship impressed me. I remember thinking that our family time of reading and prayer must be very important because nothing got in its way!

My parents did the same with Sunday worship. It was a nonnegotiable part of our family schedule. The only thing we ever did on Sunday morning was attend our church's service of worship. Even when we were on vacation, my parents would find a place for us to worship on Sunday morning. They demonstrated a commitment that pictured the importance of these spiritual priorities. We need to do the same.

GOD HAS CHOSEN US TO be his children! He has opened our eyes to his truth. He has forgiven us, adopted us, and empowered us by his Spirit. In the face of our disobedience and unbelief, he responds with patient, loving correction. We experience his amazing grace.

If we accomplish nothing else, we want our children to have hearts for God. We want them to know God, to value his love, to wonder at his grace, and to live for his glory. We want them to experience his redeeming love and to surrender their hearts to him. So we should make public worship and teaching, personal Bible study, fellowship, family worship, and ministry top priorities. We should endeavor to be parents who daily live out what it means to "seek first his kingdom" by making the pursuit of Christ our priority. In so doing, we allow God to work through us to instill a hunger for him in the hearts of our teenagers.

Questions for Reflection and Discussion

1. Which of your weaknesses and shortcomings most haunt you as a parent? What role do the perfect strength and sufficiency of Christ play as you face them?
2. What are your highest goals for your children? Who do you want them to be, and how does that desire shape your actions from day to day? Does your longing for your children to have hearts for God impact the way you live your own life?
3. The goal to help our kids to "glorify God and to enjoy him forever" is lofty indeed. What are some ways you can break that goal

down into smaller, more digestible pieces? What are some practical building blocks that lead in this direction?

4. Do you have a real sense of awe and gratitude because the Lord has chosen you to be his own? Do your children understand the gracious privilege it is to be born into a family of faith?

5. One of the most important things we can do for our kids is to continue to point them to the existence and everyday presence of a loving God. Does your teenager appreciate being known by God, being loved by him, and being chosen by him? Do you?

6. How do your family's rhythms differ from those of the Deuteronomy 6 family? Are there similarities? If your teenager does not reflect a heart for God, might busyness and separation be possible reasons?

7. Evaluate your own commitment to your faith. Is there an inconsistency between your words and your actions? Are you functionally denying the gospel by talking about the forgiveness of Christ but not confessing your own sin before your children? Are you saddling your teenagers with condemnation rather than showing them grace?

8. In what ways have you failed to represent God and the gospel before your children? Confess these things, knowing that you are forgiven and redeemed in Jesus.

9. Give an honest assessment of your teenager's heart for God. What behaviors, attitudes, relationships, and activities reflect that he or she is pursuing him? Does your teenager have a heart for God or the self-righteous heart of a Pharisee?

10. Evaluate your family worship time. Is it fun and theologically engaging? Are your children invited to ask questions, verbalize doubts, express confusion, and debate applications? What might you need to change or improve?

11. Evaluate your use of Scripture at home. Do you use it to inflict guilt or put your teenager down? Or do you use it in a way that instills hope and forgiveness, encouraging your teenager to run to Jesus for the help that only he can give?

12. Evaluate your willingness to bring your children into your own spiritual life. Do you ask them for forgiveness, accountability, and prayer?

11

Leaving Home

SHE STOOD ON THE PORCH watching him squeeze another box into the car. She tried her best to blink back her tears and see a well-prepared young man, but every time she looked, she saw the little boy wearing dirty jeans, sporting a milk mustache, and asking for just one more "chocklit cookie." She wondered how he would do a thousand miles away at a major university. They had visited the campus together earlier, but this time he wanted to go alone. Yes, she wondered how he would do, but she knew *she* wasn't ready for this.

She wanted to do it all over again. She wanted to do it better. She wanted to grab her son and ask for forgiveness for all those times she should have been there but wasn't. She wanted to apologize for all the times she had responded with irritation to another request for help. She wanted to take back all the words she had spoken in anger. She wished for another chance at the disastrous science project that had caused such conflict between them. She wanted to be there for all the Little League games that had seemed so unimportant.

She wished she had been more faithful in talking about the things of the Lord. She wished she had lectured him less and prayed with him more. She wanted to go back and be more welcoming of his friends. She wished she had gone to his room more, just to ask him about his day, simply to find another excuse to express her love. Her unspoken fear was that he would "blow up" in college like so many other children from Christian families.

Her racing thoughts and silent prayers were interrupted by his voice. "Mom, I'm all packed, and I gotta go. I can't tell you how thankful I am for all you and Dad have done. Don't worry about me—you guys have done a good job. I know what's right and wrong. I'll be okay."

They embraced. Tears streamed down her face. She didn't see it, but he cried too. Dad said, "Let's pray before you go." With that prayer and one final hug, he hopped off the porch and into the car.

She stood on the porch in the arms of her husband long after the car was gone. It seemed like a way to hold on to her son a little longer. Then her husband broke into her tearful thoughts. "Dear, this is what we've been working for all these years. He's a good kid, and he's ready. He knows the Lord. He'll be okay. Besides, he'll be back for Christmas in just a few months. I know we're going to miss him, but we ought to be happy. We can see the fruit of all our efforts. It's been worth it. We have a lot to be thankful for."

She didn't respond. It was hard for her not to imagine herself in the car with her son, giving him just a few more last-minute words of advice. Although it was hard for her mind not to run to a myriad of what-ifs, she knew her husband was right. The goal of parenting is to work yourself out of a job. The goal is to send out young adults who are prepared to live as God's children and as salt and light in a corrupt and broken world. Her son wasn't her possession. He belonged to God, and she and his father were but instruments in God's hands. She knew this was a good moment, a graduation, an emancipation, but it was hard to be happy and hard not to want him back for just a little more parenting. Yet this phase of her work in her son's life was over. She must entrust him into the hands of a better Father.

GOAL 5:
Prepare Teenagers to Leave Home

Thousands and thousands of parents have lived this scene—all knowing that it was coming, yet all a bit unprepared for the day when it actually happened. This is our final goal. God has called us to prepare our children to be meaningful contributors to the work of his kingdom, so we spend years preparing, and then we send them out.

No, they do not belong to us. They never did. They have always belonged to the God who appointed us to be his agents of growth, maturity, and preparation. We don't want them to be dependent and clinging. We want them to be able to stand strong and contribute much. We want to happily tell them, "Go free!"—knowing that they have everything they need in order to do what God has called them to do. Emancipation from the home is the important and godly goal of all those years of parental labor.

Leaving Home Too Soon

It doesn't take much of a look around to see that many teens are leaving home too soon and too little prepared. These are children who, from the age of thirteen, fourteen, or fifteen, begin to tell themselves that they are going to get away from home as soon as possible. They live for the age of eighteen, when they can graduate from high school and effect their own liberation. When these children leave, they don't say a warm thank-you to their parents. Their relationship with their parents has been broken for a long time. They leave with angry words or no words at all.

As I have counseled many teenagers and their parents, it has become very clear to me that few teenagers leave because of their parents' rules. No, they leave because of their *relationship*. The situation with their parents has gotten so bad, so angry, so confrontational, so adversarial that they cannot stand to live under the same roof with them. Sadly, this happens frequently in the homes of believers. This is not to say these teenagers are not rebellious. They usually are, but it is relational breakdown that ultimately drives them out when they are still unprepared to live godly and productive lives in a fallen world.

What happens is that parents, in their desire to get their teenagers to do what is right, allow their own anger, bitterness, and unforgiving spirits to corrupt and distort the whole process. Before long, they are almost unable to have a conversation with their sons and daughters that is not dyed with their anger. Their words become increasingly disparaging, judgmental, and condemning. They allow themselves to get sucked into battles of words, using the weapon of their teenagers' failure to win the war for power. In so doing, they forget their own experience of the love of Christ. While they were yet sinners, he died for them. It is his goodness that leads them to repentance. It is his grace that overpowers the depth and breadth of their sin. His grace never compromises what is right or says sin is okay, but it brings powerfully persevering love to those who could never earn it by their righteousness.

Parents who follow Christ's example do not correct without making the gospel of grace part of their message. They do not admonish without pointing to the reality of the love of Christ. They see every instance of trouble, failure, and sin as another opportunity to teach their teenagers to cast themselves on Christ. They never call wrong right, but they always deal with wrong in a way that depicts the glorious realities of the gospel. And they never try to do with the power of their words or the gravity of their discipline what only Christ can do as he enters into a teenager's heart by his grace. The preeminent theme of their homes is not their disappointment and anger at their teenagers' failures. The preeminent theme is Christ. He dominates times of failure as Forgiver and Deliverer, and he dominates times of obedience as Guide and Strength. In each experience, these families seek after him and give him glory. Teenagers who live in homes like these are regularly surprised at the love of their parents and the grace of Christ, who has chosen for them to live in a family where his redeeming love reigns supreme.

Four Verbs for Parents

Let me suggest four verbs that can set the agenda for parents who want to model Christ to their teenagers.

Accept

We must greet the sin of our teenagers with the accepting grace of Christ. This is not acceptance that compromises God's high standard or his call for confession and repentance but acceptance that leads to change. This acceptance holds God's standard high but does so in the context of the hope found in the cross of Christ. Our job as parents is not to condemn, judge, reject, or break relationship. Our job is to function as God's instruments of change, and the most powerful tool we have for doing so is our relationship with our teenagers. We want to conduct this relationship in such a way that God's work thrives in the midst of it.

Incarnate

As Christ was called to reveal God in the flesh, we are called to reveal Christ. As parents, we are called to *incarnate* the love of Christ in all our interactions with our teenagers. We reveal his love, patience, gentleness, kindness, and forgiveness as we respond to our children with the same (Col. 3:12–14). This must be one of our highest goals—that Christ, his character, and his gospel work would be depicted in the way we relate to our teenagers.

Identify

Hebrews 2:11 says that Christ "is not ashamed to call [us] brothers" because he suffered the same things that we suffer. He is able to identify fully with the harsh realities and temptations of life in this fallen world. He went through the process that we are now enduring. If Christ can identify with us, how much more should we be able to identify with our teenagers!

Often parents of teens communicate that they are not at all like their teenagers and, in fact, have real difficulty relating to them and their struggles. However, we *are* the same. There is no struggle that our teenagers might have that we haven't had or aren't still having. There are times when we want to shuck our responsibility and forget the things that we don't like to do. There are times when we willfully want our own way. There are times when we are defensive and unapproachable. There are times when we think we know more than we do.

We share a fallen nature with our teenagers, and we share progressive growth unto holiness with them. We must not act as if we are a different sort of person or stand self-righteously above them. We must stand alongside them as older brothers and sisters and point them to the only place of hope—Christ. We must communicate that there is no answer we can give them that we ourselves don't need.

Enter

Just as Christ entered our world and spent thirty-three years getting to know our experiences, we must take the time to enter the world of our teenagers (Heb. 4:14–15). That means we should be asking good questions and listening to the answers, not just speaking. In fact, what we say to our teenagers would be much more loving and insightful if we took the time to get to know the people, pressures, responsibilities, opportunities, and temptations they face every day. It is tragic when parents and teens quit talking meaningfully, honestly, and personally. All the correction, instruction, discussion, debate, and discipline is then done on the platform of ignorance.

Take time to enter the world of your teenager. Know what he faces every day, how he is emotionally and spiritually gripped by those experiences, in what ways he is being tempted and in what ways he is succumbing. Understand what home, school, work, and leisure look like to him. Let him know that his world and his experience of his world are important to you. Find ways to let him know that you are on board with him, that you understand, and that you care. When he says you don't understand, tell him that you love him and that you want to understand. Ask him to explain what he needs to explain to you so that you *will* understand. Ask him not to be frustrated when he thinks you don't understand but to give you help so you can.

Teenagers whose parents have *accepted* them with the grace of Christ, *incarnated* the love of Christ, *identified* with them like Christ, and followed Christ's example by *entering* their worlds do not have teenagers who are trying to get out of the home as soon as they can. Rather, these children are drawn by the powerful love and grace that have been their daily experience. They tend to treasure the one human relationship in which they have been consistently loved when they deserved it least. This gives their parents the freedom and time to prepare them a little more for their important entry into the world where they will stand with God on their own.

What Does Maturity Look Like?

Many parents have asked me how they will know when their children are ready to leave home. It is a good question. To be a functional goal, readiness needs to be defined practically. You cannot produce something you do not understand.

When we wonder what readiness looks like, we are really asking what biblical maturity looks like. Paul gives us a wonderful summary in Colossians 1:9–14:

> And so, from the day we heard, we have not ceased to pray for you, asking that you may be filled with the knowledge of his will in all spiritual wisdom and understanding, so as to walk in a manner worthy of the Lord, fully pleasing to him: bearing fruit in every good work and increasing in the knowledge of God; being strengthened with all power, according to his glorious might, for all endurance and patience with joy; giving thanks to the Father, who has qualified you to share in the inheritance of the saints in light. He has delivered us from the domain of darkness and transferred us to the kingdom of his beloved Son, in whom we have redemption, the forgiveness of sins.

Six characteristics form Paul's prayer for the Colossian church. These make a wonderful functional definition of maturity we can use to evaluate our teenagers and their not-too-distant emancipation from our homes.

But before we look at these characteristics, it is important to note that the Bible presents maturity as a lifelong goal. God is still at work bringing *us* as parents to maturity in Christ. Teenagers do not leave home as finished products. What we want to see are the *seeds* of maturity in their lives. If the seeds are there, we know they will continue to grow long after they have moved beyond our parental care.

Don't be discouraged as we examine these seeds on the pages that follow. Remember, our job is not to complete the final harvest. God will water the seeds and make them grow. Think beginnings, not final ends.

Sensitivity to God's Revealed Will

It is hard to think of anything more important for our teenagers than the knowledge of God's will regarding the varied situations of life. Teenagers tend to live with a bubble around their heads—all they seem to experience is what they think and what they want. How important it is that they get a vision for something bigger than their own happiness—a life lived to God's glory—coupled with a desire to know how the principles of Scripture apply to everyday life!

Functional Godliness

Paul prays that the Colossians would "walk in a manner worthy of the Lord, fully pleasing to him: bearing fruit in every good work" (v. 10). What a goal for our teenagers (and us)! Not that they would agree to go to church with us, not that they would be drug- and sex-free, not that they would get a job and do fairly well in school. These goals are not high enough for Paul, and they should not be for us! We need to believe that God, by his Spirit, can produce in our teenagers a desire to please the Lord in *everything* they do. We cannot settle for anything less.

Progressive Spiritual Growth

We want to see our teenagers daily growing in the knowledge of the Lord. We want to show them that every situation in life is an opportunity to know God and his Word better. Are they teachable? Are they seekers? Are they humble? Are they learning their spiritual lessons? If they are, we will see the fruit of growth in their lives. We will see strength replace weakness, wisdom replace foolishness, courageous faith replace doubt and fear, thankfulness replace selfishness and discontent, and the fear of the Lord replace slavery to the opinions and acceptance of peers.

Perseverance

What an important sign of maturity perseverance is, and what an important goal to parent our teens toward! We want to raise teenagers who both acknowledge their weakness and see that God's strength is made perfect in it. As they rely on his strength and as he empowers them, they don't give up, run away, or quit in the face of trouble. They patiently endure things that would have once caused them to throw in the towel. They no longer succumb to the pressure of peers but stand strong, unwilling to compromise their convictions. They don't quit when their responsibilities get tough, and they don't blame others for their failures. They stay in hard conversations with us even when they are tempted to shut down in anger, self-pity, or defensiveness. They are learning what it means to "be strong in the Lord and in the strength of his might" (Eph. 6:10).

An Appreciation of God's Grace

How many teenagers seem to have little or no awareness of the great privilege they have by being born into a family of faith? How many teenagers take for granted the heritage that has been passed down to them? How many fail to recognize the value of godly examples who have been around them as they have grown up? Many teens not only fail to recognize the grace of God in these areas but often wish that they were raised in families where they had more "freedom."

Paul says, in effect, "Do you realize what God has done? He has qualified you for his inheritance! You are part of his family! You are the inheritors of the riches of his grace!" Paul didn't want the Colossian Christians to miss the most phenomenal truth of their lives. We must work so that our teenagers don't miss it either. Maturity means not taking for granted what deserves to be highly prized.

Kingdom Awareness

Paul ends his description of maturity with a very important principle. Christ does not free us from the kingdom of darkness so that we can live as our own kings. He brings us from the kingdom of darkness into *his* kingdom. We go from being slaves to sin to being slaves to Christ! Our lives never belonged to us but to him. His will is our duty. His glory is to be our goal. We live through him and for him. In everything we do, we have a higher agenda—his purposes, his kingdom, and his righteousness.

How important it is for teenagers, who tend to be self-focused, nearsighted, impulsive, and emotion-driven, to have a wider focus, a higher agenda! Imagine how different the life of the average teenager would be if she lived with an awareness of God and his kingdom work. Imagine how the life of your teenager would change if she wanted to be part of what God is doing on earth more than she wanted to fulfill her own desires and dreams! (Imagine how our own lives would change!) We need to hold God's kingdom before our children so that they will grow up to see themselves as kingdom citizens, kingdom workers, kingdom builders. Our goal is for this focus to shape each area of their lives—their friendships, jobs, schoolwork, homelifes, leisure, thoughts, and possessions.

Do these standards seem unattainable? They *are* high, and I have plenty of growing to do toward them myself. But I encourage you to set your standards high. Don't give in to any perspective on parenting that convinces you that the promises and goals of the gospel are beyond your teenager's reach. Believe that God is able to do more than you could ask or think, through you and in your child. Take every opportunity to encourage your teenager toward these goals. Have a biblical vision of maturity that guides all you do as you prepare your teenager for his eventual emancipation from your home.

The Daily Fruit of Maturity

"Mom," she said, "can I ask you something?"

It was early in the morning, and everyone was rushing to get out the door. Although she was pressed for time, Mom said, "Sure, what's on your mind?"

"Well," her daughter said hesitantly, "you know that weekend camping trip that I asked you about? So, there are going to be guys there. I didn't want you to think I was sneaking around behind your back, and I wanted to know what you think I should do. I really want to go—but not if it's the wrong thing to do."

If your teenager is growing in sensitivity to God's revealed will, living an increasingly godly life, and demonstrating perseverance, thankfulness, and kingdom awareness, then his growing maturity will bear fruit in how he responds to everyday duties, decisions, relationships, and temptations. You need to know what the practical fruit of maturity will look like so that you can evaluate whether your child is ready to make his break with your home.

Let's look at the practical fruit of biblical maturity.

Acceptance of Personal Responsibility

A maturing teenager begins to step away from a view of life that says, "Life is supposed to be fun and enjoyable all the time—entertain me or

I'll get bored." (Remember that boredom tends to be one of the daily fears of youth.) As she matures, she grows to accept, and even find satisfaction in, her God-ordained responsibilities. She does not have to be threatened, manipulated, or otherwise coerced into doing what she is called to do. She doesn't excuse her irresponsibility with comments like "Oh, I'm sorry—I forgot," "I didn't know I was supposed to . . . ," or "I guess I misunderstood what you said." She doesn't need to be watched or checked up on. She begins to develop a reputation for being trustworthy and dependable outside your home.

You will see a growing acceptance of personal responsibility in several areas. Your teenager will take responsibility for maintaining day-by-day communion with the Lord. In the early years of a child's life, Christian parents are almost totally in control of the child's exposure to the things of God. At some point the child must internalize spiritual values and take responsibility for his own relationship with God. He must have a desire for the Lord that causes him to pursue Christian fellowship, Bible teaching, personal worship, and ministry.

The maturing teen will also take responsibility for maintaining healthy, productive, and God-glorifying relationships with the people in his life. This includes parents, siblings, friends, neighbors, and authority figures outside the home. Young children constantly require the intervention of adults to maintain relationships with one another. They tend not to understand how they create problems in their relationships, and they tend not to know how to solve the problems they have created. Is your teenager developing healthy, lasting relationships that do not require the consistent intervention of others to be sustained?

You should also see your teenager developing a responsible attitude toward work and productivity. In our pleasure-oriented, materialistic society, work is considered a necessary evil and an interruption—something we must do to afford the pleasures of life but that simultaneously hampers our pursuit of those pleasures. Many teens in Christian homes (and maybe their parents as well) have bought into this hedonistic worldview. The result is a disdain for work and an attempt to avoid it whenever possible.

The biblical view of work is radically different. The call to meaningful, necessary, productive, and creative labor goes to the very heart of our identity as creatures made in the image of God. Work was a significant part of God's original mandate to humanity. It was part of Adam and Eve's perfect lives in a perfect world. The fall of man into sin didn't create work; it dramatically complicated it. We image God in our work. In our work, we submit to the fact that we are creatures in his world. In our work, we find joy and meaning as we live in the way he purposed for us. We become the tools by which he maintains his world and provides for his creatures.

As we evaluate our teenagers, we look for a positive, responsible attitude toward labor both inside and outside the home. We listen for grumbling or complaining about work and look for avoidance of work. And we look for a willingness to participate in the work of the home and the results of disciplined work outside the home (the praise of the teen's boss, the thankfulness of a youth leader for his helpfulness, and so on).

Applied Biblical Convictions

As we discussed earlier, the maturing teenager erects his own moral boundaries. He does not need a lecture to force him to do what's right, nor does he need the threat of punishment to motivate him. A desire to do what is right in God's sight produces the fruit of carefulness in his life. You do not feel like you're living with someone who is always inching to the edge of the cliff or constantly trying to put something over on you.

Teens who live with conviction prove that they can be trusted. They make hard choices even when their parents aren't present and would never know what they decided to do. They tend to hang around with others who do the same. These teens may make decisions that are different from those their parents would make but that are not outside God's boundaries. After all, our goal is not that our children agree with us in every decision but that their lives be a practical picture of submission to God.

Teens who live within God's boundaries aren't hiders. They have no reason to hide. What they desire, decide, and do can be done in the open because it is consistent with the will of God. I asked my teenagers this question many times: "Is there anything that you are doing out there that you would be afraid or embarrassed to do in front of me?" This question can be a practical way of getting them to think about whether they are living within God's boundaries.

An Approachable, Teachable, Seeking Spirit

Teens who are maturing and getting ready to leave home recognize the awesome task before them. They want all the help and preparation they can get. They don't resent conversations about what they are doing. They don't get defensive when their choices are questioned. They don't put up distance with non-answers or get impatient and argumentative when drawn into discussion. And they don't turn friendly discussions into unfriendly debates as soon as the subject touches their behavior and choices. This assumes, of course, that our attitudes and interactions are what God wants them to be as we relate to them.

If we *are* relating to our teenagers in a godly way, something is wrong if we constantly feel as if we are walking on eggshells when we are around them. Mature teens are approachable. We can go to their rooms to talk without feeling like unwelcome intruders. We can lovingly challenge their thinking, choices, and actions, and they will respond without anger. They not only will allow us to approach them but will actively seek out our advice and wisdom.

Accurate Self-Assessment

Teens who are maturing have an increasingly accurate view of themselves. They have a sense of their strengths and weaknesses that guides their choices in their relationships and responsibilities. They have a growing sense of the ways they are particularly susceptible to temptation. They are not surprised when you lovingly point out a weakness that needs attention. They don't react with "What are you talking about? I never do that!" They receive your help because they have already recognized their weakness and their need for help.

I went down to my son's room one night. There was something we needed to talk about.

"Do you have a moment?" I asked.

"Sure," he said. "I wasn't doing anything important."

"I want to talk about our relationship," I said. "I have been concerned about something for a while, and I thought it was time for us to talk. It seems like you have been really defensive lately. You seem to get impatient every time we try to talk to you about your decisions. We don't look for ways to hassle you, and we don't want to wreck your life. We love you and only want you to be all that God has purposed for you to be."

I waited for him to respond.

"I guess you're right," he said. "I guess there are times when it's kinda hard to talk to me. I just feel like I should have a life of my own and be making my own decisions. Sometimes I feel like you guys forget how old I am. But I know I still need your help, and even when I don't want it, I should accept it. I'm sorry. I know I have made it tough for you lately."

"I forgive you," I said. "We don't want to make your decisions for you, and we don't want to treat you like a little kid, but we do sense that there are ways you still need us, and we are committed to giving you the help God has called us to give you. We couldn't love you and do anything less. I love you."

"I love you too," he replied, and I left his room.

This is what you are looking for. Not teens who are perfect, who do everything in the right time and in the right way. No, you are looking for teens who are mature enough to realize that they are not finished products and, because of their accurate view of themselves, are able to receive the help you are there to offer.

Proper Perspective on Material Things

We have already noted that we live in an intensely materialistic culture that worships and serves created things rather than the Creator. We tend to define success in terms of the size of a person's house and the brand and luxury level of his car. The labels that used to be sewn on the inside of clothing now appear on the outside in huge letters, announcing our good taste and affluence. It is naive to think that our teenagers can breathe the air of this materialistic culture without taking in some of its values.

As a parent, you should watch to see if your teenager is inordinately preoccupied with material things. These questions will help you recognize the signs.

- Does your teenager have a "gotta have" mentality?
- Does he have a short contentment span and quickly move on to the next craving?

- Does she tend to evaluate people by looks and clothing—and associate only with people who meet her appearance standards?
- Does he tend to describe his future goals in materialistic, monetary terms?
- Does she tend to be happiest with you and with her life when she is surrounded by the stuff she wants?
- Does he tend to leap on all the current fads?
- How does she spend the money you give her and the money she earns?
- Does he have a giving spirit and use his money to serve others and the Lord?

The maturing teenager is thankful for the things she has, but she also is learning that life does not consist in the abundance of her possessions. At the same time, she is a good steward of the things God has given her, and she is someone who can be trusted with the possessions of others. She has a sense of the proper way to think about and use the things God has provided.

SOONER OR LATER, EVERY PARENT will be like the mom and dad we saw on the front porch. Maybe we'll beg an angry teenager not to go, or maybe we'll say our tearful farewells to sons and daughters who are ready. We all know that our teenagers won't live with us forever. We all know that God's goal is for us to be his instruments in producing children who are biblically mature, ready to face life in the fallen world, ready to be salt and light, and ready to contribute to his kingdom work and who no longer need the day-by-day guidance that we have given them for so many years.

Ultimately, we need to once again face the fact that we cannot give our teenagers what we do not have ourselves. Being Christian parents does not guarantee that we are biblically mature. We too need to look intently into the mirror of the Word of God. Do we meet the biblical standard of maturity? In what areas do we need to grow? Do we model winsome, mature godliness before our teenagers? Are we living responsible lives? Are we ourselves approachable and teachable? Do we live with moral boundaries that shape our decisions and actions? Do we have an accurate sense of the areas in which we are weak and in which we are strong, and are we open to others' help? Do we hold physical things in proper balance, or do we work too much and owe too much because we have followed our culture's values?

We need to stand before God and ask if we are holding our children to standards that we are not keeping ourselves. Remember Christ's words about the Pharisees in Matthew 23:1–4. Do our lives contradict our message? Is it possible that the reason our children reject us and reject God is not because of our standards but because of our own hypocrisy? Do we humbly communicate to our teenagers that we too are in process? That we too need the grace of God as much today as on the first day we believed? That we recognize that our hearts are prone to wander away from the Creator and instead deify the created thing? That we too need God's help to remain faithful and to grow? Are we willing to go to our teenagers in times of failure, to seek their forgiveness and communicate to them a vibrant reliance on the forgiving and delivering mercy of Christ?

Do our teenagers respect the lives we lead? Do they consider being like us to be part of their definition of successful living? Do they say to themselves, "I live in a world where much is wrong and fake, but my parents are genuine. I don't always like what they say to me or what they ask me to do, but I want to be like them." Do our teenagers look at us and see truth, love, grace, faithfulness, and hope? Do they look at us and see Christ?

Successful parenting means that we admit that we, as parents, are still children in need of our Father's help. It means we go to him and say, "We cannot be what you have called us to be without the lavish resources of your grace. We have believed—help us in our unbelief! We have obeyed—strengthen us where we are still tempted to disobey! We have loved—help us when we are moved more by love of self than by love for you! Work in us, Lord, so that you may work through us to capture the lives of our teenagers by your grace. We ask this that their lives and ours may be lived as hymns to your glory."

Questions for Reflection and Discussion

1. What's the worst sin your child has ever committed? When you addressed this failure, did you primarily discipline or did you use

the incident as an opportunity to lead your child to cast himself or herself on Christ? Is the gospel of grace a part of your message each and every time you discipline or correct?

2. With the event from question 1 in mind, consider how you *accepted* your child's sin. Did your words and actions reveal the *incarnate* Christ? Were you able to verbally *identify* with your child as a fellow sinner? Did you take time to *enter* his or her world in order to better understand the trials and temptations your child faces on a daily basis?

3. If your teenager has not yet left the home, reflect on seeds of maturity you can currently identify in him or her, believing that God is able to fully complete this work. Recall the seeds we saw in this chapter: sensitivity to God's revealed will, functional godliness, progressive spiritual growth, perseverance, appreciation of God's grace, and kingdom awareness. How can you encourage your teenager to develop these traits?

4. How can you and your spouse more consistently model a theology of work and career?

5. Do you regularly evaluate whether your teenager is living within God's boundaries? Ask him or her, "Is there anything you are doing out there that you would be afraid or embarrassed to do in front of me?"

6. Does your teenager have an approachable, teachable, seeking spirit? Pray for your child's heart to be softened and his or her spirit to be open.

7. Reflect honestly on whether you are asking your children to meet biblical standards and maturity levels that you yourself are not. Does your life contradict your message? In what ways do you need to grow in maturity, humility, responsibility, teachability, and faith? Pray today for God's abundant and sufficient grace in these areas.

PART THREE

Practical Strategies for Parenting Teens

12

Three Strategies
for Parenting Teens

BILL AND JEAN SAT IN my office looking worn out and discouraged. They had looked forward to raising a family and had very much enjoyed the early years of parenting. They told of great vacations and wonderful holidays. They remembered the sweetness of reading their children to sleep, surprising them with breakfast in bed, and bringing home the occasional unexpected toy. But somewhere, somehow, they had lost sight of what they were doing and why. Now their interactions with their children all seemed to lack continuity and purpose.

They had read many Christian parenting books and even attended a weekend seminar, yet their relationship with their teenager in particular was growing more and more distant. Most of the time they corrected him out of irritation rather than with biblical purpose. They felt as if the whole process was slipping out of their grip.

"We've had so many people tell us what to do," Jean said, "but we don't know how to do it. We get excited when we read a book or hear a speaker, but then nothing works the way they described or turns out the way we expected."

Bill interjected, "We need a sense of focus or purpose. We're here because we want to have the same sense of direction with our kids that we had when they were younger. We have one teenager and two more on the way. We don't want to lose them now."

"Besides, we're tired," Jean said, "and I think it's because we complicate problems rather than solve them. There's always some mess that we're cleaning up."

Later that day, I wondered how many other couples share Bill and Jean's experience. They look back with nostalgia to the golden days of parenting. The days when their children couldn't wait until they came home from work. The days when their children carried books around, begging for them to read to them. The days when they could satisfy their children with a few moments of wrestling on the floor. How many parents secretly wish for the earlier years to return? They know that their relationships with their teenagers are not what they were when they were younger—but instead of making changes in the present, they give in to grieving the loss of the past.

In the last several chapters, we looked at five fundamental goals for parenting teens. Now we must turn to *strategies* for realizing those goals. I want to suggest three things for you to do if you want to raise godly teenagers who are prepared to live as salt and light in a fallen world. These strategies will bring a sense of purpose and focus to your life with your teen.

In all this, there is a basic truth we need to remember: what we observe about teenagers applies to us as well. These biblical insights, principles, and strategies apply to our teenagers because they apply to people in general. This exposes the core truth of this book. *Our teenagers are more like us than they are unlike us.* They face different pressures, temptations, and opportunities but deal with them in ways that mirror us. And, like us, they are not finished products.

All the spiritual needs we recognize in our teenagers are in some way identifiable in us. So we must apply these strategies with a humble willingness to identify with our teens' struggles, a humble recognition that God is still working to change us, and a humble readiness to offer our teenagers the same grace that God has given us.

STRATEGY #1:
Project Parenting

To parent with a sense of project is to know why we are doing what we are doing. Parenting without a sense of project is like going into the shop, collecting wood, glue, hardware, and tools, and starting to work, hoping that as you measure, saw, hammer, and glue, your efforts will all turn into something! None of us has ever done this because it wouldn't work. We need to know what we want to build, what materials we require, and what our process of construction will be. Yet many parents make the mistake of parenting without a sense of project in the lives of their teens.

The phrase *project parenting* refers to pursuing focused, purposeful, and goal-oriented daily encounters with our teenagers. What should we be working on with *this* particular child at *this* particular time in his life? *How* should we work on it? What themes do we need to emphasize in our conversations?

Project parenting means we parent with *prepared spontaneity*—we come to unexpected, spontaneous moments of parenting with prepared- ness and purpose. We don't just think on the fly, nor do we try to do every- thing at once. Rather, we examine our children, pray, and consider our focus. We ask ourselves where our teenagers are weak, where they are sus- ceptible to temptation, where they seem to be regularly struggling, and where we see rebellion and resistance. The issues we observe become our projects. We realize that God, in his sovereignty, gives us daily opportuni- ties to deal with those issues. Having a sense of what is of pressing impor- tance in the lives of our teenagers, we look for opportunities to deal with it.

A Biblical Model for Project Parenting

Where do we start? As he describes the mindset of the wicked in Psalm 36:1–4, David provides a wonderful model for project parenting. He helps us to understand the struggles of our teenagers so we can do the work of God in their midst, and he gives us one of Scripture's best summa- ries of God's goal for us and our teenagers. He states it negatively, but it is nonetheless clear. Let's take a look.

> Transgression speaks to the wicked
>> deep in his heart;
> there is no fear of God
>> before his eyes.
> For he flatters himself in his own eyes
>> that his iniquity cannot be found out and hated.
> The words of his mouth are trouble and deceit;
>> he has ceased to act wisely and do good.
> He plots trouble while on his bed;
>> he sets himself in a way that is not good;
>> he does not reject evil.

As David examines the heart of a wicked person, he identifies deficiencies that exist in the hearts of many, if not most, of our teenagers (and often ours as well) and gives us three goals for what our children should be.

Teens who fear God. The wicked person has "no fear of God before his eyes" (v. 1). He lacks an awareness of the existence and glory of God, and he has not submitted his life to that fact of facts.

Likewise, most teenagers do not live with the fear of God before their eyes. Their private universes are dominated by a craving for the things they are convinced they need, a desire for peer acceptance, a fear of peer rejection, or a preoccupation with identity issues. Not only does God not dominate the scene, he is not there at all! Whatever their profession of faith, God does not exist in the functional world where they live daily. They do not structure their lives around the awe, worship, and obedience that flows out of recognizing him and his glory. They do not make him the single most important reference point for all that they desire, think, do, and say.

The fear of God is meant to be *the* central organizing force in our lives—yet for many teens, it is not.

Teens who see themselves accurately. The wicked person also "flatters himself in his own eyes" (v. 2). This too describes many teenagers. Teens don't tend to live with an accurate view of themselves. They think that they know more than they actually know. They think that they are more mature, wise, and spiritually strong than they really are. They are convinced that they have outgrown their need for parenting long before they actually have. When they look at themselves, they don't use the perfect mirror of the Word of God but instead use the carnival mirrors of peer opinion, personal evaluation, and cultural norm. The self-analysis of the typical teenager is distorted by this approach. He does not see himself with clarity or accuracy. He tends to "think of himself more highly than he ought to think" (Rom. 12:3).

Teens who act wisely and do good. David says that because the wicked person lacks a fear of God and an accurate self-concept, he has "ceased to act wisely and do good" (v. 3). In this way, David tells us what qualities we should pursue for our teenagers. We want to help our children to *act wisely and do good.* Their practical, functional godliness is our ultimate goal.

Who is the wise person? It is the person who fears the Lord, whose life is organized by God's existence and his revealed will. She brings a wisdom to her everyday life that can come only from above. She seeks to bring that wisdom to every circumstance, decision, and relationship. Who is the person who does good? It is the person who has committed himself to do everything in a way that pleases the Lord and is consistent with the commands and principles of Scripture. He pays attention to God's boundaries and seeks never to step over them.

In short, the person who acts wisely and does good is always asking, "What decision, attitude, or action would best express the will of God for me in this particular situation?"

The Specificity of Godliness

These lessons from Psalm 36 must remain in our minds as we seek to parent our teenagers. Our goal is not to just correct wrong but to gain greater ground. We want our children to grow in their awareness of and submission to God and in an accurate knowledge of themselves. Thus we see each situation, discussion, problem, encounter, and interchange with them as an opportunity for us to work on the fundamental deficiencies David identifies and to pursue our goal of helping our teenagers to act wisely and do good.

As we do this, we must remember that God, in his sovereign plan, has placed each of our children in a particular life context. Each child's context is different. We need to know what God has placed on each of our teenagers' plates so that we can teach them to live with their eyes open to the particular pressures, opportunities, responsibilities, and temptations they face. What significant relationships must they deal with? Who are their authority figures? Who are the influencers in their lives, and what are they saying? What values are being promoted in their world? In what areas do they struggle daily?

We need to ask these questions because godliness is never general. Godliness is always specific. It is always lived out in particular situations and relationships. A teenager who is godly is wise and does good in the *particular setting* where God has placed him. Teenagers need to accurately understand their unique situations—and in order to help them, so do we.

If our teenagers are ever to be godly, and if they are ever to live out this godliness in their world, they need to be prepared. They need to enter each situation with an accurate sense of themselves and an accurate sense of the war within. Teenagers who lack personal insight tend to lack self-control, the internal restraint system of the heart. Teenagers who gain personal insight often have consciences that respond to their self-knowledge and the knowledge of right that God has given them. Their hearts respond to the Holy Spirit's ministry to make them humble and obedient.

There are two equally important elements to this personal insight.

Your teenager must detect his own sin. We have already observed that teenagers are not good at detecting their sin. We need to ask, "What things about himself does my teenager miss that God wants him to see?" What weaknesses, failures, sins, attitudes, values, desires, idols, thoughts, or motives does he need to see that he does not see? And how can we use the everyday situations in his life to help him to detect these problems?

Your teenager must hate *her sin.* It is not enough for our teenagers to *detect* their sin; they must also come to *hate* it. One of Satan's favorite tricks is to present sin as not so bad. This has been one of his principal schemes since the garden of Eden, and we are all highly susceptible to it.

Even when teenagers recognize wrong, they tend to color it as less than what it really is. When they fail to keep a promise, they tell us they forgot. When they disobey, they tell us they didn't understand. When they speak unkindly, they tell us we misunderstood them. When we speak to them about a failure, they refer to the same failure in one of their siblings. They don't tend to see their sin as arrogant rebellion against God—as something dangerous, destructive, and deadly. Rather than repulsing them, it sometimes even seems attractive and appealing.

If our teens do not hate their sin, they will not run from it. Our job is to work with them in the daily circumstances of life to help them to see sin as God sees it. As they do, our goal and prayer should be that they would hate that sin and cast themselves on Christ, saying, "Wretched man that I am! Who will deliver me from this body of death? Thanks be to God through Jesus Christ our Lord!" (Rom. 7:24–25).

When our teenagers gain personal insight, they know where they are weak and recognize the nature of their struggle with sin. They are sensitive to temptation. They live vigilantly, and because they do, instead of falling again and again into the same sin, they respond with self-control and, with God's help, act wisely and do good.

Project Parenting in Action

There is a war going on—a spiritual war that is fought on the turf of our teenagers' hearts every day. If they are ever going to be what God has called them to be and do what he has called them to do, they must be prepared to do battle.

Thus, we must focus all our parenting efforts on being used of God to (1) produce teens who act wisely and do good; (2) help them to maintain an accurate knowledge of their current life situations; and (3) prepare them to pursue godliness by helping them to detect and hate their own sin. We must do all this in a spirit of humility, recognizing that these things must be goals for our own lives as well. We must not approach project parenting as judges who have solved all our own problems but as those who recognize our own sin and our continuing need of Christ.

My wife and I sought to do this by sitting down a couple of times a year, usually at the start of the school year, to take a good look at each of our children. We sought to identify our "projects" for each child at that particular time. We asked ourselves, "What important struggles are present in his or her life that we need to go after? How does our child view those areas?" We wanted to know where our children were encountering temptation in their everyday lives. We sought to discern the ways in which they tended to minimize or rationalize those temptations. We sought to pinpoint how we could expose their struggles with sin and encourage them with the ever-present help of Christ. Our conversations gave us an opportunity to be honest about our own struggles with sin as we dealt with our children's blindness, rationalization, and resistance.

In project parenting, we are not working on everything at once. We are not just hoping that somehow, some way, our parenting will benefit our children. We are working with purpose, focus, and priorities. My wife and I have seen the benefits of project parenting in our children, and we have seen the benefit to us as well. Project parenting keeps us focused on God's priorities rather than the personal irritations and differences that cause so much conflict between parents and teenagers.

STRATEGY #2:
Constant Conversation

For years it was my habit to "visit" each of my four children when I came home at night. One night I went down to one of my sons' rooms to talk. I asked him how he was doing and how his day had been. He said "Okay," but he wasn't very convincing.

"You don't sound okay," I said. "What's wrong?"

"Nothing. Just the same old stuff."

"There must be something on your mind; you look discouraged."

"It's hard to explain, you know, it's just life . . . it stinks," he mumbled.

"Yeah, it can be really hard sometimes," I said. "But I still don't know what we're talking about."

Impatience edged into his voice. "Do we have to talk about this now?"

"Look, you know I love you," I said. "I come down here every day because I care. I'm not trying to hassle you. If you don't want to talk right now that's okay."

"It just seems impossible sometimes," he said. "It seems like things never turn out right. . . . It seems like you never get credit for what you do. If you do what is right, nobody notices, but there is always somebody around to catch you when you mess up. Right now I wish they would take school and my job and shove it! Sometimes I feel like I'm wearing a T-shirt that says, 'Please hassle me.' I wonder if it's worth it, why I put myself through such torture. I don't think I can keep doing this. . . . Something has got to change."

These conversations don't just happen. You make them happen by pursuing your child every day. This daily pursuit does not have to be negative, something your teenager dreads before it happens and barely tolerates as it's going on. Rather, these times can be loving and encouraging, a habit in your relationship with your teenager that both of you have grown to appreciate.

Why do our teenagers need constant (daily) conversation? Why is it dangerous for us to let days, weeks, even months pass between personal, self-disclosing conversations with our teenagers? Hebrews 3:12–13 answers this question for us and provides a model for our daily interchanges with our teenagers.

> Take care, brothers, lest there be in any of you an evil, unbelieving heart, leading you to fall away from the living God. But exhort one another every day, as long as it is called "today," that none of you may be hardened by the deceitfulness of sin.

The reason for constant conversation with our teenagers comes in the form of a warning. A falling away from God refers to a falling away of the heart. The heart always falls before the eyes, mouth, ears, hands, and feet.

Many teens who live in Christian homes attend worship services, participate in family devotions, and are active in their churches' youth groups but have hearts that long ago turned away from the living God. When they go to college and fall away from the faith, something new and radical isn't taking place. It is the fruit of a falling away from God that has taken place in their hearts months—maybe even years—beforehand.

This passage characterizes four aspects of this turning away. Each one helps us to understand the nature of the warning.

- We are warned against an *evil* heart—a heart that no longer desires to please the Lord and no longer submits to Scripture.
- We are warned against an *unbelieving* heart. This refers to a loss of faith, confidence, appreciation for, and trust in God and his Word.
- We are warned against *falling away* from the living God. Falling away is not just breaking the moral law; it is forsaking personal communion and fellowship with God himself.
- We are warned against a *hardening* of the heart—a searing of the conscience that makes it insensitive to the convicting ministry of the Holy Spirit. The heart is no longer bothered by things that would once have caused much concern and guilt.

We want to do everything we can to protect our teenagers from falling away. We want to protect them from rebellion, unbelief, rejection of God, and the hardening of their hearts. To do so, the writer of Hebrews says, we need to encourage them daily. Our teenagers (like all of us) need daily contact, daily help, daily encouragement, daily exhortation, and daily pleading. They need constant conversation.

Notice that the passage tells us why they need this daily ministry. It is because of *sin's deceitfulness*. Sin is deceitful, and guess who it deceives first? Your teenager easily sees the sins of others around her but often is surprised when her own are pointed out. This is spiritual blindness, and it is a universal problem. As long as sin remains within us, *all of us* will experience some degree of spiritual blindness.

When you think of the needs of your teenager, put the issue of spiritual blindness high on the list. It is surely one of the most significant results of the fall. Physically blind people know they are blind and structure their lives accordingly, but spiritually blind people don't know they are blind—they think they see and see well. Surely this explains why our teenagers often feel hurt and falsely accused and become defensive when we point out areas of failure to them.

It is very important to understand the spiritual dynamic at work here. We are being urged to have daily contact *not* because we have caught a person in sin and must confront him or her. This passage is not *confrontational* and *restorative* in its focus. It is *preventative*. We are urged to have daily contact because as long as there is indwelling sin in our teenagers, there is some degree of spiritual blindness as well. And since spiritually blind people don't know it, they don't ordinarily seek help. Our teenagers don't tend to seek us out because they don't think they need our counsel.

That is why you need to commit yourself to the preventative, constant-conversation model. Create a home environment where conversation is always taking place—where children cannot mumble greetings, sit at the kitchen table in silence, or spend all their time alone in their rooms. We have to be determined to talk to them and to get them to talk to us, preferably every day. As we do this, we need to face our own spiritual blindness. We are not immune to any of the sins we have discussed in these pages. In our conversations with our teenagers, God is working to open not only their eyes but ours as well.

Spiritual blindness tends to distort our view of ourselves, God, others, the past, the present, the future, and where and how change needs to take place. If our teenagers have distorted views of these things or don't see them at all, there is no way they will respond to the issues in their lives in biblical, God-honoring ways.

The constant conversation model means that you must be willing to pursue your teenager. It means not living with any distance that he has introduced into the relationship. It means hanging in through those uncomfortable moments when you're not really wanted and not really appreciated and means not limiting meaningful talks with your teenager to only those times when she has done something wrong.

Be committed to prevention. Don't settle for non-answers. Ask good questions that your teenager cannot answer without disclosing his heart (thoughts, motives, purposes, goals, desires, beliefs, values, and so on). Finally, always bring the gospel to each of these conversations. There is a Redeemer. He has conquered sin and death. He is present as the Helper in all our times of trouble. There is hope! Goliaths do die! Change—radical heart and life change—is possible!

If we as parents have our hope in the gospel, we pursue our teenagers and don't stop until they leave home. We don't wait for them to come to us for help. We don't argue with them over whether they need us or not. The call of the Word is clear. With hearts filled with gospel hope, we question and probe, listen and consider, plead and encourage, admonish and warn, instruct and pray. We awake every day with a sense of mission, knowing that God has given us a high calling. We are walls of protection that God has lovingly placed around our teenagers. We are eyes that he has given that they might see. So we converse and converse and converse.

STRATEGY #3:
Leading Your Teenager to Repentance

Secretly (and sometimes not so secretly) many parents of teenagers wish for some means of control. They wish they could wield some power over their teenagers so that they would do what they are asked to do. What many parents mourn, as their children enter the teen years, is their loss of power. So by harsh words, dramatic punishments, shame, and guilt, they try to control the thoughts and behavior of their sons and daughters.

What happens instead? They find themselves in an escalating war. The more they chase their teens, the more their teens hide. The more they beat their teens with words, the more their teens respond in kind. The more they punish their teens, the more their teens work to get beyond the boundaries they have set up. The more they probe for answers, the less their teens talk. The more they lay out what they want, the more their teens determine to do the opposite. Each side, parent and teen, is determined to break down the resolve of the other. It is a tense, debilitating, destructive way to live. Anger grows, and the only changes that take place are changes for the worse.

This is surely not God's way to prepare our teenagers for productive, God-glorifying lives! Rather than seeking to get our teenagers under our control, we want to be used by God so that they would joyfully submit to his. Rather than seeing ourselves as agents of control, we need to see ourselves as ambassadors of reconciliation. Our desire should be to lead our teens to the Lord with repentant hearts. Paul says it well in 2 Corinthians 5:17–21.

> Therefore, if anyone is in Christ, he is a new creation. The old has passed away; behold, the new has come. All this is from God, who through Christ reconciled us to himself and gave us the ministry of reconciliation; that is, in Christ God was reconciling the world to himself, not counting their trespasses against them, and entrusting to us the message of reconciliation. Therefore, we are ambassadors for Christ, God making his appeal through us. We implore you on behalf of Christ, be reconciled to God. For our sake he made him to be sin who knew no sin, so that in him we might become the righteousness of God.

God has reconciled us to himself so that we would be his ambassadors of reconciliation. It is as though God makes his personal appeal to our teenagers through us! So we seek to lead our teenagers to the Lord with words of confession, with a commitment to repentance, and with hope in the effective work of Christ on the cross. We lead them to the Lord not just once but again and again and again so that they can receive his forgiveness and help.

Our job as God's ambassadors is to make the four steps to this process of repentance and reconciliation very clear.

Consideration

As God's agents, we need to ask ourselves, "What does God want my teenager to see about herself that she is not seeing? How can I help her to see these things?" This relates to the issues we discussed regarding spiritual blindness. But many parents start down the wrong path right here. Instead of engaging a teenager in a conversation that leads her to consider things she would not consider alone, a parent *declares* what she has done wrong and what is going to happen as a result. Throughout the whole encounter, the heart of the teen remains either passive or defensive. Her eyes aren't opened at all. The parent, and only the parent, makes all the interpretations and conclusions.

Contrast this with the way Nathan confronted David about his adultery and murder. Nathan did not storm into David's throne room (as parents of teens are tempted to do) and say, "You, David, are a murderer and an adulterer, and the jig is up!" Rather, Nathan told David a story to which he could relate. Its purpose was to get David to consider what he had done, to stimulate his conscience, and to open his eyes.

When I sought to get my teenagers to look at themselves, I tried to focus on concrete situations. I would regularly ask these five questions:

- What was going on? (Situation.)
- What were you thinking and feeling? (Heart response to situation.)
- What did you do? (Active, behavioral response to situation.)
- Why did you do it? (Motives, goals, desires that shaped active response.)
- What was the result? (Impact of response on situation.)

These questions shift the focus from other people and the details of the situation onto the teenager. They were very useful for helping my teenagers to consider what God wanted them to see.

Confession

I am convinced that one of our great mistakes when we confront our teenagers is to make their confessions for them. We burst into their rooms, telling them what they have done and why. When we do this, we are not leading our teenagers to confession; we are doing it for them. In fact, it is even worse. Since we have not attempted to open their eyes, in their spiritual blindness they think we are wrong. They feel as if they have been falsely accused, and they are angry with us rather than grieved at their own sin. Instead of dispelling spiritual blindness, the encounter promotes it. The conscience of the teen becomes harder rather than softer.

We need to enter the rooms of our teenagers with the recognition that, in our own blindness, our evaluations of and attitudes toward our teenagers may be wrong. We should be willing to let God correct us as we seek to correct them.

The harsh, inflammatory words we are tempted to use at these times do not encourage repentance in our teenagers; they produce the opposite. They drive our teenagers away from us, and God, in anger. Remember, God seeks to make his appeal for the hearts of our teenagers through us! Are we acting in a way that advances his work or that gets in the way? Our goal must be to lead our teenagers to make statements of confession.

Commitment

This step must not be omitted or assumed. Commitment involves the teenager's promise to live, act, and respond in a new way. This commitment must be to God and to the appropriate people. It must involve a turning of the heart as well as a changing of behavior. At the heart of repentance is a determination to turn and go in the opposite direction. Discuss what this new commitment will look like in the particular relationships and situations that your teenager faces every day. Help your teenager to anticipate when he will be tempted to forsake his commitment and go back to Egypt.

Change

True repentance always results in concrete changes in teenagers' lives. Here again, we need to be specific. We need to help our teenagers to think about how they will do old things in a new, God-glorifying way in their particular situations and relationships. We need to keep reminding them that in Christ they have everything they need to do what God has called them to do. He will provide a way to do all that he asks.

Our job as parents is not to crank up our control but to lead our sons and daughters to heartfelt submission to the Lord's control. So we work daily to engage them in consideration, confession, commitment, and change. God has chosen to use us to make his appeal to our teenagers! As parents, we must submit to his lordship by serving with an ambassadorial spirit in the kitchens, family rooms, bedrooms, and hallways of life.

IN THIS CHAPTER WE HAVE considered three fundamental strategies for parenting teenagers: project parenting (focusing on what we need to work on at the moment), constant conversation (making daily, encouraging contact with our teens because of their spiritual blindness), and leading our teenagers to repentance (producing consideration, confession, commitment, and change). None of these strategies can stand alone. Each complements the others.

Together these strategies give focus and direction to your daily inter-actions with your teenager. They give you a daily sense that you know *what* you are doing, *why* you are doing it, and *how* it needs to be done. God will also use these strategies to restrain your own sin as you deal with your son or daughter. These strategies will expose the places in your heart where your anger, impatience, and frustration get in the way of the work God has called you to do.

Remember, the God who called us also parents us. He is with us in every situation and relationship. Our Father guides, directs, protects, for-gives, delivers, and loves us. He will never leave us alone. When we are weary and heavy laden, he gives us rest. As his strength works in us, it accomplishes more than anything we could ask or think. Our job as par-ents is not to deliver our children from sin but to be agents of the only One who can. As we parent the children God has placed in our care, we can rest in his!

Questions for Reflection and Discussion

1. Consider a recent unexpected or spontaneous moment in your parenting. What made you unprepared for what your teenager said or did? What was your response?
2. Evaluate each of your children and their unique struggles and weaknesses, along with the specific season of life that they are in. How is each different from the other? How can you keep your pur-pose, focus, and priorities in place as you work with each of them?
3. How frequently do you pursue conversations with your teenager? How easily do you give up on those conversations if your child isn't engaging? What are some practical ways that you can facilitate deeper conversations?
4. How frequently do you remind yourself that you are an ambassa-dor for Christ? Did your words and actions accurately represent the King this week to your children? Are your words and actions reconciliatory or harsh and inflammatory?
5. Memorize the five questions listed on page 206 and prepare to ask them in a conversation with your teen. Notice if your teen responds

differently to these questions than to questions you have asked in previous conversations. No matter the response, remember to persevere with the principle of constant conversation!

6. If a goal of parenting is to lead your teenager to make statements of confession, how can you lead him or her to do so by example? Are you afraid of confessing to your child? What sin can you confess today to your child before asking for his or her forgiveness? How will you model repentance?

13

Small Steps to Big Change

IT WAS THE FRIDAY NIGHT of a typical weekend seminar that I was conducting at a midwestern local church. I was laying out biblical goals for parenting teens. In the middle of my second talk, a man sitting halfway back in the auditorium raised his hand. "This is totally unrealistic," he said. "Nobody does this stuff with teenagers! You don't really talk this way to your kids, do you? Do you really think you can reach these goals? I don't know where your kids came from, but they're not like mine! I came here to get some help. . . . This stuff is just unrealistic!"

I could see the pastor slumping down in his seat, red-faced with embarrassment. I think he wanted to bail me out, but I understood the father's feelings, and I thought he had given the parents at the seminar a great opportunity to talk honestly about how discouraged they were over their relationships with their teens. It was true: what I had laid out to them looked like a huge and impassable mountain. They had no idea how to get from the valley where they were to the peaks where they needed to be. That's the way a lot of parents feel when they first hear this material. Maybe that's how you feel as you read this book. If so, don't lose hope.

The vocal father grabbed me the next morning. "I am so sorry that I attacked you as I did. . . . I was wrong to put you on the spot," he said.

"Everything you said to us was biblical and right. Your description of what our relationship to our teenagers could be was beautiful. I was just discouraged because my relationship with my son is so far from that. We seem to be angry at each other all the time. He only talks to me when he has to, and I seem to talk to him only when he is in trouble. Last night I just didn't see how to get from where we are to what you have described."

Mountains are not conquered in a single step. Relationships do not change overnight. Change is a process, not an event. God does his miraculous work of change through the small, faithful steps we take. That is what this chapter is about. We have discussed high goals for our teenagers. We have laid out three fundamental strategies for accomplishing those goals. Now we will look at the small steps you can take to change your relationship with your teenager and the changes you can make in yourself that God can use to change your teenager's life. These little steps are not presented in any particular order of importance. Each is worth remembering. Emphasize and prioritize the ones that apply most to you.

Never Think It Is Too Late

Perhaps you have read this book with remorse. You are wishing you had known this information sooner. You are tempted to think that the die is cast and there is no way you can alter the dynamics of your relationship with your teenager. You are tempted to think that God has a poor sense of timing. The opposite is true. God knows the exact right moment to teach us. He is never early and never too late.

As long as your teenager is still alive and close enough to have a relationship with you, there is hope. Go to her and start afresh. Begin by asking for her forgiveness. Admit that your impatience, unforgiving spirit, selfishness, and self-righteousness have gotten in the way of the relationship God meant for you to have with her. Be specific in your confession. Next, tell her you have determined to establish a loving relationship with her, that you are committed to talking to her, that her life is important to you, and that you want to help however you can. Then begin to follow through.

I have seen relationship after relationship between parents and teenagers change dramatically because parents refused to be discouraged. They stepped out in humility and love and began to relate to their teenagers in new, more biblical ways. Before long, the teenagers let down old walls of defensiveness and became open and communicative once again.

Stay Calm

There is a God. He is in control. All that he does is good. He knows what he is doing even when we don't! In light of this, in tough parenting situations with your teenager, there are three things you can do to avoid panicking, making impulsive decisions, and making the situation worse.

Listen Well

Make sure you listen well enough (and ask good enough questions) to get all the facts straight. Make sure you have an accurate picture of what you are dealing with. Once my parents came home after an evening out to see my younger brother's head totally covered in a makeshift bandage we had fashioned from a bedsheet. He had hit his head on a radiator. My mom immediately panicked and was ready to call the ambulance. When my dad took off the wrapping, he discovered a fairly deep but relatively small wound. My brother lived! Take the time to get the facts.

Don't Overreact Emotionally

Don't give in to the impulses of anger. Don't give way to fear. Don't be overcome by discouragement. Take time to think, pray, and discuss things with your spouse before you talk with your teenager. So much relational and spiritual damage is done by parents who don't prepare themselves for moments of trouble that are God-given opportunities to minister to their teenagers.

Don't Over-Personalize Your Teenager's Failure

Over-personalizing turns a teenager's failure into a personal offense against you. When a teenager failed two of his high school courses, his father angrily confronted him in my office with the words "How could you do this to me after all I have done for you?" He saw the failure as an act against him, not a God-given illustration of his son's struggle and need.

Because he could not get past his own anger and hurt, he was unable to minister to his son. It is hard to minister lovingly to your teenager when you are very angry about what he has done! Remember, "the anger of man does not produce the righteousness of God" (James 1:20).

Keep the Conversation Open

We were driving to the store when suddenly we entered a very important conversation. She was opening up, sharing her struggles at school in a way I had never heard before. As I dropped her off, it hit me that the most important thing I did with that conversation would be what I did once it was over. Many parents make the mistake of letting the open door of their teenagers' self-disclosure close once again. They fail to keep the conversation open. They fail to pursue their teenagers with expressions of concern, commitments to pray, and simple questions about how they are doing.

It is very helpful to get into the habit of conducting regular checkups after your teenager discloses an issue, problem, temptation, disappointment, fear, struggle, or failure. Is your teenager experiencing regular, ongoing temptation, and is she succumbing to it? Are there new situations related to it that she needs to discuss with you? Does she have new questions or doubts as time goes on? Does she feel that she has grown?

I went back again and again to my daughter to talk about the subject she introduced that afternoon. I learned more about her world, and she became less reserved in her communication. She knew I cared, and she came to believe that God did as well.

Demonstrate How the Bible Interprets, Explains, and Organizes Life

Don't resort to on-the-fly, "This is what I think about it" or "Do it because I said so" responses. Your teenager needs to have confidence in Scripture as God's source of wisdom and understanding about life. He needs to grow in his ability to use this amazing and sufficient resource. Each situation you encounter with him provides an opportunity for you to help him to realize that he is responding not simply to his experiences but to his *interpretation* of those experiences. Each circumstance also provides an opportunity for you to demonstrate how the Bible makes sense out of the things your child faces each day. Your goal should be for him to really embrace Scripture as a "lamp to [his] feet and a light to [his] path" (Ps. 119:105).

Be Willing to Bare Your Own Struggle

Many parents make the error of presenting a "just do it" view of life to their teenagers. They minimize the reality and intensity of the struggle to live pure, productive, and responsible lives by failing to reveal their own struggles. They make it seem as if it is all a piece of cake to them. They subtly communicate that it works this way: you learn what is right, and then you just do it. Their impatience and frustration with their teenagers often communicates an attitude of "I'm able to do it, why aren't you?" What comfort, instruction, wisdom, and hope comes when you share with your teenagers how you have struggled with the Goliaths in your life! (In 2 Corinthians 1:3–11, Paul models this for us.)

Keep Christ and His Work Central

The most important relationship in your teenager's life is not her relationship with you but her relationship with Christ. Your primary job is to lead your teenager to him in a spirit of worship, trust, and obedience. Be alert for opportunities to point her to the forgiveness, deliverance, and power that is found in him. Make sure that all your instruction moves her toward Christ.

Remember, sinners are hiders. They love darkness rather than light because their deeds are evil (John 3:19). They let shame and guilt drive them undercover. Christ gives your teenager a reason to come out of hiding into the light. Once your teenager begins to grasp the depth and magnitude of the grace of Christ, thoughts of hiding, denial, defensiveness, and blame shifting make no sense. Thus the message of the grace of Jesus Christ needs to color each conversation you have.

Remember too that you have been called to incarnate Christ in your teenager's life. This means it is not enough for you to speak of his grace; you must also be an example of it as you help your teenager deal with her own sins. Times of correction must not be times of speaking in a loud voice, pointing fingers, saying inflammatory things, and stomping off in parental disgust. You can powerfully and pointedly discipline your teenager in an atmosphere of grace. If you fail to speak the truth in love, the purity of its content becomes corrupted by your frustration, impatience, and anger and ceases to be true.

Don't Act Surprised by Your Teenager's Struggle with Sin

You know that your teenager lives in a fallen world. You know that he is a sinner by nature. You know that Satan is a liar, schemer, and tempter. As a parent of a teen, you should not be shocked or surprised at the presence and power of sin in your child's life. You should expect war. You should come to your relationship with your teenager armed for war—not with your teen but with the true Enemy (Eph. 6). If you are honest about your own experience, you will recognize that the battle with sin still rages within you. (Read Paul's description of this war in Romans 7.) You will recognize that it is dangerous for you to live with a relaxed peacetime mentality. And you will acknowledge that this war will be waged in your life and your teenager's until Christ returns.

This does not mean that we minimize sin. No, it means the opposite. When we respond with shock, we are minimizing the reality and power of indwelling sin. This reaction presents sin as an aberration—as something out of the ordinary—rather than as an ever-present element in every human situation, action, thought, desire, and word. The deepest issues our teenagers experience are not their pain and their loss of self-esteem but their moment-by-moment struggles with rebellion and unbelief. Wise parents expect that battle, arm themselves for it, and teach their sons and daughters to use the effective weapons that only Christ can give.

Identify the "Voices" in Your Teenager's Life

Who does your teenager listen to and respect? Who has influence in his life? What are these people saying? When a child is young, his parents are almost the sole voices of influence in his life. But when the child goes off to school and as he spends more time online, many other voices enter his world. As we interact with our teenagers, there is always a sense in which we are in a debate with the other voices in their lives. What view of life is promoted by the friend, the rock band, the coach, the video content creator, the boss, the teacher, the social media influencer, the youth leader?

You will need to expose yourself to some of these voices. Listen to the album while reading the lyrics. Sit down and watch the show. Take time to get to know the coach and the teacher. Know what you are dealing with as you have those spontaneous, casual, but very critical conversations with your teenager. Determine to become familiar with the influential voices in his life. Your goal is to encourage his willingness to stand back and biblically evaluate the voices and the fruit of their influence in the way he thinks, speaks, and acts.

When you challenge the influential voices in your teenager's life, be sure you know what you are talking about. Parents often lose credibility because they are ill-informed. If you haven't done your homework, you will resort to stereotypes, generalizations, rumors, and straw-man characterizations. This weakens your teenager's respect for the important things you have to contribute. She walks away thinking that you simply do not know what you are talking about. If you want to instruct your teenager effectively and help her to learn to filter the voices in her life, take time to do your research.

Plan for Temptation

You live with certain temptations every day, some to which you are particularly susceptible. The same is true of your teenager. She lives in a world where temptation is a daily reality. It is not enough to point out temptation after the fact and say, "This is what you should have done." We need to teach our sons and daughters to look ahead and identify the potholes in the road so they don't drive into them.

Establish a *temptation plan* with your teenager. First, find out in what areas your teen is currently struggling with temptation. Next, devise a concrete "what to do when" plan of escape for each specific temptation, always being careful to point your teenager to the resources that are found in the Lord Jesus Christ. Finally, revisit and revise the plan periodically. Are the means of escape sufficient and practically workable? Is your teenager taking the way of escape that the Lord has provided? Are there new temptations that need to become part of the plan? The result will be a teenager who is becoming wise about temptation, increasingly appreciative of your practical help, and confident in the Lord's deliverance.

Make Accountability Your Teenager's Responsibility

If your teenager admits that he is less than perfect, if he admits that he does things daily in word, thought, or deed that he should not do, if he admits that he does not yet know everything, if he recognizes that he lives in a fallen world where he is surrounded by temptation to do wrong, if he admits that at times he is blind to his own weakness and wrong, then he is saying that he is a person who is in need of help.

A teenager who has recognized that he needs help isn't irritated when help is offered. He doesn't run away from it; rather, he seeks it out. It doesn't make any sense to recognize physical sickness and avoid the doctor or to go to the doctor and refuse to follow his healing advice. In the same way, a teenager who has begun to recognize his war with sin seeks out help. He wants to have people in his life who love him enough to have conversations with him, ask him questions, and hold him accountable.

There is an important principle of personal ministry here. Accountability always works when the person being held accountable wants the help and seeks to be accountable. God's world is big. There are always places to hide. An army of people cannot successfully hold a person accountable if that person does not want the help. We need to acknowledge to our teenagers that we will never successfully follow them into the secret corners of their lives if they don't want us there. If they want to, they are able to hide from us. We need to teach them that maturity means admitting their need for help and seeking it out. Mature teenagers grow in their willingness to recognize their need, spend less time running away from help, and spend more time seeking it out.

Be a Good Listener and a Good Observer

Parenting is home-based pastoral work. Like a pastor, parents are called to watch over the souls of those under their care. People who are successful at soul care are not only good students of Scripture but also good students of their "congregation." Yet many of us lack a *soul care* or *shepherding* model of parenting. Our model is more of a "control behavior and regulate outcomes" model. Many parents of teens forget the powerful things that the Bible has to say about the heart.

If you understand your parental mission to be shepherding the heart, or caring for the soul, of your child, you will want to know that child well. You will want to model the Wonderful Counselor—the one who is able to sympathize with our weaknesses and give us mercy and grace in our time of need because he took the time to get to know us and our world (Heb. 4:14–16). To model Christ, we need to slow down our lives so that we have time to listen to our teenagers and observe their actions. Many spend little time with their teenagers and, when they do, do all the talking. This tends to be the case because they are present only to correct them.

The *words* of your teenager should be important to you. What do her casual observations about life tell you about her heart? What kind of advice does she give her younger siblings? What do her peer interactions tell you about what is going on inside her? What do you learn about her soul from the ways in which she interprets her life? When do you hear her speaking words of anger, disappointment, regret, fear, cynicism, and loss? Do you hear her speaking words of faith, truth, and hope? What is the content of her God-talk? What is the content of her self-talk? Be a student of your teenager's inner world.

The *actions* of your teenager should be important to you. How does he respond to you? To his siblings? To his friends? How does he deal with responsibilities at home, work, or school? How does he treat possessions—his own and others'? How does he respond to authority figures in his life? What does he do when he faces decisions? How does he deal with the problems he encounters? How does he respond to conflict? Do you see evidences of a heart that wants to do what is right? Do you see humility, love, and patience? Are there places where he gives and situations in which he serves? Is his life self-absorbed and self-focused? Watch, remembering that your teenager speaks and acts out of his heart. As you observe your teen, God uses his fruit to reveal to you the root issues in his heart.

Don't Give In to "Problem Allergy"

Many parents seem to have allergic reactions to the problems their teenagers bring into their lives. Their responses to those problems are swollen and inflamed. They try to avoid knowing about their teens' problems (*don't ask, don't tell*), and they long for days in which everything goes smoothly (*no muss, no fuss*). When we live this way, we are losing sight of what God is doing in our teenagers' lives and what he desires to do through us.

We need to keep two biblical principles constantly in focus. First, God is at work in every situation to accomplish what is redemptive and good. From his perspective, there are no out-of-control moments. He is good, and he is always sovereignly working for good (Rom. 8:28). Second, trial is one of the main tools God uses to mature and complete us. We cannot give in to thinking that difficulty comes because God is absent or passive. He is in the difficulty, and he is using it as an instrument to mature us (James 1:2–8).

These two principles should radically alter the way we think about and respond to problem situations with our teenagers. We have to argue with ourselves against a disaster mentality. God intends for those dark days to be times of growth and repentance. In those times, he exposes the hearts of our sons and daughters in order to rescue them from the domain of darkness and transport them to the kingdom of his dear Son (Col. 1:13–14). Rather than getting angry and frustrated—lashing out at our teenagers and telling them they are wrecking our lives—we need to see these tough times as huge, God-given redemptive opportunities. These are God's moments. We cannot lose sight of him and give in to anger, fear, and hopelessness. In everything we say and do, we need to commit ourselves to being part of what God is doing in our children's lives.

Finally, we need to be humble enough to admit that we tend to be "problem allergic" because we tend to live selfishly rather than redemptively. We want regularity, peace, comfort, and ease. We want our lives to be predictable and unencumbered. The problems that our teenagers bring home are an intrusion on our desires and plans for our lives. We tend to get angry not because they are messing up their own lives but because they are messing up ours. We get captivated by our own plan, and we lose sight of God's. We begin to think of our children as agents for our happiness rather than remembering that we are called to be God's agents of growth in godliness for them. So in times of trouble, we angrily fight for our dream instead of happily doing God's work. If we are ever to consistently see problems as opportunities, we need to begin with humble confession of our selfishness to the Lord.

Always Keep the Heart in Focus

Don't give in to a parenting style in which you deliver pronouncements and lectures with an edge of irritation. Don't settle for getting your teenager to do what you want her to do. I have watched parents embarrass their teens in front of others, threaten them with ultimatums, load them with guilt, and even use the gospel in a manipulative attempt to produce the behavior they want at that moment. Our job is to draw out the purposes of our teenagers' hearts (Prov. 20:5). In every situation we need to ask what heart issues God is seeking to expose and how we can be his instruments in the process.

We need to enter each situation with soft answers, with penetrating questions that cannot be answered without self-disclosure, and with a willingness to take the time to listen, observe, and discuss. We need to enter armed with the gospel of grace and hope. We need to tell stories that engage hearts and stimulate consciences. We need to be willing to bare our own struggles. We need to do everything we can to get our teenagers to step out of their defensiveness and look at themselves in the perfect mirror of the Word. We need to do all this with the remembrance that the words and actions we are dealing with are the fruit of thoughts and motives that have taken root in our teenagers' hearts. We do not want to settle for being fruit pickers when we can be root diggers. Lasting change in our teenagers always begins at the level of the heart.

Do Your Biblical Homework First

Our job as parents is not to clone ourselves in our children by getting them to submit to our style, desires, and preferences. Our goal is to help them to live lives submissive to God's will as revealed in his Word. Our job is not to produce *ourselves* in our teenagers but to produce Christ. So we need to prepare ourselves biblically, for our own sakes, so that our responses are not emotion-driven but driven by biblical purpose. What is biblically important in each situation, and how can we go after it?

We also need to do our biblical homework for our children's sake. We should be able to show that what we require of our teenagers is biblical. We should be able to demonstrate the way each situation they encounter can be interpreted by the commands, principles, promises, and themes of Scripture. We want to model the Word in our behavior and teach our teenagers to look at life through the lens of the Word. We want to call them to be obedient to that Word. Our hope is that our children would grow in their appreciation for Scripture and in their love for the God revealed in Scripture. Ultimately, our prayer is that they would live as people of the Word.

I am afraid that many of us fall short of these purposes because we are in too great a rush. We give in to impulsive reactions and allow our emotions to take over. We react quickly, and we want change to result quickly. We enter the scene unprepared to think and respond biblically, and we end up saying things we regret and announcing punishments we never enforce. In the process, God's purposes and the resources of Christ get completely lost. Advance biblical preparation wards off a lot of this.

Always Talk to Your Teenager Lovingly and Constructively

Acknowledge the Temptation

We need to be aware of the temptation to talk to our teenagers in a way that is less than biblical. There are several reasons for this.

First, living with a teenager means living with the unexpected—with more disorder than order. We are often hit with things we didn't see coming and for which we feel unprepared. We often give in to speaking out of our unpreparedness.

Second, as their activities, responsibilities, and relationships increase and their worlds grow wider, teenagers don't tend to be around as much as they once were. When the already busy life of the family combines with the frenetic life of a teenager, there often isn't much downtime left. We get into trouble when we try to squeeze significant conversations into brief moments along the way. We try to talk as teens are running out the door, gulping down their breakfast, or briefly riding in the car with us. When they are not receptive, we take offense, and the conversation heads in the wrong direction.

Third, teenagers are aware that they are growing up, and out of this awareness comes a desire to be independent. This is not in itself a bad thing. However, it can create tension during times of discussion. Teenagers tend to see our interventions as failures to recognize their maturity, and they often respond defensively. They start thinking they do not need the help that we are offering. (We need to admit humbly that teenagers are not the only ones who have this struggle.) When teenagers do not receive our help with appreciation, we tend to get hurt, frustrated, or irritated and lash out emotionally. Teenagers respond in kind to our disparaging comments, and conversations take a negative turn.

The final point is maybe the most important of all. Teenagers instinctively find and smash our idols. (Surely this is God's doing rather than our teenagers' intent.) If you have an inordinate love for things, your teenager will dent the car the first time she drives it alone. In her nervousness to explain what happened, she will inadvertently sit on—and break—your latest gadget while spilling her soda on your new rug! How tempting to say, "Why don't you just trash everything in the house? It seems to be the one thing you're good at!"

This is but one example of a very important principle we need to keep in mind. *Our communication problems with our teenagers exist not simply because of our children's character but because of our idolatry.* When desires for possessions, position, love, respect, appreciation, peace, comfort, and so on become the functional rulers of our hearts rather than the Lord, conflict in our relationships inevitably results (James 4:1–10).

Practice Better Communication

When we are tempted to communicate with our teenagers unbiblically, we need to examine ourselves. Paul reminds us of three important things in Ephesians 4: first, "with all humility and gentleness, with patience, [bear] with one another in love" (v. 2); second, "[speak] the truth in love" (v. 15); and third, "let no corrupting talk come out of your mouths, but only such as is good for building up, as fits the occasion, that it may give grace to those who hear" (v. 29). These commands must guide our communication with our teenagers. What do they look like in practice?

The kind of communication Paul describes avoids an adversarial "us versus them" stance. We do not stand above our teenagers as if we can't relate to their failures and are irritated by them. Rather, we stand alongside our teenagers as those who fully understand their struggles. We don't act like know-it-alls who have all the answers and none of the questions. We stand with our teenagers as those who are still being taught by the Lord and learning how to properly apply his truth to life.

Communicating biblically also means learning to respect perspectives and accept differences. Our teenagers look at life differently than we do. Our goal isn't for them to agree with us perfectly on all things but to faithfully submit to the Lord and his truth. Communicating biblically means taking the time to listen to the content, emotions, and intentions that our teenagers communicate in everything they say. It means learning to ask good questions instead of entering the room making accusations. It means learning to lead teenagers to confession instead of making confessions for them.

As we talk to our teenagers, we need to be careful to correct them without belittling them. We need to be patient, realizing that change may not be accomplished in one sitting. We need to be willing to come back again and again, giving the Spirit time to work in our teenagers' hearts. We need to learn how to accept and love them even while disapproving of their words and actions. We need to learn to acknowledge respectfully those things our sons and daughters think are important. We need to avoid clichés and overused stories that cheapen conversation and cause teenagers to hit the mental "kill" switch. We need to minimize the use of personal examples that communicate that we went through the teen years without difficulty or that we are now perfectly righteous and struggle-free. And we need to not over-personalize or catastrophize the problems we encounter with our teens.

Since it is only by the power of Christ that we can do these things, we need to greet each day saying, "Father, I want to follow your example as I parent my teenager, yet daily I find myself falling short in many ways. Today I ask that you would empower me so that I may use every situation to think, speak, and act in a way that pictures you and what you, through your Son, have done for me."

Be Willing to Overlook Minor Offenses

Not everything in your teenager's life is of equal importance. You should not go after all failures with the same intensity and seriousness. The hairstyle is not as important as the disrespect. The less-than-perfect table manners are not as important as the growing materialism that is eating away at the teenager's heart. The untidy room is not as important as the temptations toward lust and sexual sin. It's not that the hair, manners, and room are not important, but they are minor compared to the other things.

Love is willing to overlook minor offenses. It is wise to live with a sense of our priorities. Remember what we learned about project parenting in chapter 12. Our teenagers' lives are not "final exams" that we must constantly evaluate and incessantly critique. We don't want them to feel as though they can never relax and must always be on their guard. Rather, our walk with our teenagers needs to be shaped by unfailing grace, boundless love, and persevering patience. In short, our walk with them must be shaped by Christ. As we, by his grace, incarnate him before our children, we are able to greet failure with grace, and they are encouraged to live honestly and in the open.

Always Deal Honestly
with Your Own Attitudes

Remember, your teenager is not the only sinner in the house. God is still working to conform *you* to the image of his Son. Sin remains in every parent of every teenager. Because of this, it is vital that we have an eye not only toward them but toward ourselves. We need to face humbly our own defensiveness, selfishness, self-righteousness, anger, and impatience. We need to regularly go to God and our teenagers and ask for forgiveness.

Your spouse can help you here. Remember that sin is deceitful: we tend to see the speck of dust in our neighbors' eyes and not notice the log jutting out of our own. Ask for help with evaluating your attitude and actions toward your teenager, and be willing to receive it even when you have not asked for it.

Many biblical attitudes should be our personal goals as we parent our teenagers. First, we must always do what we do because we are committed to live to God's glory. This must be the desire that overwhelms all others. We must forsake bitterness and the willingness to hold a grudge. We must be willing to forgive our teenagers over and over again. We must not be only lawgivers, detectives, and judges. We must hold God's high standard before our teenagers in a patient spirit of love, mercy, and grace. We must speak carefully, promise cautiously, and always be true to our words. We must be people whom our teenagers can fully trust. We must always do what we have said and follow through with our commitments.

It is vital that we bring a spirit of humility to our relationships with our teenagers. We must commit ourselves to being approachable. We must always be willing to admit, confess, and forsake our wrongs. Finally, we must continue to examine whether our relationships with our teenagers are being shaped by a heartfelt concern for their spiritual well-being or by our own selfishness and self-interest (Phil. 2:1–11).

Expect, Welcome, and Respect Differences

God's creativity is glorious! Look at the human face. No two noses are alike! You would think that sooner or later God would run out of designs and begin to recycle old models. Yet the variety of noses is as endless as his ability to create. Your teenager won't be just like you. There will be ways in which she is very different. Don't see this as some kind of personal defeat—see it as a testimony to the glory and grandeur of God. Stand back and be amazed and amused that even within your own family gene pool there is such wide variety and difference! See differences as a cause not for consternation but for worship.

My second son is an artist. It didn't take long for me to realize that he is totally different from me. When he was in second grade, he was given an assignment to write a one-paragraph composition on the Revolutionary War with the help of a parent. He came into the house announcing that we had homework to do together. After he explained the assignment, I thought it would be a piece of cake.

I asked my son what topic he had chosen. He said, "Architecture during the Revolutionary War." I couldn't believe my ears. I looked at this scruffy, smiling little boy and wondered how he had come up with that!

So I asked him, and he said, "Today as the teacher was reading to us about the battles, I just kept thinking, 'But what did the buildings look like?'"

"*What did the buildings look like?*" I thought. "Who cares about the buildings! What about George Washington, Valley Forge, Ben Franklin, and the Declaration of Independence?"

My son ended up going to an art college. I wonder at the gift that God has given him. I am so glad that he is not like me! He has opened my eyes to parts of the world I would never have seen. He has contributed to my life and to our family in ways I could never express. I worship God for creating my son as he is and for the ways we are different. Yet I am aware of the irritation that those differences can create in me and the tendency that I still have to wish he were like me.

We need to be careful to distinguish between difference and sin, between alternative perspectives and rebellion against authority. We need to see the difference between an appropriate choice and disobedience. We need to wisely welcome and encourage differences while lovingly confronting sin.

Look for Opportunities to Put Your Teenager in the Decision-Making Role

The Bible teaches us that maturity comes through practice (Heb. 5:11–14). If we want to send out into the world young adults who are prepared to make wise and godly decisions, we need to give our teenagers opportunities to hone their decision-making skills. We tend to struggle with this for the same reason that the boss of a company struggles with delegating authority. We don't want to have to clean up after other people's failures, so we decide not to put them in situations in which they might not succeed.

We need to school our teenagers in the decision-making process (thinking, deciding, acting, reaping consequences, and evaluating). To do this, we need to resist the temptation to see achieving an ordered life as more important than developing our teenagers' ability to make wise and mature decisions. We must resist the temptation to turn back the clock when our teenagers fail and to once again take over their decision-making. Finally, we need to resist making arbitrary regulations. Our teenagers should have as much freedom as Scripture allows so that they can learn the skills of wise living.

Humbly Admit Your Limits

Always remember that you are not God. Unlike him, you and I have limits to our strength and wisdom. There is a limit to how much we can help others to change. Change in the hearts and lives of our teenagers is always the result of the gracious work of God. We must not try to do, by human force, what only God can do. We will never force our teenagers to submit and obey, because submission is by definition the willing act of a heart that belongs to God. We are not the authors of change; we will never be anything more or less than instruments in the hands of the One who creates change. We should not try to do his work but should instead be people who understand what it means to pray without ceasing.

IN ALL THESE THINGS, WE must remember the truths of God's Word. We are not alone (Josh. 1:1–9). God is an ever-present help in times of trouble

(Ps. 46). He is at work in every situation, location, and relationship to accomplish what is good (Rom. 8:28). He is powerfully at work in us to accomplish things that are greater than anything we could ask or imagine (Eph. 3.14–21).

We do not need to be afraid of our weaknesses, because God's grace is sufficient and his strength is made perfect when we are weak (2 Cor. 12:7–10). In Christ, we have already been given everything we need to do God's will (2 Peter 1:3–4). God has promised to give us wisdom without favoritism (James 1:5). He is gracious and just to forgive us and to cleanse us from all unrighteousness (1 John 1:9). Because of the victorious work of Christ, our labors in his name are never in vain (1 Cor. 15:58). A day is coming when this struggle will be over and there will be no more sin or sorrow (1 Cor. 15:50–57).

What do these promises do for us? They totally change the way we think about the job of parenting our teenagers. Our goal is not survival. That goal forgets the glorious things that God is doing in us and has promised to do through us. No, ours is a wonderful opportunity—to be a daily part of God's glorious work of redemption. We could not have a higher calling!

Our parenting task is more than a duty. It is a great privilege—and we need to embrace it with hope. God *is* here. God *is* at work! We have a reason to get up in the morning: our lives have eternal meaning and purpose! We have a reason to step out in faith and do with courage the things God has called us to do as we parent our teenagers.

May God fill you with the knowledge of his glory as you serve him by parenting those he has placed in your care.

Questions for Reflection and Discussion

1. Do you feel like your relationship with your teenager is an impossible mountain to pass over? Do you feel like it's too late for your relationship to change?
2. Identify the influential "voices" in your teenager's life. Who are people your child listens to and respects? Become familiar with all the voices—positive and negative—that are speaking to your child.

3. Identify your teenager's primary temptations and, together, come up with and pray over a "temptation plan"—a means of escape that is sufficient and practically workable for your child.

4. Does your child have a clear picture of his or her sinfulness? Does your child see his or her own need for Jesus's help and accountability from fellow believers? In his or her worst sin and shame, how can you teach your child to seek out both the grace of Jesus and the accountability of Christian friends and mentors?

5. Do you tend to avoid your teenager's problems? What do you need to change in order to see these problems as God-given redemptive opportunities?

6. Take some time to think of all the ways each one of your children is both similar to and different from you. Expect, welcome, and respect these differences.

7. Honestly examine the way you communicate with your teenager. Do you speak lovingly and constructively, with grace at the center of your message? Remember, your child is not the only sinner in the house! Are you primarily reactive, or do you come into your conversations with your teenager calm, prayerful, and prepared for anything?

Questions and Answers
with Paul Tripp

MY TEEN IS FINDING WAYS TO HIDE APPS, CONTENT, AND MESSAGES ON HIS OR HER PHONE. Do I put restrictions on my teen's devices? Do teens have a right to privacy, or can I snoop around for my child's protection?

When Steve Jobs created the iPhone, the culture of the entire world changed. Smartphones can be powerful tools for good, but many negative resources are available through these devices as well. If your teen has a smartphone in his pocket, it is harder than ever to control the influences in his life because the device makes the entire world available—the world in all its beauty and all its deep darkness. You must be concerned about this; I don't think it's possible to be too concerned. You must be proactive, and you must be ready.

There is significant pressure on parents to put mobile devices in their children's hands: pressure from other parents, pressure from their kids, pressure from their friends, pressure from celebrities, media, and advertising. These devices make your life easier, and they make it easier for you to track your kids. On the internet, on social media, and through messaging, however, there's way more foolishness than there is wisdom. It's powerful, it's attractive, and it's dangerous. So you must be careful, and you need to take charge of that aspect of your child's world. That's called parenting!

You can't hope that your child will always like you or agree with the choices you make. You must be willing to make unpopular decisions that your child won't interpret as loving, because you do in fact love him and want to protect him and guard his heart and mind. Some mobile devices function only as phones. If all you need is to have contact with your child over the phone, then use those devices. But whatever you choose, you need to know what is happening on your child's device and in his life.

I don't think you should snoop behind your child's back or parent deceptively. That leads to a lack of trust, a breakdown in the relationship, and an unwillingness of the child to listen to you in the future. This sets up an adversarial relationship that's not healthy. Instead, put the issue on the table. Be honest about what you're doing and why you're doing it. Be forthright about the controls that, out of love and godly wisdom, you need to put in your child's life.

The Christian community has been naive about the power of mobile devices, and we are losing our children. We hear about the shocking things parents discover after being way too passive and succumbing to cultural pressure when it came to allowing their children to have mobile devices. Your job is to protect your children from danger. If you want to protect your children from physical danger, how much more should you want to protect them from moral danger?

Now, as your teenager grows, his world widens, his options increase, and his desire for connectivity grows. Naturally, you will feel this changing pressure and want to adjust your approach. But you must ask, "What is it my child *actually* needs? How does God call me to protect him, and what do I need to do in order to do that?" Know that there is blessing in making these protective choices even if, at the moment, they're very hard.

How do I teach my teen about God's plan concerning dating and marriage? I know that teenagers hear the complete opposite message from their peers and from popular culture!

I don't know if you could discuss a more practically important topic with your teen than her relationships with members of the opposite sex.

When you do, you must approach the conversation in a way that keeps the sanctity and holiness of marriage in view. Other than a relationship with God, no other relationship is so weighty that it's defined as a covenant. Only marriage rises to that level of significance.

The Bible also places a weighty level of significance on the power, seductiveness, and danger of sexual temptation. These temptations arise in the teen years. If you put a seven-year-old boy and a seven-year-old girl in jeans and T-shirts, they sort of look the same. When I asked my seven-year-old son what he thought of girls, he said girls had cooties. (I still don't know what cooties are, but my boys seemed very repelled by them!) If you put a seventeen-year-old girl and a seventeen-year-old boy in jeans and T-shirts, they don't look at all the same. A seventeen-year-old suddenly becomes a cootie consumer.

Teens are very interested in the opposite sex, and that's not a bad thing. God has implanted that awareness, curiosity, and desire in us. It should be beautiful and sweet and, within the proper context, pleasurable.

Here's what is so important to teach your teenager, and it is bigger than just this issue of dating and sex and marriage: *God has designed for us to live in a pleasurable world.* That's his wise choice. This world is pleasurable, and he's given us pleasure "gates": our eyes, our ears, our taste, our touch. It's not wrong to desire the pleasures of our world. It's not wrong to find pleasure in pleasure. Finding pleasure in pleasure actually glorifies God. But the Bible teaches that pleasure needs boundaries. Pleasure without boundaries is destructive. You can't eat whatever you want to eat, whenever you want to eat it, in as much quantity as you want to eat it, without hurting yourself.

And so it is with relationships between boys and girls. The desires that grow in these relationships need boundaries. You need to address the issue of boundaries—not just the boundaries of physical behavior but the boundaries of emotions and desire. It's wrong for a boy to treat a girl like she's an object for his pleasure. It's wrong for a girl to treat a boy like he's an object for her pleasure. "Right now, this person makes me happy, and I will attach myself to him or her for a while; as soon as this person doesn't make me happy anymore, I will toss him or her away." That's a horrible thing even if no sex is involved. That's an objectification of another human being.

We need to teach our teenagers about the beauty of friendship, the enjoyment of companionship, and the way to honor others for their brains and their wisdom and the quality of their character. I don't think we talk about these things enough as parents. We need to couple that with talking about the sanctity of marriage. There are things that God, in the goodness of his wisdom and grace, reserves for this lifelong committed relationship that are dangerous to experience outside it.

This is not a conversation you have just once, in that fearful, awkward, intense, rushed talk about "the birds and the bees," then never address again. You need to offer a safe place for your teenagers to be able to talk about these things. Don't overreact. Don't quickly judge and condemn. Your teen should know that you're going to talk about this stuff with her. It should always be on the table, and if she doesn't pursue you (which she probably won't), you need to pursue her.

While the world never quits talking about sex, sadly Christian parents are silent on it. That never works. You need to talk about these things. We should not be embarrassed. Sex is one of God's good gifts. Relationships are one of God's good gifts. The creation of male and female is one of God's good gifts. Companionship is one of God's good gifts. We need to talk about this with our teenagers, and we should not expect them to be wise on their own. Be active, be involved, and look for opportunities to give guidance to your teenager that she will not come up with on her own.

I JUST DISCOVERED THAT MY CHILD IS LOOKING AT PORNOGRAPHY or interacting with other sexually explicit material. How do I approach the subject with my child? How can I protect my home from this content?

It is scary to discover that your child has been viewing pornography and may even be increasingly addicted to that content and behavior. But I want to encourage you to step back and think in broader, more biblical ways about this issue. If the Bible is accurate that your children come into the world as sinners and that their biggest issue is not just that evil exists out there but that there's sin in their hearts, it should not surprise you when sinners are attracted to sin. It's always the evil *inside* us that hooks us to the evil *outside* us. Because your child has sinful greed inside him, he may be attracted to materialism. Because your child has selfish desires, she may be attracted to illicit sexuality. You shouldn't be shocked.

There's a second important thing to remember: you should not react with such horror, condemnation, and judgment that you drive your child away from you and underground. You want to deal with this scary issue with patience and understanding and grace. How about saying, "I am so sorry that we live in this kind of world and that you have something inside you that pulls you in this direction. I'm like you. I get attracted to things that I should not be attracted to. I go places I shouldn't go. I hide things that are wrong. I share that identity with you. I can be just as foolish. But there's hope for us because there is a God who offers help to sinners, who offers power and wisdom that we wouldn't otherwise have on our own. You need help, and I need help, and I want to be part of this with you"?

It's important to understand that external protections are never enough because the issue lies within your teenager's heart. You absolutely ought to have a protective relationship with your teenager and put safeguards in place so illicit material is not readily available. But it's your teen's propensity to love what he should not love that is the main problem, not the fact that technology filters are inadequate to prevent this material from finding its way into your home and onto your child's devices. Protection, while important, is never enough. You need to find loving, patient, gentle, and kind ways of talking to your teen about the presence and power of sin and God's redeeming, rescuing grace. No matter how vigorously you act to protect your child from the outside world, if she doesn't interact with God, she won't be okay. Parenting teens in a sexually insane world doesn't end with protection; you must constantly, lovingly, patiently, and situationally preach the gospel of sin and grace to your child.

There's an even larger issue at play than the fact that your child is struggling with pornography. This larger issue of life and death and eternity is that your child naturally doesn't have a heart for God. Because he doesn't have a heart for God, he doesn't care what God says and he will go wherever his pleasure leads him. One of the things you want to do, by God's grace, is to produce in your teenager an awe of God. Talk about the glory of God with him every opportunity you can. Don't scramble an egg without talking about the glory of God. "Isn't it amazing what God created? Look at this embryo—it turns into something that you love for breakfast. God created that for you." Whether it's an egg, the sunset, or the song of a bird, you can seize opportunities to talk about God all the time. Here's why: when a teenager is in awe of God, he is predisposed to listen to the Word of God. If your child has no awe of God in his heart, it's easy for him to blow off the call of God in his Word.

You don't just fight the sex and pornography battle horizontally with protections and filters. You fight it vertically. When a struggling, tempted teenager has a desire for God, you now have the material for spiritual protection. Yes, you need horizontal protections in place, but you've got to get at the vertical issues that drive a pleasure-oriented way of living.

WHAT IS THE GOSPEL RESPONSE TO TEENS WHO ANNOUNCE THEY ARE GENDER CONFUSED OR TRANSGENDER?

We are living in a very confused and difficult period when it comes to gender. Don't ever think that somehow you can isolate or protect your children enough to prevent these powerful influences from entering your home. Particularly if your children attend a public school, they will be indoctrinated with a way of thinking about gender that is radically different from what the Bible has to say about this important topic.

After God created human beings as male and female, he stood back from his creation and said it was very good. Operating from a biblical worldview, it's impossible to think that you are mistakenly trapped in a body that is not who you are meant to be. It is very sad that this view has become so prominent and normalized in our culture. In the 1970s, the great Christian philosopher and theologian Francis Schaeffer made a statement that human rationality, apart from God's revelation, will always end in irrationality. Think about that. Human reason, if it is not rescued by divine revelation, always ends in irrational conclusions. It's not surprising that a culture that has walked away from the revelation of God would end in this form of irrationality.

If your teenager is struggling with gender issues, it could be that he or she is experiencing real emotional, psychological body dysmorphia. We should not discount that. Let me give you an example. We know that it's possible for human beings to come to the point where they hate their bodies and think they look a way they don't actually look. This is what anorexia does. Someone with anorexia looks at his or her body and does not see what you and I see. The Bible declares that sin causes us to look at our world in distorted ways, and we all have some sort of blindness to what is real. It could be that your child is struggling with this dynamic.

If this is happening, there are two things you need to do. First, you need to become an expert on gender confusion. There are wonderful books by faithful Christian writers on this topic. Do your research. Find good, solid, biblical thinkers who are writing on issues of gender. Begin to understand this dynamic in your child and in the culture. There are some very fine secular books, too, that warn about this issue. (*Irreversible Damage: The Transgender Craze Seducing Our Daughters* by Abigail Shrier [Washington, DC: Regnery Publishing, 2021] is very helpful.) Become an expert.

Second, get help for your child. If your child is experiencing gender dysmorphia, he or she needs additional help. It's almost too overwhelming for this to be a constant conversation in your family. That's why the Bible gives us the larger body of Christ. Your child probably needs to sit with a solid biblical counselor who understands the issue and who can befriend your child and address the deeper heart issues at work. There may even be dynamics in your parenting that have pushed your child in this direction, and you need to be humble and open to considering that.

It may be that your child is being powerfully influenced by media and culture. Transgenderism is a popular fad right now. I don't think it's possible that every single teen who declares that he or she is gender fluid or transgender is truly struggling with a deeper dysmorphia. What complicates this issue is that the sources of "wisdom" on this topic—the psychotherapists, pediatricians, and school counselors—are probably not going to push back against the irrationality of this trend. In fact, they will probably encourage it: "If this is what the child feels, then it must be true, so we're going to help this child to move in this new direction."

A child may talk to a school counselor who encourages him or her to make a transition. Some states allow children to move toward hormone therapy without the permission of parents. Puberty blockers or hormone therapy are anatomically dangerous for the growth and development of your child; some of what they do is irreversible. Many people who have undergone this process weep at what has been done to alter their bodies without resolving their confusion.

This is a big deal. You need to understand what is happening. You need to get a hold of the influence in your teen's life. There are many influencers out there who are fun and cool, great communicators and powerfully persuasive. They may have greater sway over your teenager than you do. You cannot get away with passive parenting. You need to be in this game. You need to become an expert and proactively address influences that shape the way your children think about who they are and how God designed their bodies.

All the while, you need to handle this with patience and understanding and grace. This is a very hard cultural moment for a teenager. It's more confusing than it's ever been. Our children need our help because we live in a world gone crazy. We've separated ourselves from the revelation of God, and we're dealing with the irrationality that results from that.

OUR TEENS HAVE STARTED TO WEAR CLOTHING THAT I DON'T APPROVE OF—or, in the case of some, nowhere near enough clothing! How do we approach our kids when they try to make a statement with their appearance and fashion?

Your teenagers will not dress exactly as you do. They won't see clothing in the way that you do. *Everybody* makes a statement with what they wear; this isn't unique to teenagers. Your statement may be "I don't care how I look because clothing means nothing to me," but that's still a statement. You need to be careful not to be legalistic about this. You may need to give your teenagers liberty about things that seem silly or look crazy to you if there are no moral issues involved.

When my sons were growing up, they were skateboarders, and in those days, skateboarders wore very baggy pants. When I took my son to buy a pair of khakis, I naturally went to the young men's aisle. He wasn't there—I found him in the men's work clothes department, holding a 50-inch-waist pair of pants, because they were baggy enough for him. That's just a fashion issue. He's turned out quite well as an adult, and guess what? He doesn't wear baggy pants anymore! We didn't stress out because we knew this would be a passing phase.

That's very different from clothing that indicates some kind of darkness or attraction to something morally dangerous or evil. And it is different from issues of modesty. For teenage girls, modesty is such a difficult thing right now. Many clothes are not designed to cover the body—they're designed to reveal the body. Even a fully clothed young woman can reveal quite a lot of her body, because that's the way clothing is being designed. It's impossible to ignore this issue. If your teenage daughter has a phone and social media, influencers are pushing products and fashion on her all the time.

Now, you must address the issue of modesty with patience and grace. Your children need protection, but they also need patient, understanding grace. You can overreact in a way that shuts down the conversation or even deepens your child's desire to do exactly the opposite of what you want. Should you ignore the issue and let your children dress however they want? No, you can't make that choice. But you ought to be involved with your children in such a way that even if they radically disagree with you, they know you love them and want what's best for them.

Don't make an issue out of things that just aren't issues. Let your children wear silly things; it doesn't make any difference. But if their clothing depicts something inappropriate, indicates some sinful attraction, or is perverse or immodest, you must be involved. Lead with grace, and watch what God will do.

I HAVE DISCOVERED MY TEEN HAS EXPRESSED SUICIDAL THOUGHTS or is self-harming. I don't know how serious he or she is about it, and I struggle to believe it. What should I do?

Perhaps the scariest thing you could ever face as a parent is your child's indication that he or she doesn't want to live anymore. How tragic, how terrifying that death looks more attractive to your child than life does. I want to state this as forcefully as I can: *you must never deny or minimize a teenager's suicidal ideation.* Good parents and good families lose teens to suicide. You must always take it seriously, and you must get that child help.

Helping teenagers in this situation needs to go beyond protecting them from the physical act of suicide, because a desire to pursue such a path reveals a deeper hopelessness of the heart. Hopelessness is a way of seeing, and it's a distorted way of seeing life. The Bible teaches us that no one is truly hopeless because there is no hole so deep that the grace of God can't reach. Everyone has hope, so you need to ask, "What is it about the way my teenager looks at life that makes his or her view hopeless and makes death more attractive to him or her than life?"

There's a difference between a child who talks about the idea and a child who actually expresses specific ways that she would do it, because that means she's progressing down the road and thinking about carrying out a plan. In either case, you need to get the child help.

And there's something else you can do: surround that child with obvious, inexhaustible, Christlike love. Love, love, love that child. Surround that child with love. I am persuaded that love is one of the most transformational forces in the universe.

I was once counseling a single person who was severely depressed and suicidal. He came to a day in the middle of his week and woke up with darker, more depressed thoughts than ever before. He finally decided that this day would be the day that he would end his life. He went down to the local drugstore, bought double-edged razor blades, went back home, filled the bathtub, and was getting ready to kill himself. But before he acted, he thought of his mom and how much she loved him. He thought of his brother, who loved, loved, loved him. As he told me later, "If I killed myself, I would get to leave earth, but they would be left with that horrible scene in their hearts and minds forever. I couldn't do that to people who loved me so much."

"What did you do next?" I asked.

He smiled and said, "I took a bath."

What stopped this man from taking his own life? For no other reason than that he was loved, he decided to continue to live. Don't make your child feel rejected and guilty because she's lost hope. Convince her that in her hopelessness, she can be sure of one thing: she is deeply and fully loved—and not just by you but by God. Love is a powerful force of rescue.

MY TEEN BATTLES ANXIETY AND DEPRESSION. How can I help?

When one of our children was in his young teen years, I opened the refrigerator door and reached for something. He stopped me. "That's expired." Now, I knew he couldn't see the label from where he was standing, so I picked up something else and asked, "What about this?" He said, "It expires next week." He had checked the expiration date of everything in the refrigerator!

I'm not surprised some people are anxious. I'm not surprised some people are depressed. In this dark and broken world, which the Bible says is groaning, it's an act of God's common grace that we aren't *all* depressed and riddled with anxiety. If you want an argument for the existence of God, it's the fact that despite the hardship of life in this world, most of us have hope.

Given all this, it's surely not a surprise that a teenager of all people might be anxious or depressed. What a hard time of life! You're in this weird moment between childhood and adulthood when you don't quite fit either world and you are going through all kinds of identity and relationship developments. A teenager looks in the mirror and hates the shape of her nose, or wishes she were taller, or wishes she were shorter. Pay attention to the significant issues at work in your teen and how she displays signs of anxiety and depression.

Depression—when not a physiological condition—is a lie. When you are depressed, you are believing things that are not true. I was once counseling a depressed person who was telling me how horrible her week had been. I said, "What you don't understand is you get up every day with a pail of black paint and a big brush. First thing in the morning, you paint your worldview completely dark, and then you step back and say, 'See, my world is dark.'" Do we live in a broken world? Do terrible things happen? Are we sinned against? Yes, but human beings operate not on the basis of the facts of their experience but on the basis of their interpretation of the facts. So, in ways that your teen is not aware of, he is participating in and compounding his own anxiety and depression. It's his way of seeing the world.

If your child is showing signs of anxiety and depression, it's important for you to get to understand his worldview and why he's seeing life the way he does. It's also important for you to get your child solid, wise, biblical help from somebody who will walk with him through his depression. (I don't mean someone who can teach him three steps to becoming undepressed; your child may be someone who lives with darkness in his life but does so with gospel hope and courage and joy.) And again, incarnate the presence and love of God in the life of your child. Make sure he never feels alone in his anxiety or depression and never feels judged or condemned because of either.

I was counseling a man who was depressed and a bit schizophrenic, and he couldn't sit in an office with me. Every morning, he would go to the local mall because he reasoned that everybody was there for selfish purposes and didn't care about or notice him, so he felt safe there. Instead of counseling him in the office, I started meeting him at the mall and walking with him. We would walk laps around the mall, day after day.

Eventually he said to me, "Paul, do you feel self-conscious walking around with me?"

"Yeah, I do a little bit," I said, "but I love you. I'm willing to do it."

"Well, I think it's pretty dumb that the only way you can talk to me is by walking in a mall," he said. "Why don't we just meet in your office?"

That's what love will do. This man realized I loved him so much that it gave him the courage to begin to share with me the darkness that was in his heart, and that was the beginning of huge change in his life. Be a loving presence like this in the life of your teenager.

Our teen is experimenting with drugs and alcohol. I'm afraid she will ruin her life and get in trouble with the law. What should I do?

If your teen has an issue with drugs or alcohol, you must act immediately to rescue her from herself. Teenagers are maturing physiologically and undergoing brain and cognition development. They should never mess with these substances. This is not to say that drugs are permissible for adults, but there's an entire body of research out there revealing the negative impact that the regular use of drugs and alcohol has on the development of a teenager in particular. Somebody who is dear to my wife and me has lived their entire adult life in a real sense as a teenager because they were stoned throughout their developmental adolescent years.

And this maturing process is not just physiological. All of us go through formative years in which we make dumb decisions—not only in our teens but even in our early twenties. We learn from the awkward, uncomfortable things we go through. If, during all this, a teen is numbed physically, emotionally, and relationally because of her regular use of some substance, she won't benefit from all the transitional hardship that would have prepared her for responsible adulthood.

This issue is extremely important. You must do what is necessary, within loving boundaries, to protect your child from herself. You must be willing to be an unpopular parent. You cannot parent teenagers biblically and simultaneously hope they will think you're the greatest and coolest peer ever. Teens *need* your wisdom and protection and boundaries, but they tend to rebel against this loving wisdom and instruction. They don't love parental intervention or restriction, but this is one of those areas in which you must intervene and place restrictions, because their physiological and characterological development will not take place in the way that God has designed if it is interrupted by these substances. So act with clarity and act with consistency. Don't give up, and whether or not your teenager ever thanks you for your intervention, you have done a good thing.

I'M CONCERNED THAT MY CHILD IS SPENDING TIME WITH THE WRONG GROUP of peers and that their bad influence is rubbing off. What should I do? Should I not allow my teenager to hang out with certain kids?

When you read through the father's instruction in Proverbs, you notice that he emphasizes again and again the impact that our companions have on us. We are always influenced by whom we hang around with.

Why is this emphasized so strongly in Proverbs? Because youth tend to be unwise in their choice of companions. I don't know about you, but when I was a teenager, I can't remember ever asking, "What is the moral impact of hanging around with these friends?" You've been there too, I'm sure. When we were younger, we wanted to be part of certain crowds that seemed cool for some reason. We were willing to do anything to be part of that social circle, even if it meant ignoring warning signs or compromising on the morals we were raised with. I've counseled thirty- or forty-year-olds who looked back on those formative teen years and said, "I wish I had walked away from that crowd, because I made decisions to be accepted by those people that I'm still dealing with today."

This is a conversation you have to have with your teenager. His companions ought to be a big concern for you. Of course, you don't want to make the conversation so aggressive or condemning that you drive your teenager into hiding. This breaks the relationship of trust, and he will stay with that crowd, but you will never know it. Instead, engage this conversation with humility, patience, gentleness, and understanding.

If your teenager isn't responding to conversations like this and making wiser and better choices, it will be necessary and appropriate for you to protect him from himself. You will have to say, "I'm not going to allow you to go here. You cannot underestimate the significance of the influence of people who have your ear and your heart. They're enormously morally influential." This is another one of those areas where you have to commit yourself to doing what's right for your teenager even if he doesn't like you, even if he doesn't appreciate you, even if he resists you. Don't get up every morning with the goal that your teenagers will just love the fact that you're their parent, or you will compromise on things like this.

I also need to say this, although I'm sure you are very aware: companions and peer influence are not just in-person anymore but now also digital. You may need to be even more concerned about this digital influence than about who your teenager physically hangs out with. Don't just be concerned about personal relationships. Be concerned about your teen's digital relationships and influences because you may win one battle while losing another. Care about both domains.

My child is not motivated to do his or her schoolwork—or any type of work for that matter. How do I motivate a lazy teen?

As a parent, you are rightfully concerned about the future and legacy of your child. If you perceive your teen as being lazy, you'll worry about his or her transition out of the home. "How is he ever going to support himself? How is she ever going to get into college? Where is he ever going to get a job? And how is she ever going to be able to perform that job if she doesn't work?" Your thoughts will spin out of control over all the what-ifs about your kid's future. And although your intention may be loving, your response should not be driven by what-if fears. Fear causes you to overreact with your child, to say things you shouldn't, to do things you shouldn't, and to drive your teenager away from the wisdom of your counsel.

Every parental response to a concern, especially a concern regarding a child's work ethic and motivation, should be born out of faith in the Lord. Here's what this faith leads you to see as a parent: *you have no ability whatsoever to change the heart of your teenager*. One of the things that we need to face as parents is the limits of what we're able to do. If you had the power—by the force of your personality, by the logic of your argument, by the threat of a punishment—to change the heart of your child, Jesus would have never had to come because change would be within the ability of human beings. Instead, the Bible teaches us that radical, lasting change of heart is always the work of God's grace. So what you have to do is ask the question "What does it look like to be a tool of God's grace in the life of my lazy teenager?" rather than "How do I keep my teenager from being lazy?"

One of the best ways to be a tool of God's grace is by being transparent. Let your teen know that you have lazy tendencies as well. You put off some things way longer than you should because you don't like the hard work of doing them. This type of confession makes you approachable to your child. How different is that from saying to your teen, "I cannot imagine ever being like that! In my day, I would have never even thought of being as lazy as you are!" That just closes the door of the heart of your child. Be transparent. Be confessional. Be humble with your child.

You can't change the heart of your child, but you can position yourself to be a tool in the hands of God. Seek to demonstrate to your child the amazing wisdom of a life of work. Accept your limits and pray that God will use you to be his tool of rescue and change in the life of your teenager.

MY TEEN DOESN'T WANT TO SPEND TIME WITH US as a family or with her younger siblings. Do I force her to spend time with us?

I remember the first time one of our teenagers asked us to pick him up from a skating party. He said, "Just wait in the car. Don't come in." I thought, *Oh, wow, my teenager does not want to be associated with me. He doesn't want his friends to say, "Look, there are your parents."* It can be very tempting to respond out of that hurt and say, "Do you know who I am? Do you know who changed your diaper? Do you know who cleaned up your vomit when you were sick? Do you know who purchased and made every meal you put in your mouth? How dare you not want to spend time with me. If it weren't for me, you wouldn't even have reached your teenage years. What's the matter with you?"

That type of response is never healthy or helpful, whether it is spoken aloud for your teen to hear or grumbled silently in your heart so that it creates bitterness and resentment toward your teen. Lashing out because your child has hurt you never heals your wounds and only wounds your child. Here's the gospel: being a parent is being called by God to share in his sufferings. Jesus was despised and rejected. He dealt with that sorrow probably every day of his life on earth. If you prioritize acceptance by or popularity with your teen, you will be endlessly bitter against your own children. You will respond out of that bitterness and drive them further away.

Think about this. Demand never produces love. It's the goodness of God—his gentleness, his patience, his kindness, his forgiveness—that draws us toward him. He's willing to reconcile with us even though we don't deserve it. Parent, model that love in the life of your teenager. Be loving, gentle, and kind. Learn to laugh at yourself, to confess when you are wrong, and to be enormously patient when your kids wrong you.

When I think of parental patience, I think of that moment when God warned King Nebuchadnezzar of his pending ruin. What amazes me is that one year later, God was still waiting, giving the king a chance to repent. Can you imagine saying to your children, "Go clean up your room right now, but I'll give you twelve months to do it"? I'm not recommending that level of leniency in your parenting, but this story exposes the impatience we have as parents compared to the patience of our Heavenly Father.

Instead of lashing out or becoming bitter, patiently and graciously ask, "What is going on that makes our teenager not want to be with us?" That question could go in one of two directions. (1) *What could be wrong in her heart that is causing her to no longer be comfortable with us?* You would want to address those heart issues. Or, fasten your seat belt, (2) *What could be wrong with us as parents that is causing her to not want to spend time with us?*

I've sat in countless counseling sessions with teenagers whose parents are bitter, angry, self-righteous, and legalistic. I've sat there thinking, "If I were this kid, I wouldn't want to be in this house either." Are you humble enough to be willing to examine your heart and behavior and ask, "Could there be things in us that are driving our teenager away?"

There will always be something amiss in your teenager's heart that makes her family no longer attractive to her—that's part of growing up. God has placed you in your teen's life to address her heart—that's called parenting! But whether you are addressing her heart or your own, either direction gives you an opportunity to move toward your child with humility, patience, grace, and confession. Demanding and forcing family time without addressing the heart never, ever solves the issue.

OUR TEENS SHOW NO INTEREST IN THE THINGS OF GOD, and they don't want to participate in family faith-based activities such as church, youth group, or family worship. What do we do?

One of the defining aspects of the teenage years is the process of spiritual rejection or spiritual internalization. As children begin to move out of the home and become responsible adults, they will either internalize all the godly wisdom they have been taught from day one in the Christian home in which they were raised, or they will progressively walk away from the wisdom of God. It won't happen at all once, and there will be fits and starts, but this process is very important.

Both internalization and rejection have their roots in love. Either love of God will cause your teen to love his Word and his commands, or love of the world will grow in your child's heart and replace the Christian values that he was raised with. This is a deep spiritual battle. It determines what love will control the heart of your teenager and set the direction of his life.

This is a critical moment in your child's life. You will be excited or afraid as your teen begins to move in a certain direction, and you will want to be involved and to intervene. But your child is only ever in the hands of God. As a parent, you literally cannot—in any way, shape, or form—create a love of God in the heart of your child. This is terrifying for every parent of every teenager because, if you love God, you long for your teenagers to love God as well. You long for them to find joy in God's Word. You long for them to love God's people and to live God's way. But you have no ability to create that love. Giving up control and entrusting your child to the Lord is one of the keys to good gospel parenting.

Now, of course, there are tools and methods to set your child up for internalization and steer him away from rejection. One of the things that God calls us to do is to be his ambassadors, to represent him in the lives of our children. That means representing his methods, his message, and his character. One of the most common ways God wins people's hearts is through his Word, so it's good and valid to have family worship and to require your teenager to participate. In my own experience, my father read the Bible to us every morning. He wasn't a teacher; he simply started in Genesis, read all the way to Revelation, and then started with Genesis again.

I'm not sure of the full impact that practice had on me, but I do have one example from my senior year of high school. I was invited to an end-of-year party that turned out to be filled with drugs, alcohol, and sex. When I arrived, I did not experience a pull toward the things of the world, a love for worldly pleasure. No, instead I experienced a powerful fear of the Lord and remembered the Word of God. I had been driven to the party by someone else, so I literally ran out of the house and walked five miles home. I didn't make that walk feeling embarrassed that I would be the unpopular kid at school; I walked home feeling thankful. I'm convinced that my fear of the Lord was born out of my family's worship routine, morning after morning after morning, as my father just read the Bible to his children.

Parent, give up control and entrust your child to the Lord, but don't underestimate the power of the Word of God to do things in the heart of your child that you could never do. Even though at times I didn't enjoy it, I am thankful to this day for early morning family worship and for a father who started with Genesis and read to Revelation and started again. At key moments in my life, I have been rescued and redirected by a fear of the Lord that I have only because of his Word. As a parent, you can never demand or instill the fear of the Lord. You can't demand or produce the love of God. But you can expose your child to God's Word and its power to do in the heart of your child what you couldn't do on your own.

How do I discipline a teen who is now physically bigger than I am? What do I do when the old ways of disciplining don't work anymore?

I remember when my two teenage sons, who are both taller than me, were getting ready to leave the house. The thought hit me, *What if they were going somewhere I didn't want them to go, and they just decided to ignore my authority? What options would I have?* I wasn't going to get into a fistfight with my sons or try to physically restrain them. Thankfully, by God's grace, they had hearts willing to submit to authority, so I gave them my final instructions and they went on their way.

I know you can't turn back the clock, but I want to go back in time a bit to answer this question. It is very important for you to fight your authority battles when your child is young. It is so important to exercise authority and implement discipline in the seemingly little moments as your children grow. Whether you're making your child eat his peas at dinner or enforcing bedtime rather than letting him stay up as late as he decides, God is using you to shape your child's heart. God uses parents to move children from naturally despising authority to seeing the value of authority and submitting to it.

Authority is a gift from God. As an ambassador of authority, you need to exercise your God-given authority in a way that makes authority beautiful. When you're given a birthday gift, it's not wrapped in garbage; it's wrapped in beautiful paper with a bow on top and a label with your name. If you exercise authority by screaming, yelling, name calling, pulling, shoving, you are making authority ugly. Poorly executed authority hardens a child's heart against authority. Instead, you should exercise authority in a way that's patient, kind, and loving while nonetheless firm and uncompromising. If you do this when your child is young, you won't have to fight the same kind of authority battles when your child is a teenager.

You may not be at that point anymore. You can't turn back the clock, and you can't treat a seventeen-year-old like he's five years old. But you do have a way to go after the rebellion that still exists in his heart, and that is to create a link between rebellion, trust, and the opportunity for freedom. Establish a relationship of trust with your teenager as a form of discipline as he gets older.

Trust is the root of the freedom your child wants. If you're going to give your child greater freedom outside the home and allow him to do things he would like to do, you have to have a relationship of trust with him. Rebellion breaks down that trust. You can say, "Until you have demonstrated trustworthiness, we can't give you the freedom to do X, Y, and Z. We would love to be able to say yes to you and give you greater freedom. When you demonstrate a willingness to obey, a willingness to work with us and to honor and submit to authority, then we can give that to you. If we can't do that, then we are not able to give you the kind of freedom you want. We can't trust you with our car. We can't trust you with that overnight invitation you have been given. Our ability to let you have an ever-increasing freedom as you get older is rooted in our ability to trust you."

But I would do more. Ask, "Why is there rebellion in your heart? Why do you struggle so hard with authority?" Be quick to confess that you still have foolishness and rebellion in your heart as well. You are more like your teenager than unlike him. Confess your need for rescue, and encourage your teenager to cry out for that rescue too. Even if he doesn't want to hear it, even if he mocks the message, give that message over and over and over again. You don't know when the wind of the Spirit will move on the heart of your child.

WHAT GOALS SHOULD I HAVE FOR MY TEENS as I seek to prepare them for greater independence after high school? When it comes to different options like choosing a college, deciding on a career path, getting a job, joining the military, and so on, how much should I try to influence them, and how much should I allow my children to make these decisions on their own?

Your first goal is for your children to have hearts for God. What could be more important than this? No, you can't create a love for God in their hearts—only God can—but you have many opportunities to talk about God and use his Word in their lives. Your teenagers were made for relationship with God, made to serve God, hardwired to love God. Your earthbound goals for your teenagers are not wrong, but an eternal relationship with the living God is most important.

After that, I would prioritize self-awareness, relationship, possessions, and long-term thinking. Are your children aware of their strengths and weaknesses, their susceptibility to sin, their foolish or rebellious hearts? Talk to them about these things—not with condemnation and anger but with vulnerability and confession. Are your teens loving, kind, generous, and caring? Do they have to be the center of attention, or do they see the beauty of the truth that "the last will be first, and the first last" (Matt. 20:16)? Do they use people, or do they serve "the least of these" (Matt. 25:40)? Are they mean, mocking, and angry, or do they exhibit the fruit of the Spirit? Does conflict follow them, or can they create peace? Are your children materialistic, constantly demanding the latest thing? Or are they content and thankful? Do they take care of their possessions? Do they understand what it means to be good stewards of what has been provided for them? Finally, do they think in a long-term way, or do they live for the moment? Are they only concerned about immediate pleasure, or do they operate with an awareness of how today's decisions will impact the future?

Self-awareness, relationship, possessions, and long-term thinking—all these are characteristics of the heart, and they will factor into nearly every single decision your teenagers make on a daily basis. If you see good things happening in these areas, then you are able to surrender decisions to your children because you know they have a basis for making wise choices. If you don't see these characteristics, you'll probably have to weigh in on their decisions and limit their freedom more than you want to, and certainly more than your teenagers want, because they do not yet have hearts that can make the kinds of independent decisions that will set their lives on the right trajectory.

As always, ask yourself, "What is going on in the hearts of my children, and because of that, what capability do they have to make wise long-term decisions?"

31 Days of Biblical Counseling

ADDICTIVE HABITS

CHANGING FOR GOOD

31-DAY DEVOTIONALS FOR LIFE

DAVID R. DUNHAM

ANGER

CALMING YOUR HEART

31-DAY DEVOTIONALS FOR LIFE

ROBERT D. JONES

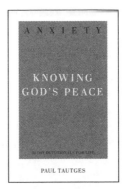

ANXIETY

KNOWING GOD'S PEACE

31-DAY DEVOTIONALS FOR LIFE

PAUL TAUTGES

DOUBT

TRUSTING GOD'S PROMISES

31-DAY DEVOTIONALS FOR LIFE

ELYSE FITZPATRICK

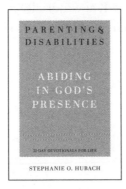

PARENTING & DISABILITIES

ABIDING IN GOD'S PRESENCE

31-DAY DEVOTIONALS FOR LIFE

STEPHANIE O. HUBACH

PORNOGRAPHY

FIGHTING FOR PURITY

31-DAY DEVOTIONALS FOR LIFE

DEEPAK REJU

In the 31-Day Devotionals for Life series, biblical counselors and Bible teachers guide you through Scripture passages that speak to specific situations or struggles, helping you to apply God's Word to your life in practical ways day after day.

Other Topics Include

After an Affair	Forgiveness	Money
Assurance	Fearing Others	Painful Pasts
Chronic Illness	Grief	Patience
Contentment	Hope	Toxic Relationships
Engagement	Marriage Conflict	Singleness

Did you find this book helpful?
Consider writing a review online.
The author appreciates your feedback!

Or write to P&R at editorial@prpbooks.com
with your comments. We'd love to hear from you.